J. P. Bean has written two non-fiction crime books, radio plays and the authorised biography of rock star Joe Cocker, WITH A LITTLE HELP FROM MY FRIENDS. He is editor of the journal *Prison Writing*.

Over the Wall

True Stories of the Master Jailbreakers

J. P. Bean

HEADLINE

First published in 1994
by HEADLINE BOOK PUBLISHING

First published in paperback in 1995
by HEADLINE BOOK PUBLISHING

10 9 8 7 6 5 4 3 2 1

ISBN 0 7472 4471 5

Printed and bound in Great Britain by
Cox & Wyman Ltd, Reading, Berks

HEADLINE BOOK PUBLISHING
A division of Hodder Headline PLC
338 Euston Road
London NW1 3BH

CONTENTS

FOREWORD

'There is a hard core of prisoners who will take any opportunity to escape,' stated the Mountbatten Report in 1966, following a series of major break-outs from British jails. This book is about that 'hard core' – the prisoner who thinks only of escape from the moment he is captured; the desperado who, no matter how slim the chance of success, will go over, under or through any prison wall to gain his freedom.

Prison escapes began to escalate in numbers in the years following the Second World War. This was not coincidental. Wartime priorities elsewhere had brought about a deterioration in standards of prison security, while the emphasis in the jails moved from containment and punishment towards rehabilitation and training. So much so that a Prison Commissioners' Report in 1947 regretted that the system should still be 'cluttered up with searches and checks, lockings and unlockings'.

By the summer of 1958, with thirty-two escaped convicts at large – including the celebrated Alfie Hinds and Frank 'The Mad Axeman' Mitchell – the public and the press were showing alarm. Criticism was mounting at

1

what *The Times* described as 'this scandalous and long-standing failure to enforce the process of law'. Commenting on the latest scare on July 9, the paper's leader column declared, 'It is no longer possible to plead as an excuse the difficulties of war and its aftermath. But the rot that set in then shows no sign of being stopped.'

The situation would get worse before it got better. The next decade, as well as bringing a continuing rise in the number of overall escapes, brought the springing of Charlie Wilson and Ronnie Biggs, both Great Train Robbers; the spy George Blake, serving the longest sentence ever imposed in a British court, and John McVicar, a robber whom the police proclaimed Britain's Most Dangerous Man. These four prisoners were serving a total of 125 years between them. They were among the most notorious criminals of modern times, they had taken a great deal of catching in the first place – yet somehow they had been allowed to escape.

The government of the day suffered great embarrassment. Something had to be done. The outcome was the Mountbatten Report, a seminal document in the history of post-war British prisons, which introduced a new regime of restrictive, maximum security. The hard line created other problems, in particular an outbreak of riots and prison protests, but it kept the danger men within the walls. Not all of them though – the household names might have been contained, but other escapers were catapulted into the news. Three people were killed when two inmates of a Scottish mental hospital broke out and only a few weeks later further tragedy followed with the murder of four members of a Derbyshire family, by a prisoner who had escaped on the way to a court hearing.

IRA propaganda was boosted by some major escapes in the eighties, with the advent of a new phenomenon, the smuggling of guns to prisoners. The biggest break-out ever from any British jail – that of thirty-eight men from the Maze in 1983 – had repercussions that continue to the present. Another first was the use of a helicopter in the airlift of two top-security inmates from Gartree. For years such an eventuality had been expected, yet nothing was done to prevent it happening.

All the jailbreakers covered in this book are men. Women escapers have always been few and far between and even Zoe Progl, who in 1960 became the first woman to escape from Holloway, is now a long-forgotten underworld name. Moors Murderer Myra Hindley came close to escaping from the same jail in 1974, but her hopes of eloping to Brazil with her prison-officer lover were thwarted when their plot was discovered. Of course, fewer women than men go to prison, but perhaps that is not the only reason for a lack of female escapers. Women are less likely to have a criminal organisation behind them and are generally less able to instill fear and violence.

Violence in the course of escaping or while on the run – be it actual or threatened – occurs in more than half the chapters of this book. Most, if not all, escapers would undoubtedly prefer to slip away and lie low without drama, but getting out of maximum-security jails and living as a fugitive does not always allow such luxury. Nor does escape always bring the better world dreamed of during long, lonely nights alone in a prison cell – Ronnie Biggs and George Blake have enjoyed the good life, but what became of Frank Mitchell? Six of the Maze escapers have since met premature deaths, as did Jimmy

Moody, while no one would wish to share Billy Hughes' fate.

Prisoners escape by a variety of means. Some are sprung by associates on the out, some assisted by friends inside, themselves content to stay behind. Most, if not all, of the escapes recounted in this book were planned in advance, at times with almost military precision. Keys, ropes, ladders and grappling hooks are made to scale walls, tunnels are dug under and through them. Weapons are stolen, smuggled in and even made in prison workshops. All in all, there is no typical method of escape.

Similarly there is no single motivation that drives a prisoner over the wall. It can be a desperate attempt to prove innocence when all else has failed; the need to provide for a family; the lure of a big job waiting to be pulled off; the old score that requires settling; the wife or girlfriend who is having difficulties – quite aside from a simple refusal to be contained. In 1992 an inmate at Acklington, a medium-security jail in the north-east, escaped to watch Sunderland play Norwich City in the FA Cup semi-final. He had applied to the Governor for home leave but been turned down.

Reactions to high-profile break-outs follow a predictable pattern. The press reflects public anxiety by increasing it, while politicians seek to score points off their parliamentary opponents. The Prison Officers' Association calls for more staff, better conditions, improved salaries. Sometimes the Home Secretary orders an inquiry; rarely does the subsequent report – if he allows it to be published – tell anyone much that they have not already learned from the media. Traditionally, official utterances following major escapes have been on the theme of an immediate introduction of 'special measures', which would ensure that no similar escape ever occurred again. But of course they have done, time and time again.

Thanks are due to the many people who have assisted in the research for this book. I am grateful for information and suggestions received from prisoners and ex-prisoners, some of whose escapes are featured in the following chapters, also to prison and police officers. For reasons which I understand, most have expressed the wish not to be acknowledged by name. For their help, encouragement and support I would like to thank personally Mike Cocker, John McVicar, James Morton, James Nicholson, Roger Houghton at Headline Books and, as ever, my family and friends.

1 RUBY SPARKS

Run, Ruby, Run

The old convicts hated Dartmoor more than any place on earth. Grim and isolated in the Devon wilderness, shrouded in mist whatever the season – a first glimpse of this grey stone fortress could bring a lump to the throat of the toughest convict. And the Big House on the Moor held the toughest convicts in all of Britain, men who were considered too troublesome or dangerous for any other jail. Hard men doing hard labour – breaking rocks, reclaiming the wild land, sewing mailbags in silence under the gimlet gaze of zealous warders. Discipline was rigid, the guards carried guns and the cat-o'-nine-tails was rarely out of use. Men were put on bread and water for the pettiest of offences, such as feeding the birds or being caught in possession of a newspaper.

In this climate of brutality and despair it was not surprising that prisoners tried to escape. In daylight and in darkness, good weather and bad, they had been trying for more than 100 years. Not one had succeeded. Some got over the wall, but the treacherous landscape and unpredictable weather of the moor meant that they were quickly recaptured. Then, one freezing January night in

7

1940, one man did break out of Dartmoor and make it to freedom. He was thirty-eight, a burglar from Camberwell in East London. His name was John Sparks, but everyone called him Ruby.

The life of villainy that would lead Ruby Sparks to Dartmoor began in Tiger Yard, Camberwell, a den of iniquity in the heart of South London. He earned his nickname at the age of sixteen after burgling the Park Lane home of an Indian maharajah and relieving him of uncut rubies worth £40,000 – which he promptly gave away, believing them to be worthless fakes.

This naivety was short-lived and during a four-year period in the mid-1920s, through cat burglary and smash-and-grab raiding, Sparks stole jewellery and other property valued at a quarter of a million pounds. His downfall came not in London, where he would have been a much-prized Flying Squad capture, but in Southport, Lancashire as he cruised homeward in his American Buick car after a spot of cat burglary in the area. Chased by the local police, the Buick hit a tree. With a post-office safe in the back and his girlfriend, Lilian Goldstein, better known as 'The Bobbed-Haired Bandit', sporting a mink recently stolen from the near-by home of Lord Sefton, Sparks was bang to rights.

Not a man to get his girl in trouble, Ruby put his hands up to all the charges and was given three years' penal servitude. But neither Strangeways Jail nor the Manchester climate were to his liking and when his girlfriend came to visit he informed her that in a fortnight's time he would be joining her on the out. As Sparks was strip-searched before leaving his clothes outside his cell each night – because he had previously escaped from Borstal –

the warder who overheard his boast did not take it too seriously. 'Son,' he told him, 'nobody has ever escaped from here.'

True to his word, a fortnight later Ruby Sparks became the first prisoner to escape from Strangeways. It cost him £400 in bribes to buy up as much mailbag thread as the other convicts could bring him, plus a knife, which he used to saw through the bars on his cell window. The thread was hidden inside his mattress and for two weeks Sparks spent every night plaiting it into a rope strong enough to bear his weight. He left a dummy in his bed, made up from a stool, a chamber pot and a blanket and, conscious that once over the wall his unclothed state might attract attention on the streets of Manchester, he made himself a suit out of another blanket.

At 11 p.m. on a wet summer's night in 1927, Ruby Sparks went over the Strangeways wall. He could not resist a dig at the authorities, so in his cell he left a note which read:

> The Cage is Empty
> The Bird is Flown
> I've gone to a Place
> Where I'm Better Known

'I signed it,' he said later, 'so the screws would know it was me who had escaped and not Shakespeare.'

In the next cell was an ex-sailor. He had persuaded Ruby to let him come along, but once in the prison grounds Sparks realised this had been a mistake. The sailor began to shake and proved more hindrance than help as Ruby broke into the carpenters' workshop and made a T-piece of wood to attach to his rope. He threw the T-piece up the prison wall, lodging it in the spikes which ran across the top.

All was going well, apart from the time. For over four hours Lily Goldstein had been waiting patiently on the other side of the wall, but the sailor's dithering slowed Ruby down. She thought that something must have gone wrong and decided that the quicker she departed the scene the better. Now, at the very moment that he scrambled up the wall, Ruby heard his girlfriend start up the car and drive away.

It was not the best way to re-enter the outside world. No sooner had Ruby's shoeless feet hit the pavement than he and his fellow escaper were challenged by a group of workmen on their way to the early morning shift. 'Have you lads just come over the prison wall?' one asked. Ruby told him not to be silly, saying that he should know that no one came over the prison wall at four in the morning, and that he and his friend were very unhappy to be mistaken for evil-doers.

Along the road Sparks and the sailor managed to thumb a lift on a passing lorry. They were hoping to get to Liverpool, but before they had travelled half way there the driver, having taken a closer look at his two oddly-dressed passengers, pulled up and said he was going no further. The escapers took cover in fields until night fell, but as they went into an orchard they were spotted by a woman. She thought they looked suspicious and raised the alarm.

Farmworkers came running and Ruby tried to get away by diving into a river and swimming downstream. The locals were not going to let him off so easily though. They did not like strangers in their orchard – they thought Ruby and the sailor were there to steal apples.

And so as he swam downstream the locals followed along the river banks, throwing huge stones at him. He decided that surrender was preferable to losing his brains, but when he climbed out of the water the men started to jab him with pitchforks. For once in his life Ruby Sparks was extremely pleased to see the police arrive.

Sparks was welcomed back to Strangeways with fifteen days of bread and water, followed by forty-two days of bread, water and cold porridge. He finished his sentence and went straight back to the smash-and-grab business, stealing and spending £8,000 in three weeks before he was arrested for robbing Mappin and Webb, the Regent Street jewellers.

At the Old Bailey the judge gave him ten years and off he went to the dark confines of Wandsworth. He never had a chance to use the bit of razor blade secreted under his lapel, with which he had hoped to slash the canvas sides of the police truck. His girlfriend followed the truck all the way in her open-topped Bentley, but he was wedged tight between warders. The famous Ruby Sparks might have made fools of their colleagues in Borstal and Strangeways with his escapes, but they were determined that he would not be making fools of them.

They were wrong. He showed the staff at Wandsworth the same disregard that he had shown others, but not for a week or two and not by escaping himself. One of the first people he bumped into was his old getaway driver, Jim Turner, a fellow who, when it came to escapes, was always keen to make one. They noticed that the prison doctor's house, which adjoined the jail, was ideally situated for an exit route and so Sparks arranged for a friend to burgle the house during the night, remain on the premises, and in the morning retrieve a sectioned ladder and a rope ladder that the friend had hidden in the garden on his way in.

The following morning, as the convicts walked round the exercise yard at 8 a.m., the rope ladder flew over the wall. Sparks and Turner broke from the line and ran for it. Turner reached the top, but Ruby had only got a short way up the ladder before he was knocked to the ground by warders hitting him with batons. Covered in blood, he was carried off and dumped in a padded cell, his face so battered that the chief officer could not recognise him.

'Which one are you?' he asked.

'Jim Turner,' replied Sparks, fuelling the expectation that he was the man most likely to have escaped. The chief officer believed him and for the next forty-eight hours the police were looking for the wrong man. When it emerged that he had put one over them, the Wandsworth warders were so annoyed that they set about Ruby with their batons again.

After these exploits there was only one destination for Ruby Sparks – Dartmoor. He had not been there long when, in January 1932, the jail erupted in a mutiny unprecedented in British prison history. Inevitably, Sparks was in the thick of it. Afterwards, when warders lined up some of the ringleaders and opened fire on them, he was hit under the collar-bone by a bullet. He considered himself more fortunate than another convict who had climbed on to the roof to wave at photographers – he was shot through the throat, knocked off the roof and paralysed for the rest of his life.

Ruby got four years added on for his part in the

mutiny, but he successfully appealed against the original ten-year sentence and it was halved on a technicality. The rest of his time passed quietly by earlier standards and he was released in 1938. But the cold, damp cells of Dartmoor Prison had not seen the last of Ruby Sparks. Only a few months after he came out he was back in – with another five stretch for house burglary. This time he intended to show the prison authorities what he was really made of.

As soon as he arrived back at Dartmoor in February 1939, Sparks began to plan his way out. He knew it would be no easy task and that the hardest part would not be getting out of the jail, but staying out and reaching civilisation. The bleak countryside with its crags and bogs had proved too daunting a course for every prisoner who had previously tried to get away. Regardless of any perimeter wall, the moor itself was sufficient security. Sparks was in no doubt about what he was up against, but he was equally in no doubt that he could do it.

He was put to work in the quarry and found himself teamed up with an old friend, Big Paddy Nolan, who had been moved to Dartmoor after trying to escape from Chelmsford. As the two of them hauled a rubble-cart like a pair of carthorses, they discussed what would be needed to make a break. The call went out for mailbag thread and a rope was begun, a few strands at a time. When they were not working on it, they hid it under the rubble pile.

This was not going to be a quick, opportunist dash for the wall with a procession of warders in hot pursuit. Sparks had to come up with a plan that would give him and whoever went with him sufficient time to put a bit of distance between them and the jail. He decided that he needed five master keys to get through the five separate sets of gates that lay between the cells and the wall. Getting hold of a warder's keys was out of the question – only the Chief Officer had them – but an eagle-eyed fellow like Ruby Sparks did not need to go that far. If he could get a good enough look he could memorise the grooves and flanges.

The only time the keys came out was when the Chief opened a gate as the convicts returned from working parties. Ruby made sure that he was always close to the officer, usually engaging him in earnest conversation. As this went on, over a period, he mentally photographed each key and back in his cell he scraped away at pieces of hard metal that another pal, Alex Marsh, had obtained for him from the machine-shop.

For almost a year Ruby worked away at his keys, testing them in the locks whenever he could divert attention for a few seconds. Sometimes he stood with his back to the gate, one hand working away behind him as he kept up his banter with the Chief about the latter's boxing prowess. Like the rope, when Paddy Nolan was not busy plaiting it, the keys were hidden under the pile of rubble.

With the keys and rope almost ready, the next step was to obtain some money. Sparks had invited Alex Marsh to join Nolan and himself in escaping, but it was obvious that they would need more than could be saved out of their sevenpence a week prison wages. Carving two dice out of a meat bone salvaged from the cook-house waste bin, Sparks and his two pals joined a gambling school run by heavies from the race-track gangs. It was a risky game – Ruby's dice were loaded and to be caught cheating in such menacing company would mean a certain razor slashing. Nolan and Marsh were apprehensive, but he consoled them with the thought that none of them was very handsome anyway, it was not as if they would be destroying works of art.

With skill and bold cunning, Ruby soon added £3 in loose change to the rope and keys under the rubble. Everything was now ready, the escape set for a Wednesday evening at a time when all prisoners were unlocked to attend a choral class in the prison chapel. As extra cover, a disturbance was arranged to take place at the appointed time.

Wednesday arrived and, once fists, boots and batons started to fly Sparks and his two pals dashed along the landing away from the trouble. Out came the home-made keys, to Ruby's relief they all worked, and through the five gates they went, stealing three warders' rain-coats on the way. They collected their rope and money from the rubble pile and ran for the final hurdle – the outer wall. This proved no obstacle. Along the way they had picked up a long bench. Now they propped it against the twenty-foot high wall, threw up the rope and climbed over.

It was a freezing January night in 1940. Icicles hung from the prison wall. Dartmoor was ice-bound, foggy and treacherous. Sparks led the other two towards the railway line, hoping to run and walk fifty miles during the night. That would have been optimistic even in ideal conditions, and when Alex Marsh fell into a bog and was almost swallowed up, all three realised why no previous escaper had ever got off the moor.

The next problem arose when they reached the railway line and took the wrong direction. Instead of heading towards London they ran straight into Yelverton station, where they were spotted by one of the search parties already combing the moor with dogs and guns. As the searchers yelled after them, the three split up, running off in different directions. Ruby did not see Alex Marsh again, but a couple of hours later he and Paddy Nolan were reunited after each called out in the darkness, using a London barrow boy's street call.

For mile after weary mile Sparks and Nolan ran along the railway track, this time in the right direction, before taking refuge in a wagon that they stumbled upon in a siding. Battered, bleeding and exhausted, they fell asleep under a tarpaulin. When they awoke it was daylight and they were slowly rolling into Plymouth dockyard.

By now their escape had been picked up by the press and their photos and descriptions were front-page news. Their bedraggled state and prison clothes should have given the game away to anyone who set eyes on them, but in spite of several close calls they managed to catch a bus into Plymouth, upsetting the conductor by dirtying the seats. Once in the town centre they bought jackets, overalls and caps from a pawnbroker, calling at Woolworth's to add spectacles to their new look. When a police car approached they dashed into a church and hid for a while under the curious but understanding gaze of a priest and nun, before slipping into the passageway of an unoccupied house to change into their new outfits. Their grey prison clothes and black warders' raincoats were found on the premises later that day, during an intensive search of Plymouth lodging houses, pubs and cafés.

After catching a bus to Torquay, changing on to another to Exeter, and buying a loaf and cheese, Sparks and Nolan were left with eightpence between them. Back in Dartmoor Jail, when news of the escape had first become known the convicts annoyed warders by constantly singing a popular song of the day, 'Run, Rabbit, Run', changing the words to 'Run, Ruby, Run'. But when the initial euphoria of seeing someone get away had faded, those left behind were not so enthusiastic. The search for the escapers meant that all prisoners were confined to their cells for four days.

Out in the cold, Ruby could not help but think that the mates they had left behind might still be locked up, but they at least were warm and fed. By now he and Nolan had found freedom to be uncomfortable and painful – they were freezing cold, without food, or money and were still 173 miles from their destination.

Two days later they arrived in London after slipping on and off trains, dodging ticket inspectors, sleeping another night out in the open and eventually hitching a lift on a lorry that took them to Slough. Within striking distance of home now, they walked as far as Hammersmith, catching a bus into the West End. There, using their last twopence, Ruby went to a phone box and called a friendly boxing promoter. He came to collect them from outside the Grosvenor Hotel in Park Lane.

Life on the run was sweet for Ruby Sparks. He had struck a blow against Dartmoor and won his own freedom. It felt much more satisfying to have come over the wall than for the warders to have opened the gate at the end of a sentence. Moreover, at this time a sentence was not temporarily suspended while the escaper was at liberty, as it is today. If he was able to stay away until the sentence expired, the authorities could do no more about it. However, if he was recaptured within his time, and all but a few were, his sentence was prolonged by the loss of remission.

Ruby went to ground in a detached house in Wembley Park with The Bobbed-Haired Bandit. It was wartime, but he lay back and enjoyed the spring air, ate decent food and lived off the £800 handout that his friend the boxing promoter had slipped into his pocket. But as always the excitement and easy pickings of crime beckoned and he teamed up with a man after his own heart, Billy Hill, for some serious smash and grab. Hill, a quietly spoken, low-key fellow with a reputation among his friends for style and generosity, and among his enemies for a ruthless use of the cut-throat razor, was already a first-division villain. A decade later, after outwitting, assaulting and retiring his arch-rival, Jack Spot, Hill would rejoice proudly in the self-proclaimed title 'Boss of Britain's Underworld'.

War or no war, and despite such priorities as the threat of blitzkreig from German bombers or the irritation of wide-boy spivs coining fortunes on the black market, the police were coming in for criticism from the press for not feeling Ruby's collar. At the same time, every significant crime in London was being laid at his door, and his notoriety escalated. The first man to escape from Strangeways and from Dartmoor, the leader of the Dartmoor Mutiny, so it was said, Sparks was now 'Public Enemy Number One' – the first British criminal to receive that dubious accolade.

No risk was too great for Ruby. When he heard that his old mother was at death's door in a Billericay hospital, he immediately hired a Bentley and drove straight there, accompanied by his girlfriend and a pal. Old Bill was expecting him and had every available man surrounding the premises, but he fooled them by getting into the hospital the same way as he had got out of prison – over the wall. Disguised as a doctor in black coat, striped trousers and black homburg, carrying his burglary tools in a medical bag, he shinned up a drainpipe and went in through a window. His exit, through the front door with a stethoscope round his neck, was a little more conventional, but he was recognised and only got away after a chase.

In April, Billy Hill got himself arrested after an abortive raid that Sparks was not on. While Hill had no qualms about working with a man who was so 'hot' in the wanted sense, other villains were not so keen. To be caught on a job with Ruby would mean going down for a long, long time. His old friends were uncomfortable when he was around, club owners, fearing for their licences, did not want him on the premises. The only people willing to work with him were tearaways seeking to make a name for themselves, young men whose lack of criminal sophistication was matched only by their eagerness to indulge in wanton violence.

His luck could not hold out for much longer. On the run in wartime, without an ID card, he could at any moment have been called upon to explain why he was not with one of the Services. Of his two fellow-escapers, Alex Marsh had reached London alone, only to be recaptured a week later, while Paddy Nolan lasted four months. But Ruby's face was one of the best known in the underworld. He was the man Old Bill wanted at any price. In a dog-eat-dog world it was inevitable that some petty criminal would put the finger on him. The surprise was that it had not already happened.

On the afternoon of June 28, Sparks broke his rule of not going out in daylight. As he was walking along a Neasden street, he noticed two large men in overcoats standing on a corner ahead of him. Looking over his shoulder, he saw two more coming up on him. He kept walking, spying a cinema across the street and thinking that if he could get in he could take advantage of the darkness and perhaps slip out through a back entrance. He never made it. Suddenly a police car bore down on him at great speed, mounting the pavement and knocking him against a wall. Two more cars boxed him in and what seemed like the entire Flying Squad fell on top of him. The police were taking no chances with Ruby Sparks.

Game to the last, Ruby protested loudly that he was an innocent pedestrian, that it was an outrage. He even tried to convince a uniformed constable that the large men in plain-clothes were gangsters attacking him. It was no good. He got twelve months added on to his sentence for escaping, the police being unable to bring any evidence of further crimes committed on the run. He was satisfied with that. He went back to Dartmoor and spent the next three months in chokey.

Ruby Sparks never escaped from prison again. When he was released he opened the Penguin Club in Soho and in later life settled down in a newsagent's shop close to London Zoo. His Dartmoor record of 170 days on the run has never been surpassed.

2 JOHNNY RAMENSKY

King of the Cracksmen

Scotland, with its own legal system and prisons, has had its share of high-profile escapers over the years. From Barlinnie to Peterhead they have cut through bars, slid down ropes and scaled walls by any means possible. In 1960 two escaped in their underwear, running along the Glasgow streets as though they were athletes in training. They have stolen bicycles, cars and on one occasion a police van to make their getaway. Few have stayed out for long, but the recapture of one 1954 runner from Saughton, Edinburgh, takes some beating. He was caught naked in a Turkish bath, spotted by an off-duty policeman.

Colourful characters, but the most colourful of all was Johnny Ramensky. A top-notch safebreaker, fitness fanatic, five times jailbreaker and wartime hero, Ramensky achieved folk-legend status in his lifetime and was celebrated in two popular songs*. His prison escapes brought him only hours of freedom, but made headline

---

* 'Set Ramensky Free' by Roddy McMillan and 'The Ballad of Johnny Ramensky' by Norman Buchan

news. When he was released he always went back to crime. Yet he captured the public imagination in a way that few villains ever do.

Ramensky's exploits brought colour into the dull lives of those around him in the Glasgow Gorbals. Ordinary folk admired the audacity of his deeds and his refusal to be crushed by the system. He did the crime and he did the time. He did not complain despite serving sentences that even in a less enlightened age were considered savage for a man who had never hurt anyone and always went quietly. By the time he died, aged sixty-seven, Johnny Ramensky had spent nearly all his adult life behind prison bars. It was a high price to pay, but in the underworld legend does not come cheaply.

Ramensky's five escapes were all from Peterhead, the toughest of Scotland's convict prisons. Like Dartmoor, at the opposite end of Britain, Peterhead is isolated, but located in even wilder, bleaker country, high on the windswept north-east coast, thirty miles beyond Aberdeen. As at Dartmoor, the regime was based on iron-willed discipline, imposed with unrelenting brutality. Prisoners were chained to the walls of their cells, floggings were commonplace and warders carried sabres until the Second World War. If a convict approached within five paces of a warder he was warned to 'stand off' and if he did not do so, the warder drew his sabre.

In the prison quarry, just as on Dartmoor working parties, warders carried guns – and did not hesitate to open fire on any prisoner who tried to escape. In July 1932 one, a Glasgow bank robber named Kynoch, did try – he was shot dead and at the subsequent inquiry the warder who killed him was found to have fired 'in the ordinary execution of his duties'. The dead man's family and the Peterhead convict population did not argue with the word 'execution', although the official account was that the warder fired to wound Kynoch and the bullet ricocheted off a rock and killed him.

As late as 1959 Peterhead warders carried .303 rifles. In that year another convict was shot as he made a run for freedom. He was wounded, the bullet passing through his arm and then ricocheting off a boulder, causing a piece of granite to hit an officer in the eye. This incident brought about changes. A shot convict was acceptable; an injured officer was not. Result: guns were withdrawn from service.

Such was the atmosphere in Peterhead when Johnny Ramensky escaped for the first time, in 1934. Ramensky, however, was not protesting against brutality or repression. He had been hardened to that as a youth in Polmont Borstal, where he went as an eighteen-year-old. Polmont was notorious for its staff's tendency towards systematic violence, while physical exercise was compulsory for inmates. Ramensky suffered the former but absorbed himself in the latter, burning off his anger and frustration and developing what would become a life-long obsession with fitness.

He escaped from Peterhead for a simple reason – while he was inside, serving five years for safecracking, his wife, Daisy, had died suddenly from a heart attack. Johnny applied to the Governor for permission to attend the funeral, albeit under escort and in handcuffs, but he was refused. In a deep depression he was transferred from his cell block to the prison hospital.

Come what might, he had to get out of jail and back to

Glasgow. The funeral went on without him, but he still wanted to go, if only to stand at his wife's graveside. In the early hours of a cold winter's morning, as everyone in the prison slept, Ramensky picked the door lock of the hospital block with a piece of wire he had put by and, barefoot, crept across the courtyard to the outer wall. There he scaled the high prison gate and hung by his fingertips twenty feet above the ground before dropping to freedom. The night was freezing cold. Like every Peterhead escaper before him, he headed south towards Glasgow, 170 miles away. And like every escaper before him, he was soon caught.

The road from Peterhead to Glasgow crosses two bridges, each spanning a fast-flowing river. On hearing that a convict had come over the wall, these bridges were the first places that the police set up road-blocks. In the past a few men had managed to cross the first, at Ellon, but no one had made it beyond the Bridge of Don on the outskirts of Aberdeen.

Ramensky fell at the first. Without warm clothing, without even shoes, he did not stand a chance. Cold and hungry, his feet swollen to twice their normal size, he was discovered in the back of a lorry as dawn broke. He went straight back to Peterhead where he was placed in a punishment cell and shackled to the wall. Cuts on his feet had turned septic, but the prison authorities took no heed. 'I was in agony,' he recalled years later, 'but leather anklets were fixed to my legs and the prison blacksmith welded rings of iron over them.' From these rings, two chains were attached, joined to a leather belt at his waist.

Ramensky endured this barbarism for weeks, with the shackles never taken off. At night it was impossible to get comfortable enough to sleep, as the loops of ice-cold chain tangled with his legs. 'When I had a bath, in a galvanised iron tub, the noise was like a shipyard.' How long he would have remained in these conditions was not disclosed, but after John McGovern MP travelled to the prison and went on to take up Ramensky's case with the Home Secretary, he was unchained – the last man in Scotland to be shackled in a cell.

In the spring of 1938 Ramensky was released from Peterhead. The next couple of months saw a wave of commercial burglaries in which safes were blown from Clydebank down to Manchester. All were top-class jobs, with Ramensky's handwriting stamped all over them, but the police had no evidence with which to charge him. Then in July an Aberdeen laundry was broken into and a safe blown with explosives. This time, with the help of an informer who pointed out his movements on the night of the burglary, and some damning forensic that turned up as a result, there was sufficient evidence to convict him. Sentencing Ramensky to another five years, Lord Russell said, 'I am sure that a man of your ability could earn a living in some honest way.'

Back in Peterhead, breaking rocks with a fourteen-pound hammer, on a staple diet of lumpy porridge and treacle-like tea, Ramensky had almost done his time when, one morning in 1942, he was summoned to the Governor's office. To his surprise he was told that 'people in high places' wished to make his acquaintance and that he would be going immediately to London, under military escort. He was staggered when the Governor shook him by the hand and wished him luck.

After swearing an oath of secrecy and travelling 500

miles by train, he was taken straight to the War Office. There he was treated with a politeness and consideration that he had never before experienced from anyone in authority. He was told that his skills with explosives were needed for the war effort and asked if he would volunteer for 'special service' in the army. In particular, would he be prepared to open safes behind enemy lines? The target would not be money, but secret documents of Hitler's plans.

Safecracking skills apart, nothing in Johnny Ramensky's previous life had prepared him for meetings with military top brass and offers to work with British Intelligence. He was born in the Lanarkshire coalfield, of Lithuanian parents, and his father died when he was a small child, leaving Johnny's mother, who was disabled after an accident, to bring up three children. He left school at fourteen and went into the mines, but lost his job when the Depression struck. His mother moved the family to Glasgow, where he drifted into small-time crime before he realised that there were richer pickings to be had by capitalising on the skills with explosives that he had acquired in the coal mines. From there it had all been downhill – until now.

Ramensky was thrilled. He did not need to ponder the offer that was put to him. 'I was proud to be striking a blow for my country,' he said. He did not return to Peterhead to finish his sentence – the handcuffs were off, the remainder of his sentence was forgotten. He swapped his prison uniform for that of a soldier and went straight into training at Achnacarry Castle in Inverness-shire, the secret base of the British Army's elite commando force.

He found commando training more demanding than

any prison hard labour. He had always been fit – once, in Barlinnie, he had climbed on to the roof and performed handstands in the guttering, waving his feet to the audience gathered fifty feet below. Now, at thirty-seven years old, he was nearly twice the age of many of the soldiers around him, but Ramensky was determined to fulfil the trust that had been placed in him. When the trainees, loaded with equipment, went on speed marches over the moors and up and down the Scottish mountains, some collapsed with exhaustion. Ramensky kept going: he completed the full commando course, the toggle bridge, the 'death ride' – the lot.

Basic training completed, he was promoted to instructor and now spent several weeks passing on his skills in handling explosives to members of the allied forces who were training with the commandos. He taught American Rangers, Free French and Norwegians, amongst others, but the most curious group of all was a squad of former policemen, who sat agog as he methodically explained the tricks of his criminal trade.

Ramensky could open any safe or vault. 'If you know what you're doing it's easy,' he told them. He explained the process: with safes he would place a quantity of gelignite over the keyhole and fix it in position with putty, then attach a detonator with a fuse and cover the safe with anything available to cushion the noise of the explosion. Ramensky's skill lay in knowing exactly how much gelignite to use, and how to pack it in a ballast of sawdust mixed with alum. From a criminal point of view, the ballast could be a handicap as traces of it often ended up on the safecracker's clothes. Such forensic evidence had convicted Ramensky on the sentence he had been serving prior to joining the commandos.

With a vault, the procedure was more complicated. Here a ring of gelignite was stuck on the door and detonated to blow a hole in the door's outer skin. He would then place a child's balloon, always purchased at Woolworth's in Argyle Street, Glasgow, in the hole, sticking a pin across the neck to prevent it falling down. The balloon was filled with more gelignite, another bang and the vault was open.

The full extent of Johnny Ramensky's wartime activities on His Majesty's Secret Service has never been revealed. What is known is that he changed his name to Ramsay and made many missions behind enemy lines, dropping by parachute and blowing safes to acquire top-secret documents. In one single day, when the Allies invaded Rome and took over the German Embassy, he is reputed to have blown fourteen safes and a strongroom that none of the other specialists could make any impression upon. Ramensky had it open in less than half an hour. In Germany, it was Ramensky who opened the strongroom and safes at Hermann Goering's headquarters in the Schorfhleide. As well as the Nazi documents, he could not resist taking a pair of silk pennants that were mounted behind the Reichmarshal's desk – souvenirs that he kept to the end of his days.

Field Marshal Rommel's HQ was another target. Here the prize included plans which contributed to the Eighth Army's advance across North Africa and victory at El Alamein. After D-Day, Ramensky spent almost all his time well ahead of the front line, breaking into premises and cracking the safes as his commando colleagues held the position until the main force arrived. But by 1945 it was all over.

Ramensky was demobbed with a discharge certificate that read: 'Military conduct exemplary. Honest, reliable man who possesses initiative and sense of responsibility.' The old lag who had the distinction of being the last man in Scotland to be shackled in a prison cell had fulfilled the trust that had been placed in him, and more. His efforts were acknowledged by the Chief of Combined Operations, General Bob 'Lucky' Laycock, who wrote Johnny a personal letter:

Dear Ramsay,
  Now that you are leaving the Army Commando, I should like to add to the many messages of farewell which you will be receiving from your contemporaries and friends, my own personal thanks to you for the part you have played in this war.
  May your gallant services to your King and country be rewarded in the future by peace, prosperity and happiness.

In reality, for a man who, by his own admission was utterly addicted to blowing safes, there was little chance of the General's hopes being fulfilled. Ramensky was demobbed in York with a travel warrant home to Glasgow, but he did not use it. A York jeweller's shop housed a safe reckoned to be robber-proof. The man who claimed, 'No safe ever defeated me,' cracked it with little trouble. He had just pulled out £2,000 worth of loot when the police arrived. His war record helped in court, but it was back to jail for another five stretch.

This passed uneventfully, but when he came out he was only free for seven days before he was caught once more, blowing a safe at Cardonald post office, near Glasgow. Again his war record was brought up in court. The judge was impressed, but it still meant another five years. Back behind the grim, grey walls of Peterhead he thought up an idea that might secure his future, a life away from safes and gelignite: he would write his memoirs and on release try to sell them to a publisher. He did so, secretly, because prison rules forbade such literary ventures, and by the time he had finished, the manuscript ran to a quarter of a million words – three times the length of an average novel.

Ramensky never saw his life story in print. On the day before his release he was called before the Governor and told that his manuscript had been impounded by the Secretary of State and that it would be destroyed three months from the day of his liberation. He had been working on it for four years, but that was the last that was ever heard of Johnny Ramensky's autobiography. Why were the authorities so keen to suppress it? Was it his indictment of the harsh conditions inside Peterhead? Was it Ramensky's knowledge of secret operations during the war? There were rumours of a D Notice, but the truth of the matter has never been revealed, nor has the fate of the manuscript. Was it destroyed or does it lie on some dusty prison department shelf to this day?

Prior to the sorry and untimely end to his book plans, Ramensky escaped again from Peterhead. By now he was in his late forties and so well known to every member of staff that he had been given a trusty's job as orderly in the hospital block – the same block from which he made his first escape. Again he went by night – he was there when roll call was taken at 10 p.m. but was nowhere to be found when it was taken again at 8 a.m. the next morning. He had gone over the wall in the night and set off down the road on a borrowed bicycle.

Inside his shirt he carried the beginnings of his memoirs, written in school exercise books, but his main motivation in going, like last time, was a woman. Although he had only been out a few days prior to this sentence, he had struck up a relationship with a widow, Lily Mulholland, and they kept in touch after he returned to prison. But there was to be no reunion with Lily just yet. At the Bridge of Ellon Ramensky was recaptured at the same spot as last time, by the same policeman.

He came out early in 1955. Despite the disappointment about his book, he had every intention of going straight. Lily had waited for him and in February they got married, the bride in a polka dot dress and the old safecracker in a hired morning suit. Of his prison past, Lily said, 'That was the last time. Johnny has changed now.' Ramensky, his stocky, five foot seven inch frame as fit and muscular as ever, said, 'I am too old to face prison again.' But the summer drew him and two pals to the seaside – and a bank at Oban.

The haul from this job – £8,000 in cash plus jewellery from deposit boxes – should have given him the new start he had often said he would settle for, but it soon went into bookmakers' pockets and in hand-outs to folk on hard times. A policeman described him as 'one of the biggest-hearted men in Glasgow' after he saved one old woman from eviction by paying off her rent arrears, and he was known to have quietly helped many families in the Gorbals at different times. Late in his life, interviewed by journalist Colin Neil Mackay, he admitted being something of a Scottish Robin Hood telling him, 'I was a crook, but I was living well. I saw men I knew trying to make a go of it the hard way, but there was no work for them. To keep their families from starving they got just shillings from the government. Yes, I helped a few of those lads – but they didn't know where the money came from.'

The Oban job was followed by another bank – and capture. In November 1955 he went up before Lord Carmont, scourge of Scottish villains, at Glasgow High Court. Carmont was not impressed by the fifty-year-old safecracker's war record, and even less impressed by his criminal record. For the one and only time in his life, worrying for his wife, alone in their Gorbals flat, Ramensky asked the judge for mercy. None was forthcoming. Carmont said he was going to send him to preventive detention, 'where you will be out of harm's way for a long time'. He gave him ten years.

So Johnny Ramensky went back to the bleak north-east, to Peterhead, to start all over again. Ten years? It was twice as long as any of his previous sentences. The judge must have made a mistake – surely his sentence would be reduced. But it was not, and three years later, in 1958, Ramensky was still eating lumpy porridge and drinking thick tea. Something had to be done to put the matter right. So Ramensky did the only thing he could – he escaped.

That year he escaped from Peterhead not once, but three times. In January he was out only a day after sloping off from the breakfast queue, forcing a skylight and borrowing a ladder to help him on his way. In October he left during the evening recreation period. A seven-year-old boy found him two days later, hiding in a barn behind bales of straw. He was weak and hungry, but when the boy's father offered to drive him back to the prison his pride would not let him give in. He set off, hobbling across fields, where the police soon picked him up.

A week before Christmas the hue and cry went up yet again. Because of heavy rain, forty-five prisoners, including Ramensky, took their exercise in a prison hall. Suddenly it was noticed that there were only forty-four. The safecracker, with the help of another inmate who devised the plot and provided a replica master-key, went into hiding in a space under the floor of the doctor's office. The authorities were baffled – every road-block drew a blank and even the policeman at the Bridge of Ellon began to wonder if Ramensky had somehow slipped across, without eating the dinner that the officer's wife had thoughtfully cooked for him. While all along the wanted man was lying doggo under the floorboards in the doctor's office, being fed and looked after by his pal as he waited for a suitable opportunity to leave.

It looked like fifth time lucky, and such was Ramensky's popularity that few people, outside or in, begrudged him his freedom. On Boxing Day he left his hideaway under the floor and took the familiar route over the outer wall. He made it to Persley Bridge at Aberdeen, not far but further than he had ever got before. This time he was picked up after a lorry driver gave him a lift, recognised him and told the police. He went back to Peterhead, where an inquiry was in progress to try to establish how a known escape risk could escape three times in one year.

The Peterhead Governor, Duncan Mackenzie, was

called to the Scottish Office to offer his explanation of recent events. Despite the problems Ramensky caused him, the pair of them got on well. Mackenzie was horrified to hear one bureaucrat suggest that Ramensky should wear a suit of canary yellow at all times, so that he would be easily recognisable when he escaped. The Governor argued that the real way to deal with him was to move him to an open prison. He told officials, 'Remove the challenge and he's got nothing left.' Neither recommendation was followed and Ramensky served nine years of his sentence.

Johnny Ramensky kept on breaking into safes, but he never again broke out of prison. Even at safecracking his day had passed. At one bank he miscalculated and used so much gelignite that two policemen, walking along the street outside, were blown off their feet. On another occasion he tried to blow up a boiler, mistaking it for a safe. In July 1970 he fell off a roof while making a getaway, crashed to the street below and spent three months in hospital before a court gave him two years in prison. His last stand came on top of a multistore in Ayr. When he appeared in court his counsel said, 'He has been on more roofs than the famous fiddler.' He was sentenced to twelve months, and in November 1972, at the age of sixty-seven, he died in hospital after collapsing in Perth Prison. His funeral in the Gorbals was a major event in the Glasgow calendar, attended by hundreds, gangsters and straight folk alike. It had been a hard life. For the King of the Cracksmen, crime did not pay.

3   ALFIE HINDS

The Learned Fugitive

During the 1950s and early 60s, escapes from British prisons increased dramatically. Between 1955 and 1961, as the prison population grew from 17,427 to 23,188, escapes from closed prisons rose from 29 to 114. In the same period total escapes shot up from 148 to 700. Crumbling Victorian jails, staff shortages and the phasing out of the old system, with its single cells, rule of silence and strict discipline, were some of the reasons put forward for this new trend. Now the emphasis was on a liberal regime. Not everyone agreed that this was such a good idea. A liberal approach was all very well, said prison officers, but without a doubt more prisoners would escape.

More did, none so famously as Alfie Hinds. Three times in the late 1950s he broke out of custody, all during the same sentence. He escaped because he maintained that he should not have been in prison. He claimed he had been fitted up by the Flying Squad and he escaped to conduct a campaign to publicise his grievances. From being a small-time criminal, unheard of outside his own manor, Alfie Hinds became front-page news as the Jailbreaker Extraordinaire who took on the prison authorities, the police and the finest legal minds in England – and gave them a run for their money.

Hinds was promoted into the big league in 1953 when the Lord Chief Justice returned early from his holiday in the South of France to try his case, which he described as 'of national importance'. It was a serious matter, certainly – £38,000 worth of cash and jewellery was stolen. But how the robbery of a Tottenham Court Road furniture store, in which no one was hurt, could be described as of national importance, Lord Goddard never explained.

At the end of the trial, which Goddard interrupted over 700 times in two days, Alfred Hinds, thirty-eight years old, was convicted by the jury and given twelve years' preventive detention, a sentence introduced five years earlier to protect society from habitual criminals for long periods. He vehemently protested his innocence. When, two years later, his appeal was turned down and a petition to the Home Office was dismissed, he was left with no means of legal redress. There were two options now – he could swallow his pride, if not his bitterness, and get on with doing his time, or he could escape. He chose to escape.

He formed a plan to go to the Republic of Ireland, from where he would conduct a campaign to prove his innocence. This idea was based on the misplaced notion that if he was picked up in Ireland the police would have to apply through the courts to extradite him. He was banking on Irish hostility towards the British authorities working in his favour.

In Nottingham Prison he met a smash-and-grab geta-way driver, Patsy Fleming. A Cockney like himself, Fleming was a man who had no intention of serving his own eight-year sentence without at least taking time out along the way. Fleming had two escape plots brewing. One involved a mass breakout with keys, while the other he intended as a private venture.

Hinds did not want to get involved in any mass incident – he was anxious not to commit one crime to prove his innocence of another, and escaping from prison carried seven years maximum. He reasoned that if someone else made the break and he simply followed, he would be guilty of breaking only prison rules and not criminal law. He knew that to be involved in a mass escape would be risky and that such an escape would be unlikely to succeed, because in all probability a prison informer would blow the whistle and the escape bid would be foiled. That was exactly what happened but, fortunately for Hinds as well as himself, Patsy Fleming, who was found in possession of a key, avoided transfer to another jail. Fleming now began to consider his fall-back position, with Hinds as his willing and ever-helpful assistant.

As far as Fleming knew, Hinds was merely helping him to get out, there was no discussion about him escaping too. That was all right by Alfie, who, ever careful to cover himself, did not want to face a con-spiracy charge if it went wrong. So, on Friday 25 November 1955, as other prisoners mingled on evening association, Fleming made his way through a stokehole and into a cellar then, using improvised keys, he climbed through a grate into the prison yard. Breaking into the carpentry workshop, he carried off two doors, propped them up against the prison wall and went over. He was hiding in a private garden when he heard a sound behind him and turned round. Having said goodbye to Alfie Hinds as he disappeared down the stokehole, he was greatly surprised to find him now standing on the other side of the wall.

'What are you doing?' he asked.

'I'm coming with you,' Alfie said.

With a lorry waiting to pick him up, Fleming did not want to arouse any unwarranted attention by arguing the matter. There was little he could do but invite Hinds to join him in the back of the lorry where, hidden between orange boxes, they passed through a police road-block and went all the way to London, dumping their prison clothes along the way, near Leicester.

By the time Patsy Fleming was recaptured in the East End three months later, Alfie Hinds was sitting comfortably in a Dublin cottage, complete with an Irish accent and the new identity of Arthur Maffia. It was hardly the most inconspicuous alias, but his new neighbours accepted it without question. 'That's a grand old Irish name,' said one, when he introduced himself. Hinds discovered later that she had thought he said Arthur Murphy.

Before leaving England he had written a series of letters to newspapers, explaining that he had escaped only to draw attention to his case and offering to give himself up if he was guaranteed a thorough inquiry into the circumstances surrounding his conviction. The press had seized on these letters and he received a lot of publicity. Now, from Dublin, he conducted his campaign through telephone calls with his wife, Peg, who kept up the momentum, even to the extent of appearing in a BBC Television interview to state Alfie's case.

While this was going on at home, Hinds began to study the basics of English law. In the National Library he met a man who worked as a porter at Trinity College and, with the man's help and posing as an English legal expert who was in Dublin doing research, he wangled his way into criminal law lectures at the college. He changed his identity again, this time to McKenna, a Belfast man, and was free for eight months. Then, as he visited a shipping company the day before his wife and children were due to join him, he was arrested at gunpoint by thirty detectives.

Hinds stuck to his latest identity and declined all knowledge of the fugitive Englishman. Much to his disgust he was visited by a police officer who he claimed had committed perjury at the Old Bailey in his case. Soon Detective Inspector Tommy Butler of the Flying Squad arrived with a warrant and Alfie was on his way home in handcuffs. Besides protesting his innocence of the charges that had put him in jail, Hinds now protested that he had committed no further offence by escaping and had thus been wrongly extradited from Ireland.

The matter was first aired in court at Nottingham Magistrates' Court, where local reporters were most surprised to see a prisoner turn up carrying Stone's *Justices' Manual* and a pile of papers. Hinds read from a prepared statement and told the court that the Director of Public Prosecutions did not want him to appear before them – he had demanded the right to be there. 'It is part of the charge against me that I escaped from prison while serving a twelve-year sentence. It is part of my defence to this charge that my sole purpose for escaping was to get before a public court proof of my innocence.' He asked for a letter to be produced, the contents of which would show that his trial had been unfair. All this was way above the heads of the magistrates, who decided that the letter ought to be a matter for a judge at the Assizes.

Alfie appeared at the Assizes, having subpoenaed various prisoners, officers and policemen. The jury, however, were not impressed by the argument he put forward; he was found guilty of escaping from prison and eleven days were added to his sentence. By now he was representing himself, but when he told the Court of Appeal judges that no common-law offence existed in the case of an escape from prison by a convicted person, Mr Justice Byrne told him his view of the law was 'completely erroneous'.

In Pentonville Prison, Hinds pored over his law books. After several false starts he found grounds for issuing a writ under civil law, suing the Prison Commissioners. The least he could get from this, he figured, was a day out to attend court, which might of course provide an opportunity for another escape.

In June 1957 Alfie Hinds went to the Law Courts in the Strand. A locksmith friend had already taped a small padlock and key under a certain table in the court canteen. Alfie had no problem persuading his two-man escort to take him for a cup of tea, and he collected the padlock as they sat at the table. After that he said he needed to go to the toilet and the warders obligingly removed his handcuffs, but insisted on accompanying him. Hinds was first to reach the toilet, where he spied two screw-eyes, one fixed to the door, the other to the jamb. With the padlock hidden under his coat, he invited the warders to go in first. They did, whereupon he slammed the door behind them, slipped the padlock through the screw-eyes and locked the warders inside the toilet.

He had worked out a getaway route on earlier visits. Dashing out into the waiting hall, he took advantage of the people milling around and soon got out of the building, knocking over a sixteen-stone messenger as he went. He had taken only a few steps along the street when he came face to face with his wife, Peg, who knew nothing of the plot and was on her way to court to hear his case. Giving her the wink, he ran down the Strand to the Temple tube station and boarded a train for Waterloo where, half an hour later he was picked up by his brother, Bert, and Tony Maffia, brother of Arthur, whose identity he had previously adopted for his alias.

They whisked Alfie to London Airport, but he had missed the Dublin flight, so they took him on to Bristol. His brother went to buy the £6.7s air-ticket, in case Alfie's description had already been circulated, but he attracted the clerk's attention when he gave her two £5 notes and did not pick up the three pound notes in his change. The ticket clerk knew the police were seeking a man for the murder of two local children and thought Bert might be this man. The police were called and he, Alfie and Maffia were all arrested, after much confusion as to whether Alfie or Bert was the wanted man – and what he was wanted for. It was a strange twist of fate, and when the clerk later said that if she had known it was Alfie Hinds she would not have breathed a word it was little consolation. By then he was back in Pentonville on hunger strike.

His two accomplices, brother Bert and Tony Maffia, each got twelve months for assisting Hinds to escape. Sentencing them at London Sessions, the magistrate said they were guilty of a cunning, ingenious and very nearly successful plan. He told them: 'We are in no way interested in either the publicity or the propaganda which is at present going on on behalf of Alfred Hinds, who has alleged grievances.' Tony Maffia, a prosperous fence and well-known gangland figure, was murdered in 1968. A Manchester coal merchant was convicted of his killing, after trying unsuccessfully to implicate Alfred Hinds.

After twenty-six days, Alfie called off his hunger strike – just in time to be put on fifteen days' bread and water for escaping from custody. Predictably, he voiced a great deal of argument about the legality of the charge, but the main thing on his mind was finding another opportunity to escape. When, without warning, he was transferred to Chelmsford, it looked as though this was going to be very difficult. On arrival there he was ordered to sleep with his hands and head outside the blankets, and an electric light burned constantly in his cell. If the night-watchman, who peered through the cell door's judas hole at regular intervals, could not see him moving in his bed, he kicked the door until he did – making sure it was a man and not a dummy lying there.

These were only the night precautions. By day Hinds wore a uniform with foot-square black and white patches sewn on. Every time he moved about the prison the warders had to sign a book which went with him everywhere. Before long he said he did not know whether he was a magpie or a registered parcel.

There was one ray of hope. His hunger strike had come to the attention of a group of MPs and thirty of them tabled a motion asking for his case to be re-opened. But anticipation soon turned to disappointment when the Home Secretary said no, so Hinds decided that he had better escape sooner, rather than later. He looked round for a suitable running mate and found one in Georgie Walkington, a Shoreditch factory-breaker doing seven years, who had been over the Chelmsford wall once already.

As he had done in Nottingham with Patsy Fleming, Hinds did not let on to Walkington that he wanted out. At least, that was Alfie's story and he stuck to it. Walkington went ahead with his plan to go on a Sunday morning, while a lot of the prisoners on the wing were at church. On 1 June 1958 he gained access to a store and, using keys he had earlier obtained, got into the grounds. Hinds used a fellow prisoner as a decoy to dodge the ever-present attention of the warders and followed him. That was all right by Walkington and the two of them climbed up the wall by balancing wheelbarrows on top of each other, scrambled over barbed wire and dropped twenty-five feet on to a path outside the prison.

Climbing up the wall, Hinds smashed a lens in his glasses, then, as he fell to the ground, he felt a sharp pain shoot up his leg. There was no time to hang about and assess injuries though, for as they perched on top of the wall they had been seen by the caretaker of the school next to the prison and he raised the alarm. Hinds crawled to the road, and a waiting Morris Minor, only to find that Walkington could not remember how to drive it. There was no alternative – bad leg or not, Alfie had to drive and, taking back lanes and country roads because he knew police blocks would be up on all the main routes, he drove all the way from Chelmsford, under the Blackwall Tunnel and deep into the Kent countryside.

They arrived at a smallholding, kept by a friend of Walkington who recognised Alfie and was not pleased to see him. He had expected Walkington to arrive alone and feared that a man as well known and wanted as Hinds would bring only trouble. The smallholder's anxieties eased when one of Hinds' friends brought some money down and the pair of fugitives moved into a caravan. After a few weeks Hinds' leg recovered and it was time to move on. Georgie Walkington went home to London, where the regulars at his local had a whip-round for him. He was recaptured soon afterwards at Wimbledon dog track.

As always, Alfie Hinds' destination was Southern Ireland, although this time he risked neither flying nor the Dublin ferry. He got a friend to drive him from Kent to Liverpool and he sailed to Belfast, moving down to Dublin by train. From there he flew to Paris, to be interviewed by a reporter from the *Daily Mail* – choosing France in order to throw his pursuers off the scent. His brother Bert had made an arrangement with the paper and Hinds received £1,000 as well as a great deal of publicity from the story which was run under the headline 'I Find Hinds In France'. With funds which his wife had saved from stories in other papers, he had around £3,000 put by. He went into business in Dublin.

William Bishop, alias Alfred Hinds, motor trader, had a small office in Kenilworth Square, Dublin. His wife and children joined him from England and life was

44

reasonably comfortable. It might have remained that way had the business not involved the smuggling of cars from the Republic to Belfast. That came to an end on 13 January 1960, when William Bishop was arrested by customs men on a Belfast street. He did not go quietly – he had been free for twenty months and had no intention of throwing the towel in without a fight. Taken to the customs office, he broke away from his interviewers and dived head-first through a glass door. Bleeding and grazed, without any idea of his bearings, he found himself running towards the basement where he was trapped.

Fortune had not yet totally deserted him, however. No one had questioned his identity as William Bishop. It was looking as if he might get a few months on the smuggling charges and serve them without being rumbled or, even better, get bail now and quickly disappear. But before he became too optimistic the authorities discovered his true identity. Next time he appeared in court he arrived in a cavalcade of police cars, handcuffed to detectives as armed police ringed the building.

Appeals, applications, affidavits and writs flew in every direction on Alfie's behalf, from mandamus to habeas corpus and back again. His knowledge of the law and legal procedure was impressive, but after serving a six-month sentence in Crumlin Road Jail he once again faced a depressing homeward journey in handcuffs. A Sunday newspaper had paved the way for him by printing his story and at London Airport he was greeted by reporters and cameramen. He went straight to Chelmsford, to escapers' patches on his uniform, a cell in the punishment block, and a by-now familiar argument with the Governor about whether he was being held as a serving prisoner or one on remand accused of an escape that he of course denied.

When he appeared in Chelmsford Magistrates' Court on the escaping charge, the authorities adopted a crafty ploy and denied him the opportunity to air his many grievances with the legal system. The prosecutor withdrew the charge, with the result that Hinds, much to his annoyance, was not allowed to speak. He went to the House of Lords next, appealing against an earlier decision to reject an application for habeas corpus. Escorted by three warders and opposed by Treasury counsel and a team of five lawyers, Alfred Hinds, self-educated in the law, represented himself better than any QC. The decision again went against him, but he battled on and two months later was back at the Lords again. This time he spoke for eighty-two minutes.

By now Hinds had been moved from Chelmsford to the new maximum-security wing at Parkhurst. Escape had become secondary to litigation in his priorities, although a further excursion across the Irish Sea was not completely out of the question. He had been in Parkhurst about a year when a group of inveterate escapers began to put a plan together. The fitting of a newly designed lock on all cell doors served only to spur them on. When the time to go arrived, Hinds declined their invitation, preferring the company of his law books, but he lost fourteen days remission anyway, because another prisoner had unbolted his cell from the outside.

In 1962, still in Parkhurst, Alfie at last got a break.

Detective Superintendent Herbert Sparks, the police-man who had led the original case against him back in 1953, published a series of articles in the *Sunday Pictorial* in which he stated that Hinds should have admitted his guilt. Three years earlier, from Ireland, Hinds had circulated a notice alleging that Sparks had committed perjury against him and pointing out that in another case in 1955 a jury considered that he had manufactured evidence against a defendant, with the result that Sparks' counsel agreed substantial out-of-court damages.

The Parkhurst Governor suppressed the newspaper containing Sparks' article, but Alfie got hold of a copy nevertheless, sued Sparks for libel – and won. It was a result against all the odds. He was awarded damages of £1,300, but the real triumph was the verdict, which amounted to a reversal of the jury's finding of guilt at his trial. A month after this case was heard, two years on from the offending articles and eleven years after he was imprisoned for the robbery he had continually and consistently maintained his innocence of, Hinds was released on the order of the Home Secretary. He went to the Court of Appeal one more time to try to get his conviction quashed, but his luck did not run this far.

Alfred Hinds earned a place in legal history as well as in the folklore of the East End of London. He was the underdog who refused to lie down, who escaped three times and fought relentlessly, until a court at last took notice. In all he represented himself in seventeen court appearances, fourteen in the High Court and three in the House of Lords. When he came out of prison he wrote a book, *Contempt of Court*, detailing his case with all its legal complexities, before building a successful business career. He left London to live in Jersey, where he became secretary of the local Mensa Society. He died in 1991 at the age of seventy-three.

4   CHARLIE WILSON

The Silent Man

The Great Train Robbery – one of the truly classic crimes of modern times – occurred in the early hours of Thursday 8 August 1963. At 3 a.m. in thick fog, fifteen men stopped the Glasgow to London night express at Bridego Bridge in Buckinghamshire. After hitting the fifty-eight-year-old driver with an iron bar, the robbers broke into a Royal Mail coach containing high-valued packages and in a swift and perfectly executed operation, departed with £2,631,684 in used banknotes.

It took Scotland Yard little time to discover the identities of most of the men they were looking for and the following year twelve of the robbers were sentenced to a total of 307 years' imprisonment. Seven of them – Charlie Wilson, Gordon Goody, Roy James, Jimmy Hussey, Bob Welch, Tommy Wisbey and Ronnie Biggs – each got thirty years. Parole had not yet been introduced and so, with a third remission for good behaviour the best they could hope for, they were looking at twenty years behind bars.

'Stiff bird' by anybody's reckoning. At a time when

the average life sentence for murder amounted to around ten years, the train robbers' sentences suggested that British justice valued government property twice as much as human life. The men appealed of course, but the thirty-year sentences stood and that, apart from rounding up the remaining members of the gang and trying to find more than £2million still missing, appeared to be the end of the matter. And it was – for a month – until Charlie Wilson escaped from Winson Green.

Charles Frederick Wilson, a Clapham man, was thirty-two years old, five foot eleven inches tall, with a fresh complexion, thickish lips and a dimpled chin. Although his only previous form worth talking about amounted to two short sentences for dishonesty, Wilson was in the top league of London criminals. In 1962 he had robbed a Clapham bank of £9,000, hitting a cashier with a pick-axe handle. He was arrested, only to be released when no one was prepared to identify him. The same year he was acquitted of a £62,000 wages snatch at Heathrow Airport, a raid set up as a dummy run to finance the planning of the train robbery.

Married with three daughters, Wilson described himself as a bookmaker. He was convicted of the train robbery through evidence of finger- and palm-prints found at Leatherslade Farm, where the gang shared out their loot immediately after the robbery. During a two-month trial he gave no evidence, called no witnesses and spoke less than half a dozen words. He was known as 'The Silent Man'.

Wilson had not said a lot more since arriving at Winson Green, an overcrowded Victorian jail two miles from the centre of Birmingham. He was regarded as a quiet inmate who caused no trouble. His share of the robbery had been £150,000 but he voiced no complaints about his routine job in the prison workshop, where his weekly wage was three shillings (fifteen pence), most of which he spent on newspapers. After he had escaped – on a Wednesday – it seemed to puzzle the authorities that he had paid for his papers until the end of the week.

When his appeal came up on 8 July 1964, Wilson chose not to attend the hearing in London. Both his conviction and sentence were upheld, but he took it all in his stride. It was if he had expected nothing better and was resigned to doing his time with as little disruption as possible.

The reality was different. For Wilson to have attended the hearing would have meant his being transferred beforehand to a London jail. There he might have remained indefinitely, or been moved on to somewhere else. Charlie Wilson did not want to leave Winson Green at the moment. He knew that within a few weeks he would be leaving anyway. Wilson had friends on the out, friends who could get anything or do anything he wanted. These friends could even get duplicate master keys for one of Her Majesty's Prisons – and break in and rescue him. It was only a matter of time.

That time came in the early hours of 12 August. Using a rope ladder, three men came over the wall into the prison and, with a key made up from a soap impression of an officer's own pass key, they opened an outer and two inner doors. As they reached C Wing, where Wilson was located, the elderly night-watchman was making his 3 a.m. patrol. He was knocked down, tied up and gagged.

Wilson had been on the escape list since arriving at

Winson Green. Every night his clothes were left on a chair, outside his cell. His rescuers did not know which cell he was in, but out of 500 men in the block, only sixteen were on the escape list, so he was not hard to locate. After looking in several cells with clothes outside the door, they soon found their man, opening him up with another duplicate key. They had no trouble from prison staff – one night-watchman was taken care of and the only other one on duty was in the kitchen, cooking the breakfast porridge. He knew nothing of any escape or assault on his colleague until the police told him later.

Wearing clothes that his rescuers had brought with them, Wilson and the three men back-tracked through A Wing and the bath-house, out into the grounds. There was not a soul about and it was a simple matter to climb back up the rope ladder, drop over the wall and drive away in two waiting cars.

Birmingham came to a standstill that morning. No one got to work on time. As hundreds of uniformed and plain-clothes police conducted house-to-house inquiries in the crowded streets around the prison, detectives and dog-handlers were turning over premises across the city. Every villain and his known associates were called to account. All routes out were blocked and traffic built up for miles in every direction as police questioned drivers.

The whole area was agog with speculation. Was Charlie Wilson still in Birmingham? Was he still in Britain? It had long been rumoured that a criminal mastermind, a Mr Big, had planned the Great Train Robbery – was the same person behind the escape?

Was it true that Wilson alone knew the whereabouts of the £2million-plus that remained unrecovered? And if so, had another gang sprung him to get to the money? Then there were the keys that had been used to unlock him – no keys had been reported missing from the prison, so how had his liberators got hold of duplicates?

Such was the level of local excitement that a large number of people believed they might know the answers to at least some of these questions. The police were inundated by hundreds of callers who claimed to have seen something suspicious, including a housewife living close to the prison who told them that two men and a blonde woman had been sitting in a car outside her house at the time of the escape. At 2.45 a.m. the woman had knocked on her door and asked the time in 'either a Black Country or a Cockney accent'.

A close study was made of all names on the Winson Green visitors' register for the previous weeks, to try to establish who might have had the opportunity to contact Wilson. His lawyers had seen him several times regarding his appeal and his wife, Patricia, had visited on three occasions. Speculation about what had taken place on these visits led to Mrs Wilson taking out a writ for libel against the *Daily Mail*.

Caravans and cottages on the banks of the River Severn were visited, along with flats, bed-sits and any likely premises, empty or occupied, throughout the Midlands. Every police station in Britain was issued with Wilson's description. As thousands of police sought the escaper and those who had sprung him, a spokesman warned, 'These are obviously desperate, dangerous men who will stop at nothing.'

And all the while, as the furore gained momentum, Charlie Wilson sat quietly in a Birmingham flat. For two days he and his liberators made no effort to leave the area. They followed developments by radio and television, and then, once all road-blocks had been removed, they drove steadily to London where, for the next few months, the fugitive train robber remained in a Knightsbridge hideaway.

Wilson's escape was the first in living memory in which a top-security prisoner had been liberated by accomplices breaking into a jail. It was audacious in the extreme, but fully in keeping with the mystery and mythology surrounding the Great Train Robbers, especially the silent, smiling Charlie Wilson. His escape was also the first of what was to become a series of break-outs by high-profile prisoners serving very long sentences. Soon, prison escapes would be a regular item on the parliamentary agenda, but for now political reaction seemed fairly muted. The Home Secretary, Henry Brooke, did admit to being 'seriously concerned', while the General Secretary of the Prison Officers' Association thought Wilson's departure 'abnormal', as he believed security arrangements at Winson Green to be sufficient to meet all normal requirements.

Within the prison there had been many rumours that Wilson was to be sprung, but rumour is endemic to prison life. Besides – had not Wilson ordered the week's papers in advance? And he had drunk his cocoa as usual before retiring to bed. Hardly the sort of actions one would expect of a likely escaper . . . so the theory went.

But the press pulled no punches in criticising the ease

with which Charlie Wilson had slipped away. 'A Monumental Scandal' declared *The Times* the next day:

> Maximum security prisons – and Winson Green is rated as one – are so-called because they are supposed to be extremely effective in stopping people from inside from getting out. On the available evidence from Birmingham to date they are not nearly so effective in stopping people outside from getting in. The audacious recognition of this tactical truth by the conspirators who early yesterday broke into the gaol to release Charles Frederick Wilson must make the prison service a laughing stock among the criminal classes . . .
>
> An act as outrageous as this would not be committed if there were not some very powerful incentive . . . The implications are sinister and this time the public has the right to demand that the authorities get to the bottom of it. That is what must be done. That the need should ever have arisen is a monumental scandal.

The Chief Constable of Birmingham, instructed by the Home Secretary, launched an immediate inquiry into the escape, appointing his head of CID to the task. The first objective was to try to establish how the intruders had obtained a master key to open double-locked doors to the cell block. Keys and locks for the prison service were distributed by the Home Office and the possibility that a set to fit the Winson Green locks had got into the wrong hands was being considered, as was the possible involvement of a corrupt member of the Winson Green staff.

Nine days of interviews with 700 prisoners and 300

members of staff produced a 50,000 word report. At the outset the Home Secretary was undecided as to whether publishing the report would infringe prison security, but he need not have worried. Charlie Wilson and his friends had already infringed security – and as to how they had been able to do it, the inquiry did not unearth one clue. Nor did a police exercise a week later. Detectives with stopwatches and notebooks stood in the rain outside Winson Green at 3.15 a.m. re-enacting the escape as it was believed to have happened. The only people missing were Wilson and his liberators.

So far there had been red herrings and wild goose chases aplenty. An advertisement in the Personal column of the *Daily Mail* the day before the escape was studied by detectives, who thought it might have been worded as a message to Wilson. It read:

W – in W almost at breaking point, Cott 11.30 today, please 4 Roser.

The explanation of this cryptic clue was not disclosed. A police spokesman said, 'We are keeping an open mind about this advertisement, no possibility is being over-looked.'

At Port Hamble, near Southampton, a yacht that went missing from a marina, six days after the escape, was thought to be a clue. It was later found drifting off the Devon coast. Similar attention was afforded a red mini-car, stolen in Devon and found abandoned near Winson Green.

Relentlessly the search continued. A report that Charlie Wilson had been seen in Burnley caused the biggest commotion in that Lancashire town for many a year. A man who approached the *News Of The World*, claiming to have helped Wilson escape, was soon turned over to Scotland Yard. A surprised resident of a Brighton hotel had his stay curtailed when the Flying Squad whisked him back to London for questioning and from all over the country more reports of Charlie Wilson sightings flooded in. They were all investigated. Every trail ran cold.

There were reports too from further afield, none more important in its outcome than that of a man in South Africa who, adding a little glamour to his life, impressed girlfriends by making them believe he was the hunted train robber, Charlie Wilson. When one went to a newspaper and a story was printed, complete with photograph of her with the 'fugitive', his real identity was found to be John Bradbury, a London villain. The South African police decided to take a closer look at him. What they saw resulted in Bradbury being convicted and sentenced to death for the murder of a Johannesburg mining engineer – a sentence that was commuted to life imprisonment after he gave extensive statements to the police about London gangs.

The police were in no doubt that the duplicate keys used to free Wilson had been obtained through the cooperation of a corrupt Winson Green prison officer. There were only half a dozen master keys within the prison and they were closely guarded. Not closely guarded enough, though, because a forensic examination of them revealed traces of soap on one. Unpalatable as the idea was to the authorities, it was obvious that an officer had taken an impression of a master key on a bar of soap and passed it on to the train robber's accomplices. The Director of Public Prosecutions considered all the evidence obtained in the police investigation, but there was insufficient to bring charges.

This situation was relished by the inmate population. Prisoners like nothing better than to see the authorities embarrassed and the escape of a Great Train Robber, followed by an impenetrable cloud of suspicion hanging over the entire staff, was enthusiastically acclaimed, not only in Winson Green, but throughout the prisons of the land.

Then, five months after Wilson escaped, a Winson Green prison officer was suspended. Fifty-one years old, married with two children and ten years in the job, he pleaded guilty to accepting £500 as an inducement to assist a fraudster to escape. He had agreed to provide hacksaw blades to cut the bars on a washroom window, a rope to get over the wall and a car outside. Sentencing him, the judge said, 'Not only did you betray a trust but the nature of the crime is in itself appalling. The maximum sentence is two years imprisonment and that is not a day too long for you.' Fingers pointed and heads nodded, but the man denied any involvement with Charlie Wilson.

As months went by in the Knightsbridge flat where he had remained since three days after his escape, Charlie Wilson realised that the only hope of any sort of freedom or even reunion with his wife and children lay abroad. His family, friends and associates – the *crème de la crème* of the London underworld – were receiving constant police attention and it was clear that the authorities' humiliation meant that no stone would be left unturned in the search for him, no matter how long it took.

In March 1965, seven months after he went over the

wall, Wilson boarded a cross-Channel ferry at Dover. His passport said he was Ronald Alloway, his appearance suggested a schoolteacher on a hitch-hiking holiday. At Calais he was picked up by a friend and driven to the south of France, where, three months later, his wife and the youngest of their three daughters joined him.

But Mrs Wilson was not keen on France and the French, so Charlie, ever the family man, applied to emigrate to Canada. He was so confident in his new identity of Ronald Alloway that, while he waited for the paperwork to be processed, he nipped over to Mexico City and spent Christmas with Buster Edwards and Bruce Reynolds, fellow train robbers who had so far avoided having their collars felt.

In January 1966 Charlie Wilson arrived in Montreal. He knew no one, he was on his own in a strange country, but at least they spoke English. He rented a flat, bought a car and looked round for a suitable place to put down roots. He had £2,000 in sterling and $7,000 in American money. The rest of his share of the train robbery was in London, invested by a gangster friend. In August, his wife and three daughters arrived, the first time the whole family had been together since before his arrest.

The inhabitants of Rigaud, a small town of 1,200 people, west of Montreal, accepted the quiet, bearded Englishman who started up a business selling silverware, china, pots, pans and glassware. 'He was a respected and well-liked member of the community,' said one neighbour later. He became friendly with the local estate agent, Perry Bedbrook, who sold him a two-acre plot of land for $4,000 and introduced him to an architect and builder.

Living in his new ranch-style home, guarded by

Alsatians, a Pontiac and Volkswagen in the drive and the children happy in their Canadian school, Charlie Wilson felt comfortable. He told Perry Bedbrook that before arriving in Canada he had been in the business of buying and renting homes, adding that he was having trouble getting money out of England and was worried about the devaluation of the pound. Nevertheless, he and the estate agent spoke of going into business together.

Wilson also had plans for an unlikely partnership with a Polish priest. They aimed to start up an investment company to hold funds for Roman Catholic parishes, reinvesting their money in Switzerland. But before these ventures could materialise, Charlie needed what was left of his share of the train robbery.

When he telephoned London he was told that his nest-egg amounted to a sum much less than he had expected. By the time his gangster friend arrived in Rigaud it was less still – £10,000 in Bahamian notes. The explanation was 'bad investments' and Wilson had no alternative but to accept it.

But the friend from London brought more than Charlie Wilson's money. He also, indirectly, brought Chief Superintendent Tommy Butler of Scotland Yard, accompanied by fifty Mounties. Butler, known as 'The Grey Fox', had a personal mission to arrest all the Great Train Robbers – and re-arrest those who escaped from prison. The information that led him to Rigaud came not from the London underworld, but from the French Riviera, where a detective had overheard a female relative of Wilson's mention Canada in conversation. When Butler heard this he had a watch put on all the train robber's close contacts, thus the

London man was followed all the way to Rigaud.

At 8 a.m. on Thursday 25 January 1968, as he drove his children to school, Charlie Wilson stopped to help the occupant of a car that appeared to have slid off the road into a ditch. When he got out of his car, he discovered to his cost that the man in the ditch did not need help. It was Tommy Butler. 'Hello Charlie,' he said. 'You're nicked.' The Mounties moved in, but they were not needed. The hunt that had lasted three years and five months was over.

The true identity of their neighbour Ronald Alloway came as a shock to the good people of Rigaud. They took the line that he could have told them he was one of the most wanted men in the world. Perry Bedbrook, the estate agent, said, 'All his friends are dumbfounded and a little mad because he conned us.' The recaptured train robber, he said, had a reputation for counting every penny and not being a man of wealth.

After three days in custody, Charlie Wilson went from his new life in Canada back to his old one in prison. It was an eventful journey which began before the plane left Montreal when an official of the Quebec Superior Court tried to serve a subpoena on him. Had the document been served, Wilson would not have legally been able to leave Canada, but the Scotland Yard men had travelled too far to fall for a simple trick like that.

At Heathrow, as the plane touched down, every corner of the airport was guarded and the tarmac ringed by police. Eighteen other passengers disembarked before Wilson was hurried down the steps with a raincoat over his head, handcuffed to a detective. On the flight he had been surprisingly cheerful, chatting to detectives, eating a continental breakfast and enjoying the last gin and tonic he would see for a good number of years. The other passengers were warned by cabin crew to keep away from him, but one told reporters at Heathrow, 'If they had train robbers on every flight I would fly BOAC every time.'

Wilson was hustled between two Flying Squad men into the back of a Rover police car for a high-speed dash to Parkhurst Prison on the Isle of Wight. It was almost too high-speed – at Cosham, close to the ferry terminal, the police car crashed into another vehicle, causing a five-car pile-up. No one was hurt and Wilson was transferred to another car for the last leg of his journey to the most secure jail in Britain. There, in the special security block, he was welcomed by five of his associates in the Great Train Robbery gang.

For Wilson's parents, news of his recapture came as a relief. His father, William Wilson, a bus driver, said he was glad his son was back in prison, 'At least he can't get into any more trouble. My wife, Mabel, has been worried to death about him since his escape. We haven't known for more than three years whether he was dead or alive.' He said he had not seen his son for ten years or more. 'I hardly recognised him when I saw the pictures in the papers last week.'

Charlie Wilson did not try to escape again. Whenever the subject was broached, on prison landings or in recreation rooms, he said that his wife could no longer face life on the run. He was paroled from Pentonville in 1978 at the age of forty-six, having served twelve years. In 1982, £2million VAT fraud charges, relating to the sale of krugerrands, were dropped after he paid £400,000 to Customs and Excise. Two years later he spent four months on remand for armed robbery, but was freed after allegations of police corruption. Soon afterwards he went to live in Spain.

On 23 April 1990, Charlie Wilson answered a ring on the doorbell of his hacienda-style villa at Las Mantanas on the Costa Del Sol. He let in a pale-faced young man and the two of them walked across a patio towards the swimming pool. There the man kicked fifty-eight-year-old Wilson in the testicles and smashed his fist into the train robber's face, breaking his nose, before taking out a 9mm Smith and Wesson revolver and shooting him twice at point-blank range.

Six months after Wilson was murdered, a London drug dealer, Roy Adkins, who had allegedly ordered the £5,000 contract killing after being wronged by a friend of the train robber, was gunned down in an Amsterdam cocktail bar.

5   RONALD BIGGS

The Loser who got Lucky

Ronnie Biggs was nothing grander than an unsuccessful petty criminal before the Great Train Robbery. He was not one of the leaders of the robbery gang, but he nevertheless got a thirty-year sentence. Biggs had served less than two years when he became the second train robber to escape and, ever since, his ability to remain free and his colourful lifestyle have meant that he has become the best known of all the robbers. Any would-be prison escaper looking for a role model, need look no further than Ronald Arthur Biggs.

Biggs' early life gave no indication of the infamy he was to achieve. Unlike some of his train robber colleagues he had no impressive criminal pedigree, no reputation as a hardman or fearless blagger. He made his first court appearance at fifteen for stealing pencils, was sent to a remand home for thieving his brother's watch and at nineteen he exchanged a dishonourable discharge from the RAF for six months' porridge. Two months after he came out he went to Borstal, absconded, and ended up at the Old Bailey on a string of charges that sent him down for three and a half years.

In Wormwood Scrubs, Biggs became friendly with two men who were to play important roles in his life. One was Bruce Reynolds, a sophisticated villain with an ability to plan and organise serious crime. The other was Eric Flower, with whom Biggs set about trying to escape. On this occasion they were caught in the early stages, chipping a bar out of a toilet window. Next time they would have better luck.

Biggs was only out six months before going back for another six months and on his release this time he met his wife-to-be, Charmian. They took a ride in a stolen car and Charmian, eighteen years old and a headmaster's daughter, was put on probation while Biggs went back inside for a year. In 1960 they got married and for a while Biggs settled down to legitimate work as a self-employed carpenter. All was going well until a customer for whom he had done an expensive job told him he could not pay. Needing money, Biggs approached Bruce Reynolds and asked him for a loan of £400.

Reynolds had a better proposition: the opportunity to pick up a minimum £40,000 by taking part in a job he was helping to put together. Ronnie Biggs could not resist that sort of temptation. His criminal career so far had been a catalogue of failure, this time everything would be different. This was to be the Big Tickle that would set him up for life. But Reynolds' proposition turned out better and worse than anticipated. Biggs came out with £148,000 – and a thirty-year sentence.

Ronnie Biggs was in Wandsworth when Charlie Wilson escaped from Winson Green. He was delighted to hear the news, but, along with the other train robbers, soon found that he would be picking up the bill for Wilson's freedom. That same morning the Home Office announced a tightening of security measures. At night Biggs had to leave all clothing outside his cell and to sleep with the light on throughout. He was subjected to frequent moves from one filthy cell to another, checked every fifteen minutes and new constraints were placed on visits, recreation and work. After three weeks all this was grating on Biggs' nerves. He wrote to his MP, explaining the situation and asking for help.

Biggs listed his complaints: he was not allowed open visits, which meant that a prison officer sat in and could hear everything that he and his visitors discussed; he could not attend evening classes or the occasional concerts held in the prison; he was allowed to work for only two hours a day and to take one hour's exercise, thus he was out of his cell for only seventeen hours each week. This lack of activity – when he did work it was only sewing mailbags – had caused him to become three stones overweight.

He told the MP, as he had told the Wandsworth Governor, that he was anxious to settle down and keep out of trouble and to earn maximum remission. 'But,' he said, 'the extra aggravation I am being subjected to is making it very hard for me.' Rather than finding it more difficult to escape, he concluded, he was finding it difficult not to. Whether or not the MP regarded this as idle talk, subsequent events would prove it otherwise.

When Marcus Lipton did not reply to his letter, Biggs became more despondent. He appealed to the Wandsworth Governor, but he was under strict Home Office orders and could do nothing to relax the security. It was clear to the train robber that prison was going to be very uncomfortable for a long time to come. His mind now moved urgently towards escape.

Through his wife, Biggs contacted the gang who had sprung Charlie Wilson, but they were not taking further commissions. One Great Train Robber was enough for the time being. Then he got to discussing his predicament with a fellow prisoner, Paul Seabourne, who was soon to be released from a four-year sentence on which he had lost all his remission.

Seabourne was no novice at getting out of prison. In 1961 he had organised a mass escape from Wandsworth, when ten prisoners attacked warders in the sack shop and went over the wall. Well-respected in the jail, he had no love of authority and saw helping Biggs get away as the least he could do for a man serving such a long sentence. He took no persuading.

Over the next few months, various ideas were discussed. Biggs discounted a helicopter air-lift on the grounds that as soon as a helicopter was seen above the prison he would be swiftly hurried indoors. Seabourne suggested an armed, commando-style raid on the prison at night, but Biggs rejected that too. He had no wish to leave in a wave of violence. If he was going he wanted a clean escape, not a bloodbath. All aspects of security at Wandsworth were studied for a loophole and eventually they hit on the outer wall that bordered on the exercise yard.

But how to get over it? As a maximum-security prisoner Biggs was always under observation, even while walking round the yard. The operation would have to be pulled off in seconds rather than minutes, it was not going to be a case of throwing a rope over the wall and hoping the prisoner was in the vicinity. Between them, they came up with the idea of a furniture van. If part of the roof was cut away, a hinged platform could be built inside and, when required, the platform could be raised to the height of the prison wall. The van would be driven up alongside the wall and from the top of it ladders could be dropped down into the yard. Since exercise was held at the same time each afternoon, there was no problem about knowing when Biggs would be on the yard.

Seabourne was released from Wandsworth in June 1965 and immediately set about the plot, financed by £10,000 provided by Charmian Biggs. He brought in two friends for £2,500 apiece and bought an old removal van for £240. Once this was repainted and converted, he obtained a rope ladder, a tubular ladder, an axe and a shotgun.

Biggs, meanwhile, had been joined in Wandsworth by his old friend Eric Flower, who was awaiting appeal against a twelve-year sentence for armed robbery. He had escape plans of his own, but when Biggs invited him to join his, he jumped at the chance. Flower's impending appeal meant that he could have daily visits, so it was now easy to pass messages in and out of the prison.

The escape was set for 3 p.m. on Thursday 8 July 1965. Charmian Biggs was to make sure she had an alibi by taking the children to the zoo and, to prove it, getting a time-stamped ticket for her new Rover 2000. When the day came, Biggs and Flower went out for an hour's exercise at 2.30 p.m., along with twelve other men on the escape list. They had been walking round the yard, with growing apprehension, for over half an hour when a red furniture van drew up outside the wall, in full view of prison officers' houses. Biggs, aware that it was already 3.05 p.m., heard the van draw up with a mixture of relief and anxiety. Seconds later he saw Paul Seabourne's

69

hooded head appear over the top of the wall and two ladders were thrown down into the yard. As two prisoners, who had each been paid £500, held off warders, Biggs and Flower dashed to the ladders. Directly above them, atop the wall, sat Seabourne, brandishing a loaded shotgun.

At the crucial moment Biggs froze. He stood at the bottom of the ladder, unable to move a muscle. From somewhere he heard a voice shouting to him, 'Get going!' and he was jolted out of his trance. Up one ladder he went, as Flower took the other. They reached Seabourne on top of the wall and dropped over on to the raised platform, through the hatch and down into the furniture van. They were out!

But there was a complication. No sooner had they landed inside the van than two other prisoners, not involved in the plot, appeared on the top of the wall. The sight of ladders coming into the exercise yard had proved too much of a temptation for them to resist. Never a mean-spirited man, Biggs waved them on and all four, plus Seabourne and his accomplices, sped away in a hired Zephyr.

Immediately a massive manhunt swung into operation. For nearly a year police at home and abroad had been seeking one escaped train robber, now they were seeking two. When the alarm went up that Biggs had gone – the prison had to dial 999 as there was no direct link with the police – every police car in London was mobilised and an immediate watch set up on all sea- and airports.

This time there was a little more to go on than there had been when Wilson escaped. The furniture van was left behind, plus the rest of Seabourne's equipment, including a loaded shotgun. The original plan had been to set fire to the lot, but just as petrol was being sprinkled the unexpected gatecrashers appeared on top of the van. Their opportunism proved costly to Biggs' rescuers. In the haste to get away, evidence was left, including fingerprints that later convicted them.

At their trial, Paul Seabourne admitted organising the escape, but said none of the five men who stood in court with him knew anything about it. He was alleged to have received 'rich financial reward', although he had only twelve shillings on him when arrested and told the court, 'That is how I stand now.' He was sentenced to four and a half years' imprisonment. It is a generally held view amongst villains who knew him that Seabourne's motivation in springing Ronnie Biggs was based more on his sense of loyalty and justice than on money.

Official reactions to the escape were rather muted. There seemed to be great care on all sides not to say anything that might upset the prison officers of Wandsworth. Detective Chief Superintendent Richard Lewis, head of West Division CID, told reporters, 'The escape was engineered without a doubt with collusion inside the prison. This does not suggest that there are any prison officers involved.' Sir Frank Soskice, the Home Secretary, visited Wandsworth and said, 'I can find no reason to think that any blame attaches to the prison service.' It was left to *The Times* to remind readers that, after the Wilson escape, a Winson Green prison officer had been convicted of helping another prisoner in an escape attempt, and to point out that British prisons had been 'built in a horse and buggy age'.

71

Four days after the escape the Home Secretary again absolved the prison service from any blame. He told the Commons that the report of the Home Office inquiry disclosed 'no reason to think that any member of the prison service was guilty of misconduct or negligence'. At this, a Labour MP said, 'The over-whelming majority of the people find themselves sympathising with the men who have escaped, and the reason is that a property-owning judiciary has imposed sentences ten times as heavy as they would for the most brutal crime against a child. While this kind of sentencing goes on you cannot have public sympathy behind it.' As politicians on both sides of the House shouted, 'No, no,' the Speaker ordered him to with-draw his remarks which were, said one Tory member, 'a slur on the judiciary'.

But if no one knew who was to blame for the latest escape, or where the escaper might be, former Home Secretary Henry Brooke knew the way to prevent fur-ther escapes. He told the Commons that the only way to stop long-term prisoners from escaping was to hang them. The Murder (Abolition of Death Penalty) Bill was about to become law, but he said that the case for retaining hanging had been strengthened by the escapes of Wilson and Biggs, 'The five or six people now serving sentences of more than twenty years could not be deterred from further crimes if they escaped, by any-thing short of the death penalty.'

The men who had freed Biggs were not hard to find, but as to the train robber's whereabouts, the police were clueless. Flying Squad informants were put under pres-sure to come up with the names of those who might be hiding him, with rich rewards offered for any information leading to his recapture. Figures as high as £10,000 were mentioned.

Just as it was in the aftermath to Charlie Wilson's departure, the homes of villains everywhere, as well as those of their friends, families and next-door neighbours, were enthusiastically turned over by the police. And once again the search wandered – albeit at high speed and with urgency – down a number of blind alleys.

A tip-off the day after the escape led armed police with dogs and tear gas to Winterfield House, a mansion near Cranleigh in Surrey. A cordon was placed around the house and all roads in the area were blocked. Three hours later the mansion was discovered to be empty.

A similar turn-out, but supplemented by a helicopter and a contingent of Royal Marines, swamped Upton House, the Poole home of Prince Carol of Rumania. Coincidentally, the prince was a director of the property company involved in purchasing the Cranleigh mansion, raided two days earlier. Both prince and property company suddenly became the focus of publicity of a most unwelcome kind – until the Home Secretary's private secretary cleared Prince Carol of any involvement with Biggs or his escape.

From Wandsworth Jail, Ronnie Biggs and Eric Flower were driven at breakneck speed to Dulwich, five miles away. The two gatecrashers were given thirty shillings each and left to make their own way in the hired Zephyr as Biggs and Flower switched to a Cortina and went straight to the safety of a top-floor flat rented by a friend of Paul Seabourne. They celebrated their first night of freedom drinking champagne as they watched news of their escape on television.

They kept on the move, staying with a docker in Bermondsey and a private detective in Putney, before moving into a rented holiday home at Bognor Regis on the south coast. Here they had brief visits from their wives and children before returning to a Kennington flat owned by a friend of one of the police officers on the Great Train Robbery investigation.

For £40,000 Biggs had done a deal with a top-level criminal fixer to get himself and Flower to any part of the world that took his fancy, plus plastic surgery and passports. They had been on the run three months when they were smuggled out of England to Antwerp in a Dutch freighter. From there they were driven to Paris, where, apart from an eventful trip to the Folies Bergère, they spent day after boring day in a flat, with a minder who refused to let them venture out. They had gone to the French capital primarily to undergo plastic surgery, which was intended to make them unrecognisable. After the operation Biggs was left suffering excruciating pain with 140 stitches and serious doubts as to whether he had made a mistake.

With his new appearance and a passport in the name of Terence Furminger – writer – Biggs was ready for what he hoped was to be the last leg of his journey to a new life. Some time earlier he had read a book, *The Weird Mob*, which had impressed him by its portrayal of a beer-swigging life Down Under. On New Year's Eve 1965, with £700 in his pocket and the rest of his ill-gotten gains back in England, he flew in to Sydney Airport. He met up with Eric Flower, who had travelled separately, and they rented a house. Biggs got a job in a furniture factory and six months later he was joined by his wife Charmian and their two children.

The Biggs family settled in Adelaide and Ronnie decided that a straight, no-crime, no-risks life was the only way to stay free. To come under the eye of the local constabulary for even the slightest misdemeanour could put an abrupt end to the good life. He got a job as a roofing contractor and, when a third child was born, the family's new-found happiness was almost complete. Then a whisper came from England that Scotland Yard knew he was in Australia. Biggs could take no chances. He put wife, children and furniture into a $600 truck and did a moonlight for Melbourne.

His £148,000 fortune had all gone. £30,000 of it had been left in London with a crooked solicitor – so crooked that he would not give it back. Another name change – to Terence Cook – and Biggs found work as a carpenter at Channel 9 TV studios. His finances were so low that, after getting The Seekers pop group to autograph a $10 note, he had to cash the note soon afterwards.

Again the net began to close. Word reached Britain that the train robber had been picked up by Australian police on a drunk and disorderly charge – but released before his true identity was known. Then a home movie which supposedly showed him swimming off the Australian coast was broadcast on British television. In October 1969 Eric Flower was arrested in Sydney. The law descended on the Biggs residence – but Ronnie had already gone. He had heard from the television news that Flower had been taken. Worse, he had seen his own photograph right there on the screen. He had to leave, very quickly. When the police swooped, his wife Charmian was taken into custody but soon released, to pick up $65,000 from a newspaper story.

Biggs had to find a new hiding place. He settled on Brazil, impressed by a travel brochure photo of the Sugar Loaf Mountain and the fact that the country had no extradition treaty with Britain. Using a passport in the name of a friend, Michael Haynes, and $2,000 of Charmian's money from the newspaper, Biggs set sail for South America on the *Ellinis*, a passenger liner. He was the life and soul of the party aboard ship, organising games for the other passengers and enjoying a fling with a young English woman. Amazingly he revealed the truth of his identity to her. Even more so, she kept it to herself.

In Rio de Janeiro, Biggs dropped into an agreeable routine of wine, women and samba. Once again his life was in limbo, but he had known worse places than Copacabana Beach. Then in February 1971 he received bad news from Charmian – their eldest son, Nicky, had been killed in a car crash. The family, still in Australia, had been constantly in the glare of publicity, much of it hostile, since Biggs departed. Now the pressure on his wife, alone in her grief, was close to being unbearable.

Biggs thought about giving himself up, but came to the conclusion that this would not help his wife and two remaining children. Instead he remained incognito in Brazil, tempering his despair in the jazz clubs of Rio, with no shortage of female company to take his mind off his family far away. Three years passed and little changed, until in early 1974 a London journalist, Colin

Mackenzie, turned up in Rio with an offer of £35,000 for Ronnie Biggs to tell the latest episode of his story to the *Daily Express*.

Mackenzie discovered Biggs' whereabouts by a chance conversation with a man he hardly knew. The man had recently returned to London after some time living in Rio and told him of a man he knew as Michael Haynes, who had one day revealed that he was actually the escaped train robber, Ronnie Biggs. Mackenzie phoned Biggs, confirmed he was who he said he was, and set off for Rio and the scoop of his career.

Biggs was wary – another train robber, Jimmy White, had been nabbed after reputedly coming to an 'arrangement' with the *Express*. He was right to be wary, but it was too late. Mackenzie's editor had covered his own back by informing the police of the journalistic mission. No sooner had Biggs begun recounting his story, reclining on the bed wearing only a pair of red trunks, when who should tap on the door of Room 909 of the Hotel Trocadero, Atlantic Avenue, but Old Bill, in the form of Detective Superintendent Jack Slipper, his sidekick from Scotland Yard, Brazilian plain-clothes men and the British consul.

'Hello Ronnie,' Slipper greeted him. 'Long time no see.'

'Fuck me!' replied Biggs. 'How did you get here?'

Slipper's offer – a pair of handcuffs and a one-way ticket to Wandsworth – looked like an offer that Biggs was not going to be able to refuse. Biggs was taken into custody by the local police and it seemed only a matter of getting the paperwork sorted before he would be on a plane back home. But the Brazilian authorities were not going to be rushed. They were bound by no obligations of international diplomacy – Britain had no extradition treaty with Brazil – and having discovered they had one of the Great Train Robbers in their country, they wanted to have a good look at him before letting him go. Deadlines came and went, Biggs stayed in jail and Slipper of the Yard became very frustrated.

Meanwhile, without paying Biggs, the *Daily Express* ran their headline scoop – and the world's press descended on Rio. The story now was not just about a train robber having his collar felt, it was twisting and turning like the last act of a racy melodrama.

Centre stage was Biggs' former girlfriend, Raimunda, an athletic good-time girl whose announcement that she was expecting his child caused all bets to be suspended. Under Brazilian law the father of a Brazilian child could not be deported and so Ronnie's prospects took a definite upswing. That he and Raimunda had parted and his affections were now focused on another nubile local beauty, Lucia, did not matter.

As the pregnant Raimunda revelled in the publicity, blowing kisses one minute and bursting into tears the next, Biggs cheerfully gave press conferences in jail for the benefit of the international media. Then the inevitable question arose – what about Charmian? She was, after all, Biggs' wife. No sooner was the question asked than Charmian arrived in Brazil to answer, flown from Australia by the Sydney *Daily Mirror*. Tears were shed and photographs taken. Mistress and wife posed together, with Raimunda aiming a bow and arrow at Charmian's head, the most recent lover, Lucia, relegated to the background. No scriptwriter could have invented such ballyhoo. The press were loving every minute.

For Slipper of the Yard, Biggs' good fortune was a cross he had to bear. One of the last of the Great Train Robbery investigation team to still be serving in the Metropolitan force, he stayed only four days in Brazil and had no option but to fly back to London empty-handed. He faced considerable, if undeserved, criticism from the British press and, as 'Slip-Up of the Yard', was the butt of cartoonists for some time to come. To his credit, he took it all in good part.

Neither Scotland Yard nor the press emerged unscathed from the Brazilian fiasco. Questions were asked as to how the police and a national newspaper came to be working in such collusion. In the Commons a question was put to the Home Secretary calling for an inquiry into the affair, in the light of a statement from the Melbourne Police Commissioner, who claimed that he had sent detailed information about Biggs' movements to Scotland Yard three years earlier, including his alias Michael Haynes and his route and destination after he left Australia for South America.

Biggs stayed in Rio and Charmian flew home to Melbourne for good. Raimunda gave birth to a son, Michael, and then left for Switzerland to work as a stripper. Biggs brought up his son and became a familiar sight on the beach and in cafés and bars, always available for interview if the price was right. In 1977 he was in the headlines after a drinking session with sailors aboard HMS *Danae* in the Rio docks, and the next year he recorded a song, 'No One Is Innocent', with punk band The Sex Pistols. Shortly after that he survived a kidnap attempt by mercenaries-cum-bounty-hunters.

In 1981 Biggs published his autobiography, *His Own Story*, in which he expressed the hope that one day he might be pardoned by the British Government and allowed to travel to Australia to see his family. This hope was repeated, with more urgency, in June 1992, two months before his son's eighteenth birthday, an event that at the time seemed likely to deprive him of the protective status that had allowed him to remain in Brazil. The train robber told reporters that he would have to appeal to Prime Minister John Major for leniency, saying that he had heard, 'He is a very affable fellow.' The crucial date passed uneventfully and he continued to enjoy life to the full in his spacious three-storey apartment.

A condition of Biggs' licence to stay in Brazil is that he does not work for money, but this has not prevented him from managing the pop-singing career of his son, Michael, or appearing in TV commercials, advertising such products as coffee, safety locks and burglar alarms. When the Earth Summit took place in Rio in July 1992, he was recruited to offer advice to visitors on avoiding becoming the victims of crime. Ronnie Biggs, convicted train robber, said that people take too little notice of safety recommendations, but if he warned them, they would take more. His advice was to avoid taking expensive cameras to the beach and 'not to dress like gringos'.

On the thirtieth anniversary of the Great Train Robbery, in August 1993, Biggs held a party in Rio for 150 guests. As ever, the wine flowed and sixty-four-year-old Biggs was surrounded by beautiful women, many young enough to be his granddaughters. A couple of months earlier Jack Slipper, long retired from Scotland Yard, had visited him in Rio, seeking to finally establish which member of the robbery gang had bludgeoned the train driver, Jack Mills. Biggs welcomed Slipper like an old friend, but evaded all questions that could incriminate his former associates, even thirty years on. They spoke of what might lie ahead if Biggs turned his back on the fugitive life and returned to Britain, but that is most unlikely. Ronnie Biggs has twenty-eight and a half years of his sentence left to serve. Prison lore has it that if he does ever return he will go straight back to Wandsworth, where his old cell and his prison clothes await him.

6 GEORGE BLAKE

The Spy in the Scrubs

Wormwood Scrubs was an unlikely prison to hold a man doing forty-two years. A typical Victorian jail, outdated and overcrowded, it was close to busy streets, backed on parkland, and was only twenty minutes from London Airport. Furthermore, within its walls was a pre-release hostel from which up to fifty prisoners were allowed to leave each day to work at jobs outside the prison.

George Blake arrived at Wormwood Scrubs in May 1961. He had been sentenced to the longest term of imprisonment ever imposed by a British court*. A Foreign Office man, he had admitted spying for the KGB while working for MI6 and was given three maximum sentences of fourteen years, to run consecutively. So much for pleading guilty!

Blake was no ordinary spy and his sentence reflected the damage he had done to British Intelligence. This, together with his intellectual powers and resourcefulness, his experience in manipulating people and the

---

* Since superceded by the forty-five-year sentence imposed on Jordanian terrorist, Nezar Hindawi, for an abortive bomb plot against an El Al airliner in 1986.

strength of his ties with the Soviet Secret Service, should have marked him out as a major escape risk for many years to come. He had more motivation to escape than probably any other prisoner in Britain. But he was sent to Wormwood Scrubs.

The Scrubs had lost a lot of inmates over the wall in the previous couple of years. Twelve escaped in 1959, the following year the exodus continued and in 1961 six went before Blake arrived in May. The numbers slowed down, but it was still remarkably easy for any agile convict with a fancy for freedom to nip over the wall and along Du Cane Road, where he could be picked up by a waiting car.

In contrast to Wormwood Scrubs, other prisons holding maximum-security inmates had been upgraded following the authorities' embarrassment at the Wilson and Biggs escapes. The style of the two break-outs, and the financial and criminal resources known to be available to their associates still behind bars, brought home the fact that this was a new class of prisoner – one able to take on the state and win. The Home Office acted quickly – wings at Durham and Leicester were hastily converted to accommodate escape-risk prisoners and a new Special Security Unit was constructed at a cost of £250,000 at Parkhurst on the Isle of Wight. This prison-within-a-prison was segregated from the rest of the building by high fences and security gates. It had electronic warning devices and closed-circuit television to monitor the inmates' movements. At night the entire perimeter of the jail was floodlit. It opened in February 1966, but George Blake was not transferred there. He remained in the run-down Wormwood Scrubs.

★ ★ ★

Blake was sent to the Scrubs straight from the Old Bailey, because it was convenient for MI5 and MI6, who were to interrogate him for many months to come. He settled into prison life and gave every impression that he was resigned to his sentence and had no intention of even considering an escape. This was a deliberate smokescreen to hoodwink the authorities, for at the same time he was keeping his mind and body active so that if an opportunity to escape did present itself he would be ready. He did yoga exercises in his cell and studied for an honours degree in Arabic, while enjoying popularity among other prisoners by helping illiterates to read and write and giving French and German lessons.

His front worked. On arrival at the Scrubs he was placed on the escape list, but after only five months he was taken off because it was felt that he was not likely to escape. A month later, with his interrogation at an end, the security services recommended that Blake be moved to Winson Green – but the Prison Commissioners said that to move him so far away from London would be a great hardship for his wife.

Such consideration seems surprising when one thinks of the much longer journeys imposed on the families of the Great Train Robbers. As their wives, all London-based, hauled children to Leeds, Liverpool, Aylesbury, Manchester, Parkhurst and, worst of all, Durham, they might have wondered if there was one rule for the middle-class traitor, whose dirty work had reputedly led to the deaths of many British agents behind the Iron Curtain, and another for the blagger who hit the jackpot.

Although Blake was not giving out escape hints, it was

inevitable that rumours of plans to spring him would surface. In 1964 alone, four such alleged plots were investigated. The first came about when a prisoner informed the Scrubs Governor of a detailed plan to get the spy away by helicopter. The prisoner was a qualified pilot with a history of mental instability, a combination that did not help those responsible for assessing the credibility of his story. His flying abilities were certainly not in question – some years earlier he had landed a plane in the Atlantic off New Jersey and hitched a lift to England on a passing ship.

According to what this man told first the Governor and then MI5, Blake was to be flown from the prison direct to East Germany and then onwards to the USSR. The plan also involved an ex-Scrubs inmate – a man who had been expelled from Eton and sent down from Oxford University. This man was to break into the jail and, posing as a trusty, fetch Blake from the mailbag shop where he was working at the time. The ex-prisoner was acquainted with a Foreign Office official who would arrange Blake's reception by the Russians.

After questioning the pilot, the security services came to the conclusion that he had invented the whole story. The Home Secretary commented that the story was fantastic but not impossible, adding that great care should be taken over Blake's custody, and asking whether he ought to be moved to another prison. It was a good question, but the Head of Security Services said that he doubted whether a move was necessary.

A couple of weeks later another prisoner was released from the Scrubs and immediately told the police of conversations he had held with Blake, speaking in French and Dutch. Blake, said the man, had asked him to act as an outside contact and he agreed as he felt forty-two years to be a harsh sentence. He told Blake that he would do what he could to help, but as soon as he was released he told Special Branch the same. Neither senior officials in the Home Office nor the Governor of Wormwood Scrubs were made aware of this situation.

In October a prisoner happened to mention to a passing officer that Blake was to be sprung from D Hall on Christmas Day. The story this time was that he was paying £1,000 to those who were aiding him and he wanted only to be taken to an address in Kensington. Investigations were pursued, but nothing came to light and George Blake spent the season of goodwill in the Scrubs.

The fourth and final alleged plot began shortly before Christmas, with the return to Britain of Patrick Meehan, a Scottish safebreaker who had once been apprenticed to Johnny Ramensky. Meehan knew a thing or two about escaping – in 1955 he helped a prisoner get out of Peterhead and in August 1962 he himself had taken a break from an eight-year sentence by escaping from Nottingham Prison.

Something of an adventurer, Meehan fled to East Germany by way of a quick trip home to Glasgow, a plane to Dublin, another to Frankfurt and, eventually, a bicycle on which he was caught pedalling across the East-West border. Interrogated by the East German secret police in Berlin, he offered his services to them, saying he could arrange the escape of any spy from any British prison. At the time there were quite a few to choose from, but, according to Meehan, the East Germans were only interested in Peter and Helen Kroger, convicted the previous year, and George Blake.

When Meehan was eventually handed over to the British authorities at Checkpoint Charlie, he was flown back to resume his sentence in Wandsworth Jail. His first visitors were the men from Special Branch. He refused to see them, then and on several further visits, but after he was moved to Blundeston, in Norfolk, he agreed to talk to MI5. Later, Meehan told Chapman Pincher of the *Daily Express* that he had warned his interviewers of the East Germans' interest in getting Blake out. Pincher confirmed that Meehan's warning had been passed on to the Director General of MI5 and to the Home Office. However, the later Mountbatten Report, referring to Meehan but not actually naming him, claimed that he had given no such warning. On the contrary, according to Mountbatten, he had told MI5 that his communist interrogators were not interested in George Blake. A mysterious business . . .

Patrick Meehan was at the centre of further controversy a few years later. In 1969 he was wrongly convicted of murder in Scotland and served seven years before being granted a Royal Pardon, following the identification of the real killers.

In the face of all rumours of impending escape, and suggestions that George Blake should be moved to a more secure prison, the spy remained in Wormwood Scrubs. Neither the conversion of the maximum-security wings at Durham and Leicester, nor the opening of the Special Security Unit at Parkhurst, caused Blake any inconvenience at all. Most remarkably, even when the Governor of the Scrubs was asked if he had any recommendations for the transfer of prisoners who posed a high security risk – and he submitted Blake's name – he received no explanation as to why his recommendation was not acted upon.

In mid-1966 the Prison Department received what should have been the most obvious hint yet, that to keep a security risk in Wormwood Scrubs was to almost invite him to escape. On 3 June, the Metropolitan Police informed the prison that two specified D Hall men planned to escape at 7 a.m. on 6 June. Not only were names, dates and time provided, the method to be used was also helpfully described. When the inmates were unlocked that morning, the men would make their break during 'slopping out'.

Sure enough, come 7 a.m. on 6 June, the two men, plus three others, walked away from the 'slopping out' queue, went through a first-floor window – the bars having already been cut – and sprinted twenty yards to the perimeter wall. One was caught, but four of them got over, using a rope to which they had attached metal hooks made from handrail supports off the prison landing.

In an amusing sequel, one of the men, an armed robber, sent his prison clothes, wrapped in a brown-paper parcel and addressed to the Governor of Wormwood Scrubs, to a north London magistrates' court. A note was attached:

Dear Guv,
    I don't want you to think I'm so low as to steal your clothes, so I am returning them except for the shoes, as it hurts to walk barefoot in London.
    Love, D. W. Barnard

He, like the other three, was back inside within days, but

the fact that they had been able to carry out the escape after the authorities had been so clearly tipped off, showed that almost any prisoner who so wished could escape from Wormwood Scrubs.

From Blake's earliest days in prison he kept his eyes and ears open for anyone who might be willing and able to help him escape. At a music appreciation class he met Michael Randle and Pat Pottle, anti-nuclear campaigners who were each serving eighteen months for their part in organising a demonstration at a US Air Force base. They took pity on Blake and when the topic of escape was broached they told him that they would help in any way possible. Before arrangements could be made, Randle and Pottle finished their sentences and were released, but they did not forget Blake and he did not forget their offer.

Blake had no doubts about Randle or Pottle's reliability, but he needed someone to act as a go-between. He found the ideal man in Sean Bourke, an Irishman who edited the prison newspaper. Bourke was coming to the end of an eight-year sentence for sending a bomb to a policeman who had insulted him. He was a trusty and he was also about to move to the pre-release hostel, which meant that he would be allowed out of the prison each day to work, returning at night. Even though the hostel was quite separate from D Hall, messages could easily be passed by other trusties who had access to both parts of the prison. Sean Bourke was eager to help Blake – he was impressed both by the way he did his bird and by the way he got on with other prisoners and he felt sorry for a man who, with full remission, would not be released until he had spent twenty-eight years inside.

Ruby Sparks, first man to escape from Dartmoor.

Johnny Ramensky, Scottish safecracker, war-hero and five times escaper from Peterhead. (*Scottish Daily Record*)

Alfie Hinds and his wife, after a High Court jury had awarded him £1,300 libel damages against Ch. Supt. Sparks of the Flying Squad. (*Press Association*)

Patsy Fleming, who led the way for Hinds to escape from Nottingham Prison in 1955. (*Press Association*)

Charlie Wilson arrives
at Heathrow from
Canada in 1968, to
resume his 30 year
sentence. (*Press
Association*)

Charlie Wilson, Great
Train Robber, who
escaped from Winson
Green Prison in 1964.
(*Press Association*)

Ronnie Biggs, before
undergoing plastic
surgery following his
escape from Wandsworth
Prison. (*Press Association*)

George Blake, spy. (*Topham Picture Library*)

Sean Bourke.

Michael Randle (right). (*Press Association*)

Pat Pottle. (*Press Association*)

Frank 'The Mad Axeman' Mitchell.

Walter 'Angel Face' Probyn, photo issued after he escaped from Dartmoor in 1964. (*Press Association*)

John McVicar, 'Most Dangerous Man'. (*Press Association*)

The Carstairs Killers

Tom McCulloch. (*Scottish Daily Record*)

Robert Mone. (*Scottish Daily Record*)

Billy Hughes, shot dead by police while on the run. (*Press Association*)

Chesterfield women protest at Hughes' funeral. (*Sheffield Newspapers Ltd*)

HOLY GROUND NOT FOR KILLERS

By now, besides impressing other inmates, Blake had ingratiated himself so well with prison staff that he had moved from the mailbag shop and was in charge of the canteen. He had no trouble in finding a place to hide the walkie-talkie set that Bourke purchased and smuggled in. Now the spy in his cell and the accomplice in his hostel room could talk to each other in comfort. Soon Bourke was released and went to live in an outside bedsit. Radio reception was poor, but he got round that problem by going on to Wormwood Scrubs Common, adjoining the jail, and calling Blake from there.

The break-out of the five men from D Hall in June 1966 caused the conspirators some anxiety. Not surprisingly, they feared that security and vigilance among staff would now be tightened. They need not have worried; nothing changed. But two months later, the murder of three policemen in near-by Braybrook Street did put the escape plan on hold and for a while Bourke dared not go on to the common with his walkie-talkie because of the intense police presence in the area.

Bourke bought a car, a Humber Hawk, with £60 provided by Randle and Pottle, whom he had contacted at Blake's behest while he was in the pre-release hostel. The three of them discussed plans for Blake's escape, and possible ways of getting him out of the country afterwards. One Saturday tea-time in late August, Sean Bourke did a test run, sitting in his car outside the prison, speaking to Blake on the walkie-talkie. For good measure he held a bunch of chrysanthemums, as though he was waiting to visit someone in Hammersmith Hospital, the next building along Du Cane Road. All went well and the date of the escape was now fixed.

★ ★ ★

On Saturday 22 October 1966, George Blake ate his tea as usual at 3.30 p.m., watched some wrestling on television and had a bath. There were few prisoners about, most had gone to a film show. At 6.15 he put on his plimsolls, got out the walkie-talkie and called Sean Bourke, who was already in position beyond the wall. Getting the go-ahead, he walked to the landing on the floor above and climbed through a glass panel in the church-like window that took up most of the end wall. A metal bar, which released the panel, had been broken a few minutes earlier by another prisoner. Blake was now twenty-two feet above the ground, but was able to break his fall by dropping on to a covered doorway and a bin. He called Bourke, but the Irishman had hit a problem. Just as he was about to throw his rope ladder over the wall a courting couple pulled up across the road from him and the road was so well lit by other car lights that he was scared the couple would see him.

Blake waited. He had come so far and could not get back into D Hall now. Then, as a transfer to the Parkhurst Special Security Unit flashed before his eyes, the rope ladder came over the wall. Bourke had gone ahead regardless of the courting couple. Up the ladder went Blake, to freedom on the other side. He fell awkwardly, hurting his head and an arm. He and Bourke jumped in the Humber car and sped away. Three minutes later they were sitting in a rented flat in Highlever Road, W10.

Back in D Hall, association ended at 7 p.m. and all prisoners were ordered to return to their cells for the routine roll call. There was no initial concern at Blake's absence for it was common for stragglers to delay the procedure, requiring a second check. When ten more minutes passed and there was still no sign, a call was made to the main gate. The grounds were searched, but if Blake had still been about, he might not have been apprehended, for it later transpired that some officers had never heard of George Blake, let alone knowing what he looked like.

The authorities' worst fears were confirmed when a rope ladder, reinforced with knitting needles, was found hanging from the wall. And so, forty minutes after he was first noticed missing, over ninety minutes after he left D Hall through the window, Scotland Yard was notified that George Blake, serving forty-two years for espionage, appeared to have escaped from Wormwood Scrubs Prison.

Within five minutes nine police vehicles, including dog vans, arrived at the scene and began to search the immediate vicinity. As well as the rope ladder, another clue had now been found – a pot of pink chrysanthemums wrapped in florists' paper. Bourke had been holding it as he stood on the pavement, purporting to be a hospital visitor. Later the Humber Hawk would be found abandoned in Kilburn and tracked back to Bourke.

Once the alarm was raised, a panic alert went out. All the London airports and any small airfield where a light aircraft could land or take off were put under close watch. Special Branch and customs officers at all manned seaports were given instructions. Ships were searched at London docks and particular scrutiny was placed on Eastern Bloc embassies and their staffs.

But in the search for the missing spy the police faced a serious difficulty: few people outside Wormwood Scrubs knew what Blake looked like. As soon as Scotland Yard heard the news of his escape, the Blake file was raised – but amazingly it contained no photograph. Fortunately the Scrubs had one – the one and only photo taken of Blake in the five and a half years since his conviction, despite Home Office instructions that long-sentence prisoners should be photographed regularly and prints sent to Scotland Yard.

Frantic activity ensued. Even though it was now established that a photograph of George Blake did exist, the crisis was not over. It was Saturday night and the prison photographer was not available to make a print from the negative held at the Scrubs. A senior police officer was summoned urgently, but while this was happening Scotland Yard discovered that it was too late for the photo to be reproduced in the next morning's Sunday newspapers, which had already gone to press. All the reporters had left their offices with the exception of one man at one paper. Arrangements were made to hold the front page so that George Blake's photograph could be included. So it was that at 1 a.m. on 23 October 1966 every police force in Britain received an express message calling their urgent attention to the front page of that day's *News Of The World*.

Sprung and hunted, George Blake was much more important to the authorities than he had seemed to be while inside. Saturday night television programmes were interrupted by news-flashes of his escape and the Prime Minister, Harold Wilson, was notified immediately at Chequers. Press speculation as to who had got him out and where he was likely to be hit fever pitch, while leader writers without exception demanded the head of whoever was responsible for the security shortcomings that had allowed such an outrage to happen.

The Times feared that Blake 'probably with alien contacts still in Britain' might have slipped away even before the security net tightened at ports and airfields. The *Guardian* went along with this, ranking Blake on a par with earlier traitors Philby, Burgess and Maclean. Overall, the consensus of opinion was that he had probably crossed the Channel in a small boat and was now well on his way to the USSR.

In the Commons there was uproar. All questions focused on how it could be that Blake was in an ordinary prison like Wormwood Scrubs when there were security units at Durham, Leicester and Parkhurst. With MI5 and MI6 acutely embarrassed and their US counterparts, the CIA, incredulous in their anger, Quintin Hogg MP declared the escape 'delivered a swingeing blow at the national prestige at a time when this country could not afford further blows'.

One explanation put forward for Blake being in the Scrubs was that he had told his interrogators all he knew and was therefore of no further use to the Russians, even if he did escape. Lord Butler, Home Secretary at the time Blake was sentenced, was not impressed. He said, 'Quite extraordinary, I simply do not understand it. It is deserving of some criticism. They should have sent Blake to Parkhurst. I think it is a matter which should be raised in public to find out why.'

Amid many calls from the Conservative Opposition for an independent inquiry, Home Secretary Roy Jenkins appointed Lord Mountbatten of Burma to head an inquiry into prison security as a whole, the Blake escape to be an integral part of his investigations. At this, four MPs, including Quintin Hogg and the Leader of the Opposition, Edward Heath, tabled a censure motion, deploring the Home Secretary's refusal to go along with their wishes. The censure motion failed and what had been an attempt to gain political capital rebounded badly when it was revealed that it was the now-critical Lord Butler who, as Home Secretary, had put Blake in the Scrubs in 1961, in full knowledge of the jail's escape record in preceding years.

What evil force had spirited Blake away nobody knew, though the KGB were odds-on in the betting. And if they could spring him and enjoy the resultant propaganda, as the British Government squirmed in embarrassment, what was to stop them trying to spring others? After years of being regarded as not much different from any other convict, spies were suddenly Hot Prison Property. Less than a week after Blake's departure, three men convicted under the Official Secrets Act were transferred to Durham's maximum-security E Wing. Harry Houghton, five years into a fifteen-year sentence, had to move from Winchester, while William Vassall, four into an eighteen, and Frank Bossard, who had only just begun his twenty-one years, could not be risked a moment longer in the relative ease of Maidstone. For Peter Kroger, five years into a twenty at Wakefield and allegedly named by Patrick Meehan as the one man besides Blake that the Russians wanted out, there was a different destination: he went to the Parkhurst SSU.

In a typical exercise of locking the door after the horse bolted, 'new measures' were announced for Wormwood Scrubs. The prison walls were to be patrolled by day and night. Police with dogs were to be brought in especially to guard D Hall's 320 long-term prisoners. The building of a watchtower was under consideration, as was the use of surveillance cameras for all maximum-security inmates.

None of this could deter the adventurous escaper. While the new measures were still being worked out, one Scrubs inmate hit upon an ingenious idea. He forced apart two bars on a window and fastened a piece of strong elastic between them. He then attached a length of twine to an arrow, which he fired over the boundary wall. A home-made rope was fastened to the end of the twine and the line and rope were pulled tight by two accomplices who waited outside the jail.

Unfortunately for this enterprising fellow, a prison officer saw the rope stretched between window and wall. He raised the alarm, whereupon the two accomplices fled, leaving a stolen car in the street and a frustrated prisoner in his cell.

Theories poured forth as to who got Blake out and where he was now likely to be. No one could rule out the possibility that he had been flown abroad soon after the escape. Every tip-off was acted upon – like the one that he was bound for Sydney on an aircraft from Bangkok. When the plane landed, Australian police checked all disembarking passengers for wigs, dyed hair, false beards and other modes of disguise.

It was suggested that he had been sprung for money by a criminal organisation; that he was a double-double agent who had been acting for Britain all along; that the man who had served five and a half years and gone over the wall was not George Blake at all, and that his escape had been arranged by the security services to delude the communists.

The pot of pink chrysanthemums found at the scene was never likely to be ignored. All manner of significance was attached to that. It was, claimed one Canadian pundit, the crowning touch, the trademark of British Intelligence. 'What makes Britons such marvellous commandos or secret agents is their mischievousness,' said Philip Deane. Even spy novelist John Le Carré had his say; he expressed the opinion that the Russians were behind the escape and had done it for the propaganda value.

George Blake was not in Bangkok, Sydney or Russia. He was still in London, barely a spit away from the Scrubs and in need of a doctor to set the wrist he had broken as he fell during his escape. Michael Randle, his friend from prison, came up with one who was willing to visit the bedsit, even though he knew the identity of the patient.

Soon afterwards Blake was moved to another hideaway and then to Pat Pottle's flat in Hampstead. By now Sean Bourke was well in the frame, following a bizarre and reckless telephone call to the police, telling them where he had dumped the Humber car. Ownership of the vehicle had been traced to him and he was being urgently sought all over Britain and in his native Limerick. Unabashed, he joined Blake at Pottle's flat and plans were laid for the next stage – getting out of Britain.

A week before Christmas, Blake was smuggled to Germany in a Commer van, hidden in a secret compartment beneath the seating. Michael Randle, together with his wife and children, drove him there. All the way from London and across the English Channel the spy was confined in the narrow space, until they reached Ostend. Every time the van approached a border, Blake would disappear back into his hiding place, reappearing when they hit the open road.

Finally, after thirty-six hours without sleep, Randle drove the van into Berlin. There Blake got out, bade them farewell and walked the last few yards to an East German checkpoint and a new life behind the Iron Curtain. A few weeks later Sean Bourke joined him in Moscow, but the Irishman soon became disillusioned with Blake and with the communists.

Bourke returned to Ireland after two years to publish a book about his experiences. He died, an alcoholic, in 1982. Michael Randle and Pat Pottle kept quiet about their role in the Blake affair until 1987. After much press speculation they were prosecuted for assisting with the escape. Both were acquitted after a protracted trial in 1991. Their account of their part in the affair had been published a year earlier. George Blake remains in Moscow, living with his second wife on a KGB pension of 400 roubles a month, in spite of the fall of communism which brought rumours that he could face extradition back to Britain – and Wormwood Scrubs.

7 FRANK MITCHELL
The Mad Axeman

Within the space of just over two years, three of the most infamous prisoners in Britain had gone over the wall. All three escaped with relative ease and the authorities did not have a clue where to begin to look for them. Men whose arrests and trials had dominated the news were once again in the headlines – but now the triumph was theirs. Prisons as a whole were having difficulty keeping their charges within the walls – in 1962, 249 prisoners escaped; by 1966 the figure had more than doubled to 520. Press, public and Parliament demanded action of Labour Home Secretary, Roy Jenkins. Something had to be done. And so, with the post-Blake atmosphere in the Scrubs still, as one prisoner put it, 'like Christmas Day after Santa Claus has been', the Mountbatten Inquiry began.

Earl Mountbatten of Burma, Admiral of the Fleet, aide-de-camp to the Queen and last Viceroy of India, was an unlikely choice to conduct an inquiry into prison escapes and make recommendations for improved security. He had no previous experience of British prisons. Nevertheless, assisted by three assessors, he set about the task immediately, visiting Wormwood Scrubs and studying the route taken by the departing spy.

The Mountbatten Inquiry ranged over all implications of prison security. He or members of his team visited twelve more closed prisons in England, primarily concentrating on the escapes of Wilson, Biggs, Blake, and an incident in May 1966 when nine prisoners got out of a coach returning them to Parkhurst from Winchester Assizes. If he did not learn much that was new about these escapes, Mountbatten would at least be able to highlight some serious security flaws, and recommend ways in which they could be rectified to avoid escapes in the future. For seven weeks the inquiry went on and by mid-December it was complete, the report due for publication any day. Then 'The Mad Axeman' went on his toes from Dartmoor.

Frank Mitchell was one prisoner whose escape could not be treated lightly. His name might not have been as familiar to the public as that of a train robber or a spy, but he was serving a life sentence and he was extremely dangerous. A giant of a man with enormous strength, Mitchell was a thirty-seven-year-old psychopath who had spent most of his adult life behind bars of one sort or another. Sent to Borstal at seventeen, he escaped, was sent back and escaped again. From then on prison sentences of three months, six months, twenty-one months and three years followed with hardly a break.

He had barely settled in at Pentonville for the three years when he attacked a warder and was flogged with fifteen strokes of the cat. Any other prisoner would have slowed down after such punishment, but Mitchell was not a man to be cowed. Physical pain held no fear for him – on the contrary he relished it, wore the weals and scars like medals and proudly boasted that he could withstand anything the prison authorities threw at him. Before long he had outstayed his welcome even in punishment blocks and in July 1955 he was certified mentally defective and sent to Rampton, a secure hospital in Nottinghamshire.

Mitchell thought Rampton would be easy. He later wrote in a letter, 'I thought, Frankie boy, you've made it now – a nice cushy hospital. Let them see you're sane and then in weeks out you go.' He misjudged the situation – 'I had walked into a hell on earth.' In January 1957, after eighteen tempestuous months in the madhouse, he escaped with another inmate. They stayed ahead of the chase for two days by breaking into three houses and forcing the occupants to hide them and to provide them with food. One elderly man argued – until Mitchell hit him with an iron bar and threatened to kill him and his wife with an axe he rested across his knees as he sat watching their television.

This weapon secured Frank Mitchell's nickname – The Mad Axeman. Police warned householders in the area around Rampton to keep doors and windows locked – and to arm themselves if possible. Mitchell had made it clear to his earlier victims that he would kill if necessary as he had nothing to lose. But his freedom was short-lived – the following day he was recaptured by a police motorcycle patrol on the Great North Road. After a display of strength at a special court hearing in Retford, when he lifted a massive oak table and threw it at the magistrates, he got nine years at Nottingham Assizes for wounding with intent to murder. He went back to prison, but within weeks he was certified once more –

this time as insane – and sent to Broadmoor.

He had said that if he was put back in a mental institution he would escape again. He did not break his word. July 1958 saw him climb the Broadmoor wall, after placing a dummy in his bed and opening his cell door in the maximum-security block with a key he made out of a bedspring. For a man who since early childhood had been classed as of sub-normal intellect, Mitchell was no slouch at working out ways to escape from custody.

It was a summer for manhunts – Alfie Hinds had gone from Chelmsford five weeks earlier and thirty other fugitives from Her Majesty's Prisons were currently being sought. None, not even the elusive Hinds, received more attention than Frank Mitchell. As the Broadmoor siren blasted across the Berkshire country-side, a nation-wide search swung into operation. 'DANGEROUS MAN OF BROADMOOR HUNTED' ran one headline, 'CRIMINAL LUNATIC AT LARGE'.

Escapes from Broadmoor had risen in numbers in the 1950s and were a sore point among local residents. It was only six years since John Thomas Straffen, a double child-killer, had escaped and killed a third child, close to the institution. With that tragedy still fresh in many people's minds, the police tried to allay anxiety with a statement that Mitchell was not likely to harm children and was 'not sexually minded'. But, living up to his nickname, he was armed with an axe as well as a billhook when he burst into the home of a couple near Woking-ham, telling them, 'I'm an escaped convict from Broad-moor and I've got nothing to lose.' The sixty-four-year-old husband tried to grapple with him, but was no match for the huge, super-fit Mitchell, who knocked him unconscious.

For an hour and a half Mitchell held the couple in a state of terror. At one stage he set about strangling the wife, but suddenly gave up and sat on the settee, complaining that his feet hurt. With great presence of mind the woman offered to bathe them as well as making him some cheese and pickle sandwiches. Rested and fed, taking ten shillings from the couple for petrol, he then left in their car, ordering the man to start it up because he did not know how. Mitchell had never been at liberty long enough to learn to drive. He weaved about the road and meandered along until he reached Sandhurst, then he abandoned the car and made his way onward to Bournemouth, where he slept on the beach.

The next morning he boarded a London-bound coach, but he had been recognised from his photograph in the morning paper by two men on the beach. They informed the police and the bus was stopped as it approached Camberley. Mitchell tried to bluff it out, but his unmistakeable size and tattoos on his arms gave him away. He said, 'I've had a good run. I'm not hungry but I would like a cup of tea.'

The other passengers were almost sorry to see him get off the coach. Far from instilling terror and mayhem in their midst, Big Frank was the model of courtesy, opening a window for one old lady and reminding another not to forget her handbag.

He was in more rumbustious form the next day when he appeared before Wokingham magistrates, charged with robbery with violence. All was well as he arrived, handcuffed and smiling at the large crowd which waited outside the courthouse. Inside, his handcuffs were removed and he sat quietly in the dock, flanked on either side by his Broadmoor escort.

The first hint of trouble came when the magistrates entered the room and Mitchell was told to stand by a police superintendent. 'Why should I stand for these people?' he asked, but after some grunting he eventually got to his feet. The hearing lasted only three minutes, the chairman saying, 'After careful consideration, my colleague and I have decided that as the Broadmoor authorities did not carry out their duty to hold Mitchell safely, he will be remanded to appear before us next Tuesday. The remand will be to a place where escape is virtually impossible – Brixton Prison.'

This appealed to Mitchell's sense of humour. He threw his head back, roared with laughter and said, 'OK Guv – yes!' Still grinning, he took a few casual steps to the end of the dock platform, swung a right hook at a police inspector, and leaped towards the bench.

The country magistrates, more accustomed to the occasional poacher, or schoolboys who rode bicycles without lights, than escaped madmen, went into rapid retreat as two Broadmoor nurses and five policemen flung Mitchell to the floor. They pressed him down, two others removed his shoes and four more held on to his arms, with Mitchell struggling and shouting, 'I'll get you, you bastards.'

Battle raged on the floor of the courtroom for ten minutes, as the giant escaper, summoning every ounce of his enormous strength, punched and kicked as only a wild man fighting for his freedom can. But he was outnumbered by twelve to one and once his hands were manacled it was all over. Carried out – feet first and still shouting – he was thrown into the back of a van and taken to Brixton.

Brixton was not as secure as the Wokingham magistrate believed. In recent years it had lost its share of prisoners, as Frank Mitchell was no doubt aware when he erupted with manic mirth. He remained there though, until he went up to Berkshire Assizes on the robbery with violence charge. Pleading guilty, he was asked if he would like to say anything before sentence was passed. Mitchell said, 'I stand here through my own folly. All I can say is I'm very sorry I've been to a place where I have. I do not consider myself insane, I just jumped from the frying pan into the fire.'

Mitchell's own assessment of his mental state – that he was not insane – was supported by two doctors who gave evidence. One said he was an aggressive psychopath, but not insane, but the real surprise came from the Medical Officer at Brixton Prison, who said that Mitchell had the average intelligence of any other twenty-nine-year-old and that there had been a great improvement in him since his treatment at Broadmoor. Mr Justice Byrne was unmoved. He told Mitchell, 'Having regard to your record and to the fact that this is not the first time you have been guilty of crimes of violence, I must take steps to protect society from you for some long time to come.' He sentenced him to life imprisonment.

So The Mad Axeman was no longer insane, but he was still dangerous. He went back to jail and a year later was charged with attempted murder of another prisoner, only to be acquitted when the one witness willing to give evidence against him vanished before the case got to court. Soon after that he received another fifteen strokes of the birch for attacking two warders, maiming the hand of one and slashing the other with an improvised knife, so that he required seventy-five stitches.

In September 1962 The Mad Axeman arrived at Dartmoor. Here, after the mayhem of earlier years, he seemed to calm down and to settle into a routine of sewing mailbags in the workshops and pursuing hobbies in his cell. He repaired watches and clocks, made model cars out of scrap materials and took great care of his cage birds. He was also reunited with an old Borstal mate, Fred Benson, one of the few real friends Mitchell had in prison.

Such was the improvement in his behaviour that within nine months of his arrival Mitchell was taken off the escape list and by May 1965 he was allowed out of the prison to work in the quarry. In September 1966 he gained further privileges when he was allocated to the honour party, clearing Ministry of Defence ranges and repairing fences. Each day a warder drove Mitchell and four other prisoners twelve miles or so along the Dartmoor lanes and then left them to get on with their work with the minimum of supervision.

This relative freedom was irresistible to a man who had been locked up and kept down as long as Frank Mitchell. Part of the reason for his new-found good behaviour was the Dartmoor staff's inclination to humour him, rather than direct him. Terrified of his size, strength and reputation, they would give in to his outbursts and demands rather than risk assault. If Frank Mitchell had changed, Dartmoor Prison had changed too. The hard years of Ruby Sparks and co. had passed. The Big House on the Moor had gone soft.

★ ★ ★

Mitchell kept himself at peak fitness, spending hours in the prison gym and more hours doing press-ups and sit-ups in his cell. He liked nothing more than to display his physical prowess and could lift two fifteen-stone men off the ground at the same time, one in each hand. He is reputed to have once picked up the Governor, Dennis Malone, lifting him off his feet. Malone murmured, 'Now Frank, be a good chap and put me down.' At other times he single-handedly lifted out cars that had become stuck in the Dartmoor mud and on special occasions he would lie underneath a full-sized billiard table and raise it off the ground.

Outside the prison, away from watchful eyes, Mitchell took full advantage of the trust and privileges he was allowed, visiting several public houses in the locality. Never short of cash, he took away bottles of whisky, vodka and brandy, as well as flagons of cider, for later consumption in his cell, where they were kept under the bed. Some afternoons were spent in an isolated barn, drinking with the other prisoners in the honour party, others with a woman who met him there. On one occasion he ordered a taxi to pick him up at the Elephant's Nest in Horndon and take him to Tavistock to buy a budgerigar. Another time he went to Okehampton to buy one for his friend, Fred Benson. Frank Mitchell had no complaints about working on the honour party.

He did, though, have complaints about his life sentence and about the uncertainty of ever being released. In a letter to his sister in 1964, he wrote, 'I could have been out years ago if I had not been such a mug, but I got myself such a bad record that it's going to take a good few years to live down. I've done that much cutting and knifing over the years, people take one look at my record and say "Next please".'

He had spent half his thirty-seven years in one form of custody or another and he yearned for a life outside. Despite, or perhaps because of, the honour party, he had become more and more frustrated by his situation, especially after he petitioned the Home Office for a release date and none was forthcoming. He had served eight and a half years and thought that was more than enough, but the Home Secretary thought differently. In a recent speech on the subject of long-term prisoners he had said, 'There may be some who are likely always to be a menace to society, and whom it may never be possible to release. For these a life sentence will mean exactly what it says.'

Mitchell always maintained that he escaped from Rampton and from Broadmoor to prove his sanity. The victims of his terror on the run might not have been convinced, but after Broadmoor did nothing to curb his violence the psychiatric profession came to agree with him. Now he decided that the only way to draw attention to his current plight was to escape from Dartmoor.

In prison Frank Mitchell had a retinue of runners and lackeys, also-rans in the criminal stakes, who did as he bade them. At the other extreme, on the out he had some very powerful friends, none more so that the Kray twins. He and Ron Kray had first met years before in Wandsworth Prison and the twins looked after Mitchell, sending him boxes of clock and watch parts, arranging visits for him and making sure he was provided with cash. Now they would do him the ultimate favour – get him out of prison.

110

Ron and Reg Kray felt sorry for The Mad Axeman. He was a good pal who had been inside too long. He ought to be given a chance. They pondered the matter and came to a decision – if the Home Secretary would not free Big Frank, they would. When all was said and done, it would hardly be difficult. He was halfway out already.

The afternoon of Monday 16 December 1966 was wet. It was too wet for the honour party to repair fencing on Bagga Tor rifle range and so the five prisoners sheltered in a hut. Shortly after 11.30 a.m. Mitchell left the hut and set off across the moor, running nine miles to an isolated telephone kiosk, where he had arranged to be picked up by members of the Kray Firm. No one took much notice of his absence in the hut. Such was the freedom that Mitchell enjoyed that there was no reason to think he had not merely trotted off for a pint, or a cosy afternoon in the hayloft with his female friend. It never crossed the mind of the officer in charge that he should raise the alarm. This officer told the Mountbatten Inquiry that he had given Mitchell permission to take bread to some horses half a mile away at 3.30 p.m. Later he admitted he had not seen Mitchell since 11.30 a.m. 'I did not really think he had run away,' he said.

It was 4.40 p.m. before anyone at Dartmoor saw fit to inform the police at Okehampton that The Mad Axeman was once more on the loose. Immediately all available resources were thrown into the search. As moorland farmers were told to lock their doors and Westward TV broadcast a public warning about Mitchell, a police spokesman said, 'He is an extremely dangerous man who will stop at nothing. He is not to be trifled with.'

Hindered by rain and high winds, marine commandos

joined 200 police in forming a three-ring cordon around the prison, spreading outwards over the desolate countryside. For two and a half hours a RAF Whirlwind helicopter flew overhead, prompting a crew member to tell reporters, 'If Mitchell is there I should think he is very cold and miserable.'

But Frank was not there, nor was he cold and miserable. He was warm and happy in a Barking council flat, sitting down to a meal of steak and chips. He and his rescuers had left Dartmoor long before the alarm – and road-blocks – went up and they had swiftly driven to London. The weather-battered search parties were wasting their time.

Two days later Mitchell's prison clothes were found where he had dumped them, in a lay-by near Exeter. The hunt now switched from Dartmoor to the main road and railway line between Tavistock and Okehampton and the commandos withdrew. In their place came a company of Argyll and Sutherland Highlanders, who caused much merriment among the Devon locals when they began their search to the music of bagpipes.

In Parliament, the by-now mandatory 'immediate inquiry' was demanded by Tory back-benchers, in a motion that asked the Home Secretary 'why a prisoner with Mitchell's history and character was allowed on an outside working party, by whom and on what advice?' Roy Jenkins replied that a former Governor had pressed the Prison Department to give Mitchell a release date. The general view of the authorities was that he had 'matured substantially' and it was thought that 'the fire had burned out'. Jenkins said it was considered that Mitchell would not abuse the trust he was given. He added, 'I very much regret that this trust proved mis-founded.' The Opposition, as usual, called for his resignation.

The Home Secretary did not resign, instead he ordered an immediate inquiry, as an extension of the Mountbatten investigation. Robert Mark, one of Mountbatten's assessors travelled forthwith to Dartmoor, with a brief that he examine charges that prison officers were opposed to Mitchell being allowed on outside working parties, and that he had wreaked terror among their ranks. Pub landlords, summoned to the prison to be interviewed by Mark, told of Mitchell's visits to their hostelries and one farmer said he had let The Mad Axeman ride his ponies, even lending him a saddle. 'He was a jolly chap, very mild and pleasant,' he said. 'I knew all about him and that he was a prisoner.'

In London things were not turning out as Big Frank had expected. He had been looking forward to a coming-home party, to meeting old pals and in particular to being personally welcomed by his good friends Ron and Reg. He was disappointed – the twins were busy and he was stuck in the flat, passing the time playing cards and watching television with other members of the Firm. There was one bright spot during the first evening when the ten o'clock news showed police and commandos scouring Dartmoor. He roared with laughter at that.

One of the men assigned to keep him company was, like Mitchell, known by a nickname that cast doubts on his mental well-being. But Mad Teddy Smith's interest in gangsterism extended to the might of the pen as well as the gun and only recently the BBC had accepted a play written by him. Smith had an affinity with Mitchell and now he applied his literary talents to help him compose letters to the Home Secretary, offering to give himself up if he could be promised a release date.

Letters were sent to the *Daily Mirror* and *The Times*. In one Mitchell wrote:

> Sir, the reason for my absence from Dartmoor was to bring to the Notice of my unhappy plight. to be truthful, I am asking for a possible Date of release, from the age of 9 I have not been completely free, always under some act or other.
>
> Sir, I ask you where is the fairness of this. I am not a murderer or a sex maniac, nor do I think I am a danger to the public. I think that I have been more than punished for the wrongs that I have done.
>
> Yours sincerely,
> Frank Mitchell

In another letter to the *Daily Mirror*, Mitchell apologised for the criticism the Home Secretary had received and spoke of the kindness and hope he had been given by the earlier Dartmoor Governor, Dennis Malone. He said, 'I can only repeat my appeal to the humane thinking people of this country. If I must be buried alive give me some reason to hope.'

The escape of any prisoner known as The Mad Axeman could not fail to create a stir, now his letters ensured that he remained front-page news for days to come. Yet, for all the alarm and anxiety that a fugitive with Mitchell's history aroused, there was some sympathy and support for this feeble-minded giant.

Even a group of prison officers urged him to give himself up. Through the *Daily Mirror* they urged him to contact them, saying they would ask permission of the Home Secretary to collect him and take him back to Dartmoor. All very well, but from Mitchell's point of view, for how long? For the rest of his life? This would not resolve the matter that led him to escape in the first place.

The Home Secretary did not ignore Mitchell's letters. In an unprecedented appeal to an escaped prisoner, a Home Office spokesman said that his offer to surrender if given a date of release had been noted. He said the fact that he was on the honour party at Dartmoor was an indication that his release was under consideration, as the Home Secretary had told the Commons the day after the escape. He added that account would have to be taken of the escape and of Mitchell's conduct while at large, but if, after he returned, he was found to not constitute a danger to the public then 'fresh consideration will be given to fixing a date for his release'. The spokesman concluded by saying '. . . by remaining at large, Mitchell can only damage his own interests. He will be well advised to give himself up immediately.'

This statement was published in the *Daily Mirror* on 23 December, accompanied by a comment from the editor offering Mitchell what he called 'man to man advice'. Summarising the coverage and appeals, he said, 'Now it only remains for you to keep your word – and surrender at once . . . We've given you a fair hearing Frank Mitchell. Now give yourself up.'

There was no chance of that happening. Frank had better things to do than throw in the towel for a Christmas in chokey. He had fallen in love.

The recipient of his affections was a blonde club hostess,

provided by the Firm when he got restless sitting about in the flat doing nothing. She arrived in a taxi direct from the West End at 2 a.m., and was promised £100 and 'the gratitude of the whole East End' if Mitchell was satisfied. It seems he was – after insisting on being paid immediately, she and The Mad Axeman went to bed and stayed there for the next two days, their love-making interrupted only by Frank now and then hopping out of bed for a quick fifty press-ups.

At 8.30 p.m. on 23 December 1966 Frank Mitchell was collected by members of the Firm from the Barking flat. It was the last time he was seen alive. A subsequent Old Bailey trial was told by Albert Donaghue, the one name to consistently surface in all the accounts of who had helped him to escape, that Mitchell was told he was going to a farm in Kent and that the woman, from whom he did not want to be parted, would follow on later. He walked outside to a waiting Thames van and, according to Donaghue, as it pulled away he was shot a number of times in the head and body.

Donaghue was alleged by the club hostess to have returned to the flat and telephoned Ronnie Kray, saying, 'The dog's dead. We gave him four injections in the nut.' Initially charged with Mitchell's murder, alongside the Krays and other members of the Firm, he crossed the line and turned Queen's Evidence. His uncorroborated account was rejected by the jury and all defendants were acquitted of the murder charge.

What did become of Frank Mitchell? For years rumour and speculation abounded as to whether he was alive or dead. Was he living incognito in some foreign clime, his features radically altered by plastic surgery paid for by his underworld friends? Or was he dead, murdered because he had become an unmanageable burden? Had his huge body really been chopped up and fed to pigs, or was it buried deep in the concrete foundations of a motorway flyover?

By the first anniversary of his escape, the strong word in knowledgeable circles was that Big Frank was dead. The appearance of one newspaper article headed 'AXE-MAN MAY HAVE BEEN MURDERED' caused his anxious parents to contact journalist Norman Lucas. They told him, 'We are worried sick. We cannot under-stand why Frank has not been in touch with anyone if he is still alive.'

Then in March 1968, fifteen months after his escape, his parents' hopes were raised by another letter to *The Times*. Signed in block capitals it said he was alive and well and would be prepared to discuss his whereabouts if James Callaghan, now Home Secretary, would repeat on radio and television the offer to review his sentence.

Scotland Yard, who had received dozens of 'sightings' of Mitchell, seized upon this lead. It was a red herring. Just as Old Bill was getting his head down for some serious forensic and handwriting tests, a pupil at Down-side School in Somerset admitted to his headmaster that he had sent the letter.

Whatever happened to Frank Mitchell, his body has never been found. And that, in official terms, means that he is still on the run from Dartmoor Prison.

8 WALTER PROBYN

Angel Face

He was 'The Dimpled Demon', the East End slum kid who stole a tin of peas at nine and stabbed a policeman at fourteen. He was 'The Hoxton Houdini', always looking to escape. And he was 'Angel Face', the eight-stone youth whose pleasant features masked his true evil. That was the name that stuck.

As a criminal, Wally Probyn was a failure – as a prison escaper he is a legend. Thirty of his first forty-four years were spent in custody of one type or another – and he escaped sixteen times. No amount of security and no degree of punishment could deter him. Whatever the effort required, Probyn was equal to it. The long weeks and months of planning, watching, checking, acquiring and hiding tools, often under close scrutiny from warders – to Angel Face it was a way of life, a challenge he could never resist.

Probyn was first sent away to approved school at the age of ten, after breaking a probation order imposed for stealing the tin of peas. For the next three years he was constantly on his toes, running away from every approved school and remand home, returning to his family and being dragged off again by the police. Savage beatings and gratuitous violence from staff, offended that he should choose to reject their wisdom and hospitality, only served to increase an anti-authoritarian attitude that would at times in the future be the very strength that enabled him to survive.

At one remand centre he stole a bunch of keys before he had even got out of reception, but could not use them because staff were watching his every move. He soon shook them off by handing the keys to the headmaster, admitting that he had stolen them with the intention of escaping, and saying that he now realised it was best to do his time. So impressed was the headmaster that he gave Wally his coffee cup and told him to take it to the staff kitchen. There the bars were wide enough for a thin lad to squeeze through – Probyn did.

Squeezing through bars became a regular activity. By the time he was fourteen Probyn had been locked up by the police at Old Street Police Station, at Hackney, at Victoria and at Rochester Row. He escaped from them all – Old Street on five occasions – by getting through the small hatches in cell doors.

Eventually he was sent to an approved school in Wales, too far away from London, so it was thought, for him to even contemplate absconding. Little did the authorities know that by now Wally Probyn had developed a homing instinct on a par with a racing pigeon – no matter where they put him he would have found his way home. He loved the sense of adventure, the exhilaration of reclaiming his freedom. No sooner had he arrived in Wales than he departed, running through fields and woods until he reached Carmarthen Bay, noted for its treacherous quicksands and currents. Probyn knew nothing of these hazards and swam straight across to the other side. Finding a railway line, he boarded a train to London, only to be caught by the ticket inspector and handed over to the police at Paddington.

Back in Carmarthen he was beaten, but in no time at all he was off again, despite having to sleep naked in a locked room. In his birthday suit and without shoes he broke out one midsummer's night and trotted through the Welsh countryside until he again reached Carmarthen Bay. This time he was more cautious about the dark waters. He had heard how dangerous they could be. He did not fancy his chances again so he found a small dinghy on the beach and put out in that, only to discover the bung-hole open and the boat disappearing from under him. Like it or not he had no option but to brave the currents and swim to the far shore.

The first time Wally Probyn was sent to prison he was fourteen years old and four feet ten inches tall. He had appeared in the juvenile court with two black eyes, two split lips and marks all over his face and body, charged with assaulting a six-foot, seventeen-stone policeman. He got three months in Wormwood Scrubs. Released at the end of it, he was returned to approved school, from where he soon did another runner – his fourteenth – and when cornered by the police he stabbed one of them.

Still only fifteen, it was now, in the build-up to his trial at the Old Bailey, that Probyn was dubbed Angel Face – by police and press eager to ensure that his benevolent appearance did not deceive the public, or defeat the course of justice. It certainly did not do the latter – Mr Justice Stable said he was too young for Borstal so he gave him four years' imprisonment without remission.

Stunned and bemused by a sentence that seemed like a lifetime, Probyn soon focused his mind on positive matters, in particular trying to find a way out of the Scrubs. Every day, after sewing mailbags, he was locked up in his cell, whereupon he set about digging through the floor with a spoon, camouflaging his handiwork in between times with black wax stolen from the workshop. The rubble that he removed was thrown out of the cell window, on to the prison garden. He was making steady progress towards the basement below when suddenly, without any warning, he was moved 180 miles away to Wakefield.

Angel Face was not happy in Wakefield, a jail then as now noted for a high proportion of sex offenders. He was put to work in the tailors' shop where he spent much of his time fighting off homosexual advances, although he did manage to appropriate two sharp knives, which, with their edges serrated, were ideal for sawing through cell bars.

Already Probyn had spent a considerable part of his time at Wakefield in the punishment block. The next two years brought almost permanent residence there after another convict grassed on him for trying to saw through his bars. Worse than that, the authorities then decided that prison was not the place for a young man as troublesome as Wally Probyn. In an action that seemed as unwarranted and outrageous in the late 1940s as it does today, he was certified under the Mental Defective Act and removed to Rampton, the dreaded Broadmoor of the north.

Wally Probyn was rebellious, defiant and an undoubted

embarrassment to the authorities, who could not handle him. Mentally defective he was not. He had served nearly three years of his four-year sentence and should have been due for release – instead, at eighteen years old, he was plunged indefinitely into the nightmarish bedlam of a madhouse, amongst severely disturbed and dangerous people, not many of whom had much hope of ever coming out.

After a few weeks at Rampton, Probyn found an inmate with whom he had something in common – escape plans. One December day in 1949 as the patients went on to the exercise yard, Probyn and his running mate each made for a drainpipe, shinned up and climbed on to the roof. With patients and staff running about in all directions below them, they leaped a fifteen-foot gap between two roofs, raced along the top of a workshop to the female side of the institution and got over a wall to freedom. Only one guard pursued them and he followed the other inmate as the pair of escapers split up, dashing across open fields. Once he was clearly ahead, Probyn hid in a ditch and covered himself with vegetation, freezing in the ice-cold conditions and waiting for nightfall.

Under cover of darkness, he eventually hopped on to the back of a lorry which, as luck had it, took him all the way to London. He was at liberty for five months, experiencing a number of near misses when police officers spotted him and gave chase. While on the run he rescued a small boy who had fallen in the canal at Victoria Park, puzzling the child's grateful parents by his haste to get away from the scene. He could not hang about, in case a policeman turned up seeking details.

When he was recaptured, after police surveillance on a

girl whom he was taking out, the parents of the rescued child went to court to speak up in support of Probyn's plea not to be returned to Rampton. It made no difference – back he went to the madhouse. Soon a hacksaw went missing and the finger pointed at Angel Face. It was a fortnight in solitary followed by another fortnight sleeping on a stone floor.

Brutality at the hands of Rampton staff was commonplace at this time and for many years to come. Beatings, kickings, spine-dropping, being rendered unconscious with a wet towel twisted round the neck, or held under water in a cold bath, were regular happenings – from time to time made public but always allowed to continue. Many inmates were broken by this savage and sinister regime, but Probyn had no intention of joining up with the soulless, burnt-out wrecks around him. His reaction to the so-called treatment provided by Rampton Institution was an increased determination to escape. Once more he made a bid. Scaling the wall he got away, but was caught by staff only a few fields away – and kicked and punched all the way back to Rampton, along the corridors to his ward and for a long time afterwards.

Wally Probyn spent nearly three years in Rampton. Even then he was only released because his family threatened a writ of habeas corpus, following independent psychological reports that confirmed his above-average IQ and balanced state of mind. He had been locked up for six years on a four-year sentence that was imposed because he was not old enough to do two years' Borstal.

He had gone inside a boy, he came out a man, but it was hard to settle in the saner world. He had seen too much of life's dark side to know that there could be light. Before long he was arrested and sent down for three months and while serving that got a further three years on a belated shopbreaking charge.

This sentence passed without him venturing beyond the walls of Wandsworth, then in 1958, serving another eighteen months for office-breaking – and with only four weeks left to do – he absconded from an outside working party at Maidstone. His girlfriend was in financial difficulties and worried that her two children might be taken into care, so Probyn took his leave of Her Majesty's Prison to provide for them in the only way he knew. Scotland Yard immediately put out an all-force alert – 'This man is violent and dangerous.' But even they did not know how dangerous.

Probyn went underground for a month as Old Bill turned over his family and all known associates, with irritating regularity. He came to notice quite by chance, when an off-duty constable, on his way to get his boots repaired, happened to spot him looking at cars on a garage forecourt in Stamford Hill. Recalling the warning that Probyn was violent, the constable rang for reinforcements, but as they arrived the wanted man ran off, hotly pursued by three policemen. They cornered him in a cul-de-sac but stopped in their tracks when Probyn pulled a gun out of his jacket pocket. As the policemen froze, Probyn got away by leaping over a low wall. Large numbers of police swamped the area, cordoning it off and doing house-to-house searches, but Probyn, living up to his Hoxton Houdini nickname, had vanished.

Twenty-four hours later they caught him on his home turf in Shoreditch. He had been upset by the *Daily Mirror*'s coverage of the previous day's chase and contacted a reporter to give his side of the story. A meet was arranged, but when Probyn turned up he walked straight into a police trap. The *Daily Mirror* man had betrayed him. It was bold headlines and a photo of the infamous Angel Face – held in a neck lock – right there on the front page of the paper. Wally did not have a lot of time for the press after that.

Back to jail he went, this time Wandsworth, to do two and a half years for using a firearm with intent to resist arrest. Growing restless and with another domestic crisis brewing, he faked appendicitis symptoms by swallowing carbolic soap and rolling around with apparent stomach pains. Taken to St James' Hospital in Balham, he hopped off a trolley in casualty, dived through a window, climbed the hospital gates and disappeared down the street, barefoot and in his pyjamas.

He was free for two and a half months, only to fall into the arms of the Flying Squad in Christmas week, as he visited a garage to get a punctured tyre repaired. Seventeen charges followed, all for offences committed on the run, including possession of a long-handled axe found in the front of his car. He got five years, despite an appeal from his girlfriend, Joan, who told the court, 'If you give Wally a real chance I know he will go straight.' He also received a message from a disgruntled prison doctor that he would die if he ever had appendicitis in prison.

In 1961 Walter Angel Face Probyn arrived at Dartmoor. He found the Big House on the Moor as grim and depressing as its reputation. But to a man with escape uppermost in his mind it had a lot of possibilities that he felt should be explored and exploited – when the time was right. Since Ruby Sparks became the first man to get clean away from Dartmoor back in 1940, there had been many attempts, some spectacular, but only a few that could be classed as successful. Probyn aimed to join the latter category.

Stan Thurston was one of the ones who made it, a couple of years after Sparks. The press called him 'The Man No Prison Can Hold' after earlier break-outs from Liverpool and Lewes. Roy 'Rubber Bones' Webb was another, but he only lasted a week, while Cyril Michael Bond, who tried to get away to America, was arrested within hours, as were the two bent warders who had helped him.

William Day was even less fortunate. He got over the wall in driving rain and dense fog on a January afternoon in 1959. He was accompanied by Dennis Stafford, who had earlier escaped from Wormwood Scrubs, set up a lucrative but criminal trading company in Newcastle and then retired to Trinidad, only to be extradited. Stafford got away from Dartmoor to London – but Day was found six weeks later, floating in Burrator Reservoir, four miles from the jail.

In the early 1960s escapes from Dartmoor Prison became so frequent that it was suggested *Which?* should publish a guide as to the best method. By far the most spectacular was that of Jimmy Jennings, a twenty-two-year man, who in June 1964 hi-jacked an oil tanker as it delivered to the prison and, with two other convicts aboard, smashed through the gates and drove along the Devon roads for a spell of liberty that lasted only hours.

Wally Probyn admired these escapers and others, men who refused to bow down and kow-tow to a system they despised. They were men after his own heart, but the plain fact was that while their exploits had made them

heroic figures among their peers, few of them had
achieved much in the way of freedom. Before Probyn
got around to making his own move in August 1964,
there had been thirteen unsuccessful escape bids that
year.

It was not surprising that they tried – the crumbling
wall was in such a bad state that not even ropes or hooks
were needed to go over it. But few runners got away
from the vicinity of the prison, and the reason for this, he
concluded, was that they were frightened of the moor.
They were intimidated by its wild terrain and unpredictable weather. More than that, they were afraid of the
darkness. For Angel Face, who enjoyed being on his
toes at dead of night, that was all the more reason to give
it a go.

He had little to lose. The five-year sentence had by
this time been doubled, following a week's home leave
to get married. He had wed, not Joan, whose financial
problems had caused him to run off from Maidstone, but
another woman, Beryl. The honeymoon was curtailed
when the pair of them were arrested for shopbreaking
and Angel Face ended up looking at ten years instead of
five. To make matters worse, as he languished in his cell
he learned that back home Beryl was being terrorised by
a previous lover and local ne'er-do-well named Punchie
Hines.

Because of Dartmoor's isolated location, and the
difficulties that faced anyone who did run off, even
long-sentence convicts were allowed to work outside the
walls. Probyn was put in a group repairing prison officers' houses at near-by Princetown. When the group set
out on the morning of 24 August 1964 it looked like rain
and so he was allowed to carry a white mackintosh.

Unbeknown to the guards, he had a compass hidden in one of the houses he was working on. As an afternoon fog began to close in, Probyn slung a bag of plaster on his shoulder and, with the mackintosh over his prison overalls, he marched through the streets. No one would suspect he was escaping while carrying a bag of plaster. When he reached the end of the street he just kept walking, dropping the bag and quickening up his pace.

Visibility was down to twenty-five yards and road-blocks were set up all across the moor as hundreds of police with dogs, two army helicopters, troops and prison officers began to search. They were not expecting too much difficulty, it was usually only a matter of an hour or two, but they underestimated Wally Probyn. He was in a higher league than the thirteen men who had tried in previous months. Probyn, as one prosecutor described him, was 'a past master of the art of escapology'.

He soon appreciated the benefit of his compass and once he reached the reservoir where the unfortunate William Day's hopes of freedom had expired, he knew he was heading in the right direction. By dawn the following morning – his thirty-third birthday – without any food or drink, Probyn had covered fifty miles of the most treacherous countryside in Britain, on foot. Seeing a mini-van in the drive of a house, he removed his prison boots before creeping up the gravel drive, but he was disturbed by the house owner. He had no option but to dash off, barefoot, knowing that the police would now know exactly where he was.

Resting by day and walking by night, Probyn struggled eastwards. Exhausted, starving with hunger and burning inside from a raging thirst, he pushed on, determined that he would die before he gave up to his pursuers. After five days he reached Porton, a small village near Salisbury. Barely able to speak, he made a reverse-charge call. His ordeal was over. He was picked up by car and taken to London to be reunited with and looked after by his wife and friends.

Probyn was free for seven weeks. During that time the man who had been troubling his wife, Punchie Hines, was summoned out of a Shoreditch pub, the Royal Standard, by a woman in dark glasses. When he followed her out of the bar into an alleyway he was shot in both legs by an unseen assailant. Hines recovered after operations on his legs, but refused to give any information to the police. Old Bill did not like it, but there was no evidence to link Wally Probyn with the shooting.

There was plenty to link him with the shooting that preceded his recapture – and there was plenty of shooting. The police received a tip-off that the wanted man had plans to meet someone outside a post office in the East End at 8 p.m. on Friday 16 October and when Wally and Beryl Probyn arrived for the meet in a Ford Zephyr, they drove straight into a Flying Squad ambush. Getting out of the car, Probyn realised it had all come on top and, dragging Beryl behind him, he darted into a fish-and-chip shop, with six detectives hot on his heels.

Yet again he lived up to his Houdini nickname – the police turned the back room and basement upside down, but he had vanished. He could only have gone one way – out of the window, so his pursuers did too – to find Mr and Mrs Probyn crouching on the roof only feet away. A chase worthy of any thriller movie ensued, with Probyn firing at the police as he and Beryl stumbled across the

Shoreditch rooftops, through the window of a tobacco-nist's shop and down the stairs into the street. One detective got close enough to hit the fugitive with a broom that he had grabbed along the way, another brought him down with a rugby tackle, but Probyn slipped away again.

Beryl Probyn was seized and screamed at her husband to help. He tried – firing a shot that whistled past the head of the sergeant who held her. Seeing that he was now on his own, Probyn dived into a parked car, at which the detective with the broom smashed the wind-screen and tried to press him down. Another shot was fired, another policeman got close enough to hit Probyn with his truncheon – but Angel Face struck back, hitting him with the gun. Again he broke away and leaped a fence into the gardens of houses, but he was tiring and this time his pursuers ran him to ground.

Miraculously, during all the mayhem and flying lead no one was hit by any of the shots from Probyn's .22 revolver. The police, four of whom were later awarded the George Medal for bravery, said that he fired at them nine times – Probyn said twice, and only then because he did not realise they were police officers. He said he thought he was being pursued by Punchie Hines and his gang. Nine shots was bad, but the outcome could have been worse – when they got Beryl Probyn to the police station and turned out her handbag it contained 174 bullets.

Wally Probyn never looked less like Angel Face than when he appeared in Thames Magistrates' Court, hob-bling in straight from a hospital bed where he had spent five days vomiting blood. He was minus his front teeth and had an arm, a shoulder and several ribs broken.

Nevertheless he was handcuffed to a detective. At the Old Bailey, Mr Justice Melford Stevenson, the judge who later told Ronnie Kray that society had earned a rest from his activities, weighed Probyn off with twelve years for shooting to commit grievous bodily harm. He went to Wormwood Scrubs, where it was found that his broken arm required a bone-graft operation. But while the arm was still in plaster he attempted yet another cunning break-out.

As a Special Watch prisoner, Probyn wore a uniform with bright yellow patches sewn all over it. Wherever he went in the Scrubs he had to be signed over from the custody of one officer to another. Opportunities to escape were few and far between and the task was made even more difficult by the fitting of a new type of lock on the wing, besides the ever-present risk of being grassed.

Against these odds, Probyn and another prisoner got hold of a rope and grappling tackle, a trusty's armband and a set of ordinary prison clothing. They made their break from the bath-house, helped by a pal creating a diversion. But with an injured arm and a partner who lacked sufficient strength to throw the tackle to the top of the wall, the attempt was doomed to failure.

Next stop was Parkhurst and the new security block, the prison-within-a-prison built to hold the Great Train Robbers. Probyn had served eight years inside and was looking at another ten. He had begun to seriously wonder if he would ever see freedom again. Parkhurst was like entering another world, a science-fiction world of electronic doors where a warder had to address a speaker panel before the door opened, where closed-circuit cameras followed prisoners' every movement and staff watched through bullet-proof observation panels. It was the ultimate prison and to Wally Probyn it seemed like the end.

But he still had a few tricks up his sleeve. More accurately, he had five hacksaw blades, concealed in a folder which he had brought with him from Wormwood Scrubs. Somehow the state-of-the-art security had missed these essential components of every escaper's tool kit. To his dismay he found that the blades were useless – the security block window bars were made of manganese steel. A hacksaw blade would not even scratch them.

Once more, it was back to the plotting table. Of all the notable prison escapers, Wally Probyn was probably the most meticulous when it came to patiently calculating the obstacles to be beaten. He would later say that a would-be escaper does not need a lot of patience because in prison he has nothing else to do anyway, that prisoners have twenty-four hours a day to scheme and plan. So with the hacksaw blades redundant, he came up with a bigger and better idea.

This time he teamed up with a prisoner whose notoriety made Angel Face seem like an upright citizen. Only a year earlier Harry Roberts had aroused national outrage by cold-bloodedly shooting two policemen in Shepherds Bush, soon after the abolition of capital punishment. He was sentenced to life with a recommendation that he serve at least thirty years, but few would put money on him ever coming out.

Probyn worked out a complex plan whereby he and Roberts were to get out of the security block through a sealed double-door entrance by dropping through its roof, from the landing above. He had found what he believed to be the one chink in the security block's armour. He and Harry Roberts worked for weeks in their cells, making replica Luger pistols out of wax and cotton reels. By the time they were finished, copying the Lugers from photographs in Roberts' case papers, the guns looked perfect.

Roberts had been thinking of escape plans since arriving at Parkhurst, it was all he had left to hang on to. When the chance presented itself he panicked, leaving the replica Lugers in a toilet, where they were found by a warder. The whole block was turned over and in the leg of Wally Probyn's bed they discovered an Ordnance Survey map of the Isle of Wight and a naval map of the Solent. At 4 a.m. the next morning Angel Face was dragged from his bed, handcuffed, and bundled in the back of a police car, to be ghosted 350 miles to Durham in a high-speed, five-vehicle convoy, lights flashing and sirens blaring all the way.

On arrival at Durham, Probyn spent six weeks in solitary, time well spent for it gave him a chance to work out that, while cell bars could not now be cut, they could be removed from the masonry in which they were set. Out of chokey and on the maximum-security E Wing, he got hold of a serving-spoon handle which he shaped into a chisel, acquired water-colour paints and suddenly discovered an all-consuming interest in papier mâché modelling. Each day he made grotesque masks, which he hung on his cell wall to disguise his real use for the materials – patching up around the window after he had spent long sessions each night scraping cement from around his bars.

After much careful endeavour, all under the eyes of

warders who knew – or should have known – that he would always be working on some escape plan, somehow Probyn got the window bars to a stage at which he could remove them. This, despite constant searches of his cell, including checking on the bars by shaking them. One ploy he used to distract the searchers was to leave soft-porn magazines on his bed; by the time they had looked through them they had spent enough time in the cell and moved on to search another.

Physical fitness is, generally speaking, essential to prison escapers and Probyn always kept himself in peak condition. Unfortunately the same could not be said for the man he invited to escape with him. Once they got out of the cell window they were faced with an arduous route, descending the outside of the wing with a rope made from mailbags, climbing a drainpipe and crossing rolls of barbed wire, before they got anywhere near the outer wall.

Probyn was up to it, but when the day came his running mate failed the test. His arms were not strong enough. In an effort to help him, Probyn fell from three floors up, landing stiff-legged with a shock that shot up his spine and knocked him unconscious. He was picked up by warders and dropped in the strong box – a bare concrete cell with a wooden slab for a bed, and no other furniture. Two blankets were thrown in and he was left to lie there, unable to stand and unattended in an agony that would last for many weeks to come.

Most men would have called it a day at that, concluded that they were not destined to beat a system that now held all the aces. The old days had passed. The sensational escapes of the Great Train Robbers and spy George Blake had introduced a new concept to prison life – maximum security – which was widely believed to be foolproof. But if the authorities really believed that another failed attempt, serious injury, loss of remission and all the other punishments they threw at him would cause Wally Probyn to forget about escaping, they were well wide of the mark. Next time he would pull off the Big One.

9   JOHN McVICAR

Most Dangerous Man

The Mountbatten Report contained fifty-two recommendations for the improvement of prison security. Most had been aired before at one time or another, but successive Home Secretaries had chosen not to act upon them. The report was published without much real controversy – apart from one proposal, for a custombuilt superjail on the Isle of Wight. The idea of a fortress holding 120 of the most dangerous convicts in England was greeted with anger and dismay by the local residents. Alcatraz was the word on many lips. They had enough trouble with escapers from the two jails already on the island, Parkhurst and Camp Hill, and had no wish to see the place turn from a holiday resort into a penal colony. They preferred visitors who came for a fortnight, to those who came for thirty years.

The superjail proposal never materialised, but another of Mountbatten's ideas, to divide all prisoners into four categories, A-D, according to security risk, was adopted and operates to this day. At the top of the list were the Category A prisoners – 'those whose escape would be highly dangerous to the public or the police or the security of the state'. In early 1967 a total of 138 men were assessed as fitting this category – 'young, violent professional criminals who are both dangerous and persistent in their criminal activities'. Many had posed acute control problems for the authorities and, of the 138 total, 51 had escaped or attempted to escape during their present sentence, while a further 83 were suspected of plotting to escape.

John McVicar was a Category A man. A career criminal of the first order, who in his own words became a 'professional prisoner', his progression to the underworld elite began as a youth in East Ham, London. Neither remand home nor Borstal could hold him and from the age of sixteen he spent all but a few short months either inside or on the run. Convicted of robbery in 1964, two years later he was among a group of prisoners travelling in a coach from Winchester Assizes back to Parkhurst Prison. The party had been called to the court to give evidence in the trial of a Parkhurst prisoner who was charged with stabbing another inmate. It had not been too good a day for law and order – the jury failed to agree and a re-trial was ordered. What the jury could not know was that the whole case was a sham – a set-up planned to get a group of prisoners out of Parkhurst and called to court, thus providing an opportunity to escape. Ironically, the prisoner charged was later found guilty, despite being innocent, and was sentenced to five years.

Thirteen convicts – nine of them known to be violent and escape-risks – and seven prison officers were in the coach when it left Winchester at the end of the trial. Three of the convicts were handcuffed to officers while

138

the other ten were handcuffed in pairs. They were all searched before setting out, but were still able to smuggle three improvised keys on to the coach. Protected by the high backs of the seats, it was easy for the ten men to free themselves.

Prior to leaving Winchester, the officer in charge had received a tip-off that trouble could be expected on the way back. He telephoned Parkhurst and as a result extra police were drafted to the Portsmouth ferry terminal, the place where a break-out attempt was thought most likely to happen.

The coach never reached the ferry. The prisoners made their move before it got there. As they passed through Bishops Waltham one shouted, 'Right!' and the others, now free of handcuffs, jumped from their seats. Some leaped on officers while one made a grab for the steering wheel. As he struggled with the driver, who refused to let go of the wheel, the coach slewed about the road before coming to a halt. The door crashed open and nine men ran in different directions.

Immediately behind the coach was a police escort car. Assistance was summoned by radio and then two police officers gave chase. They were soon joined by 120 of their colleagues and fourteen tracker dogs, as roadblocks went up and a RAF helicopter flew in to scour the area.

The swamp operation worked. Seven of the runners were picked up within a few hours and another lasted two days, living rough. Two men slipped the net. John McVicar made it to London and enjoyed a summer at liberty. The Flying Squad put an end to that after four months when they recaptured him after a botched raid on a security van.

★ ★ ★

McVicar was doing eight years when he escaped. He went back to do twenty-three, as a result of his activities on the run, one in particular where shots were fired at the police after an attempt to rob a security van. Sent to Chelmsford, he broke through the roof but could not get over the wall and from there he was despatched post haste to Durham's maximum-security E Wing, from where escape was said to be impossible.

E Wing had been converted to maximum security after the Wilson and Biggs escapes, to house other Great Train Robbers and long-term prisoners. Soon after it opened controversy erupted when the Chief Constable of Durham called in the army to protect the prison from the friends of the train robbers who, he said, were preparing to launch a full-scale military attack to spring them, 'even to the extent of using tanks, bombs and what I believe are known as limited atomic weapons'.

According to the Chief Constable, a report had been received that bogus police were to be involved in the attempt and the rescuers would have a helicopter standing by. Once armoured vehicles had breached the main gates of the prison there would be nothing to stop them, he told incredulous newsman. 'A couple of tanks could easily have come up through the streets of Durham unchallenged . . . Nothing is too extravagant . . . they can go to any lengths, irrespective of risk to life or limb. If that happened there would be a pitched battle and a lot of people would be killed.'

Drastic action was called for, there were no half measures: a Bren gun was reported to be fixed to the roof of the jail, while soldiers of the 1st Battalion Lancashire Regiment were clearly visible outside E

Wing, with bayonets fixed to automatic rifles. Police with dogs guarded the outer wall as two patrol cars circled continuously. To no one's surprise zero hour passed without an escape party – or the arrival of the rescue helicopter that had been rumoured to be hovering ever since the Great Train Robbers' trial.

The Chief Constable's utterances alarmed the Home Office who issued a statement distancing themselves from all talk of atomic weapons and tanks. His response to this rebuke was to explain that his choice of words had been 'the Greek in me coming out' and to add that he was merely trying 'to unglamourise people who have been glamourised'. With talk of bombs, atomic weapons and tanks rolling through the streets to collect them from jail?

This was the climate in Durham E Wing when John McVicar arrived in late 1967. Tensions and frustrations were already running high and, when a new Governor arrived to introduce a series of additional petty rules, the prisoners showed their dissatisfaction in the time-honoured way – they revolted. In February 1968 E Wing was taken over by its inmates, who barricaded themselves in the office, rang the *Daily Mirror* and spent the night reading reports and records compiled on them by staff.

In a file a foot thick, McVicar was astounded to read that on the out he had been a cohort in crime of fellow inmates Charlie and Eddie Richardson, remarkable since he had never even known them. As well as their files, which they tore to shreds once they had read them, the rioters found another document – the contingency plan for dealing with escapes from Durham Prison.

Code-named Operation Seagull, it showed the locations where all police road-blocks were to be set up in the area around the town. This information would come in very useful later in the year.

The rioters' barricades did not come down until a Home Office man travelled up from London to negotiate. An eight-day hunger strike and a statutory stint in chokey followed. The grievances that had caused the riot had not been resolved, and now McVicar conducted other running battles with staff, one in particular over a pair of trainers that had been taken from him. He won this one after enlisting an unexpected supporter – the Home Secretary, James Callaghan, who, on a post-riot visit to the jail made a point of talking to McVicar and intervened on his behalf.

McVicar was twenty-eight years old and restless. He was looking at a long, long time behind bars; he was also looking for a way out. No Category A prisoner had so far come within a whisker of escaping, but he was determined. It was most fortuitous that one of his fellow inmates on E Wing happened to be Wally Probyn – if anyone was likely to be able to plan an escape from E Wing, it was Angel Face. McVicar knew that he was a dedicated escaper, but felt his motivation was directed more at embarrassing authority than gaining liberty. He had a word and made his own position clear – he wanted to get out, and if the master escaper had any ideas he would be very interested.

Wally Probyn had been let down by accomplices in the past, but in McVicar he recognised a commitment to escaping first and putting one over the authorities second. Despite the failure of his recent attempts, and the serious injuries he sustained on the last occasion, Probyn had lost none of his spirit or determination. Even as McVicar spoke, Angel Face had half a dozen possibilities running around inside his head.

As he walked about the wing barefoot, Probyn made a discovery. Parts of the floor were warm, and when he stamped his feet, he could tell that other parts were hollow. To a man with his hard-won grasp of prison architecture, this indicated a cellar and hot-water pipes underneath the wing floor. When he discovered a space behind a wall in the shower-room, his curiosity would not let him rest until he satisfied himself that it was, as he had hoped, a ventilation shaft. Did the shaft run down from the wing into the cellar? There was only one way to find out.

Tools were required, especially chisels to bore the hole. It was convenient that Probyn worked in the wrought-iron shop, but security measures meant that everyone leaving the workshop had to pass through a metal detector. To anyone else this obstacle might have been insurmountable, but to Probyn the solution was simple. The metal wheel in his hamster cage – manufactured earlier in the workshop – kept breaking down. He took it in and out of the workshop for repairs, and every time it came out, in a secret compartment he carried long spikes which could be used for poking at bricks and mortar. Another time he bolted two chisels to weight-lifting equipment, which he handed to a warder to carry through the detector.

Probyn worked for weeks on the hole, one bit at a time, with the shower turned on, filling the room with steam. If an officer bothered to look in he would not hang about to get his uniform damp. After each stint the hole was plugged with papier-mâché. All the while, as Wally scraped and dug, outside the shower-room, McVicar deflected attention lifting and dropping weights with as much noise as was reasonably possible. By this stage of the plot, all of E Wing knew that a break-out was on and the possibility that someone would blow the whistle was ever likely. Wally Probyn had been through too many campaigns to let that bother him now.

Instead, he took the battle into the enemy's territory, telling a prison officer who gave him a parole form to fill in that he didn't need parole, he was making his own way out. Complimented by the Assistant Governor on the weight-lifting equipment he and McVicar had installed – the night before they were due to go – he said, 'It's no use to me. I'm off tomorrow.'

He was, too. At 7 p.m. on Thursday 28 October 1968 Wally Probyn and John McVicar went. They took with them Joe Martin, a lifer who had only arrived on the wing the day before, from the Leicester block. The idea of him escaping from Durham, within hours of being transferred for security reasons, appealed to their sense of humour.

Making their way to the shower-room, they went through the hole in the wall, down the air-shaft and through a grille and gate that Probyn had forced during an earlier reconnaisance. Up a rope they climbed, on to a plastic roof. As they ran across it, every step rang out – they were making so much noise that inmates were coming to their cell windows to see what was happening. Worse, Charlie Richardson, the London gangleader who had wanted to be in on the escape and now suddenly discovered he was not, began yelling abuse after them.

The alarm was now well and truly raised. Joe Martin was soon grabbed by staff as Probyn and McVicar ran from roof to roof, not knowing how they were going to be able to drop to the ground where prison officers were already gathering in wait. They made it to the roof of the courthouse which adjoins the prison and they parted company. Probyn forced a trapdoor and descended through the roof into the court building, but he could go no further. He was trapped, the place surrounded by dogs and police. Two hours later when they went in to get him he was sitting patiently in a waiting room. He got fifty-six days in chokey and never tried to escape again. He was eventually released from his seventeen-year sentence in 1974.

John McVicar stayed on the roof when Probyn took the downward route. He made his way along for seventy yards until he reached a spot where he could drop down into the gardens of a row of terraced houses. No sooner had he hit the ground than a group of policemen ran towards him. Dodging away he dashed along the wet streets, passing by a police station and through the town until he reached the River Wear.

At every turn expecting someone to try to grab him, he went to ground among trees and shrubbery on a piece of waste land, but fell and sprained his wrist. Too late, he realised that he had lost a shoe, so he threw off the other one and swam twenty yards across the river. Dogs were barking and searchers calling to each other. For a few hours he sheltered in the backyard of a student house, then he decided to brave the waters once more and try to swim out of the city.

The River Wear on a bitterly cold November night

was no place for even a super-fit desperado like McVicar. His plan had been to avoid the streets, but the freezing water proved too much. He swam a few hundred yards before climbing out and for the rest of the night he lay shivering, trying to dry out his clothes as he waited for morning to come. The following day, which he would later describe as one of the biggest days of his life, passed with agonising slowness, until darkness allowed him the cover to move on again.

In his book, *McVicar By Himself*, he writes of his feelings during the three days and nights that he lived rough: the cold that froze him to the bone; the pain of cut and bleeding feet; the hunger and thirst; the need to keep constantly on the move and the emptiness and desolation he felt at seeing other people going about ordinary lives. Most poignant of all are his comments on the two men who drove up to Durham from London to collect him, once he managed to make a reverse-charge call to his girlfriend. 'The two guys who picked me up in their car had never met me before and received nothing for doing it. If I had offered payment they would have been insulted. What can you say or do about people like that, except name your children after them?'

John McVicar had achieved the impossible, or what was supposed to be impossible. He had escaped from the escape-proof Special Security Block at Durham Prison. So much for the vast sums invested in state-of-the-art electronic devices, cameras, dogs, extra manpower and the strictest regime in the British penal system. What had gone wrong? That was a question the Home Office could not answer.

The SSBs were designed to meet the threat of organised escape attempts planned from inside or outside. Now a prisoner whom the police and press were labelling extremely violent had got away by the removal of twenty-three bricks in a shower-room and a route down an air-duct and over the roof. When the alarm sounded McVicar was still on the roof. Within three minutes a police cordon surrounded the prison. How had he escaped? As the General Secretary of the Prison Officers' Association said he believed security at the prison 'could be toughened' and the Home Secretary ordered an immediate inquiry, the police warned the public to be wary of McVicar, saying, 'If any member of the public meets him they should take extreme caution. He has a record for violence.'

This was good news for the press. Away from prison yards and landings, McVicar was not a household name. Few people beyond the London underworld had ever heard of him – but he was the first Category A prisoner to escape and the police said he was violent. Bold headlines were ordered: 'DURHAM WALKS IN FEAR OF McVICAR' declared the local paper. Soon he would be described as 'The Most Dangerous Man In Britain' and given that rare accolade awarded only a select few – among them Al Capone, John Dillinger and Ruby Sparks – Public Enemy Number One.

For three days and nights, more than 100 police, some on horseback and others with dogs, searched the area round Chester-le-Moor, a pit village near Durham. They were following all reported sightings in response to the police description – 'McVicar is five feet nine inches tall, he has brown hair, a fresh face, a muscular body carrying no surplus fat, and thin, snarling lips.' They were still searching long after the wanted man had been driven to London.

As so often happens when the first week fails to turn up the fugitive, John McVicar dropped out of the minds of press and public, if not the police. From time to time there were reports of him being seen in various corners of the land, but nothing transpired. If McVicar really was The Most Dangerous Man In Britain, he was being dangerous in a very quiet and unobtrusive manner.

In April 1969, six months after his escape, Scotland Yard took the unusual step of making a public announcement that he need fear no violence if he gave himself up. 'John McVicar has no cause to be apprehensive of the police. The remedy lies in his own hands. He can go alone or accompanied to any police station in the country and surrender himself.' Darkly, the statement continued, 'If he does not surrender it is the duty of every member of the police service in this country to take all possible steps to effect his arrest.'

The no-violence assurance was given, said the Yard, following receipt of a letter 'believed to have been written by McVicar, voicing his fear that the police might use unnecessary violence in an attempt to arrest him'. What was beginning to look like a propaganda campaign gained momentum a couple of months later in the sort of setting beloved of dramatist and mystery writer: a murder case.

Giving evidence in preliminary proceedings at Old Street Magistrates' Court, a senior detective told the bench, 'Police have received information that a man named McVicar, unlawfully at large from Durham Prison, might have murdered Mr Frank Beiring, aged sixty-seven, in a London jewellery shop.' Three men were committed for trial. There was not a shred of evidence to link McVicar to the case, but it was Friday the 13th.

Twelve months passed before the next flurry of activity. In the summer of 1970 many addresses were turned over following supposed tip-offs, the search for an escaped prisoner as ever providing a good reason for Old Bill to take a look in places that generally arouse his curiosity. On 16 July a Devon farmhouse was raided. McVicar, believed to be staying there on a skin-diving holiday, was nowhere to be found, but the thirty-five-year-old chicken farmer was arrested and charged with assisting an escaped prisoner, a £237,000 security van robbery being thrown in for good measure.

The pressure was on. Police forces throughout Britain, together with Interpol, stepped up the search. *The Times* reported, 'A squad of men, all with experience of handling firearms, has been assigned to track him down.' Three days after the Devon farmhouse raid, the search switched to a flat in Manor Park, East London. The wanted man was not at home, but a sawn-off shotgun and seventeen cartridges were found and McVicar's common-law wife was arrested. The net was closing in.

In the game of cat and mouse, the police had most of the advantages. McVicar could not go back to his chosen trade – armed robbery – because other professionals would not work with him. The Flying Squad had spread the word loud and clear that anyone caught with McVicar would be liable for the same fate, whatever that might be. At the same time, he was extremely vulnerable to being grassed, should the grapevine throw up news of his whereabouts. The chances of the latter were increased when Security Express put up a reward of £10,000 for McVicar's recapture, on the basis that his continuing liberty was an encouragement to crime. Ironically, after a two-year search, it was not the lure of cash that brought about his downfall.

The 'official' account of McVicar's recapture centred on a supposed tip-off that he had recently had a telephone installed. The Flying Squad checked all known aliases and one – A.Squires – just happened to be the name in which a telephone had been installed at a flat above a Blackheath dress shop. The name appeared on the Electoral Roll and when a photo of McVicar was shown to a neighbour the response was, 'That's Mr Squires.' McVicar dismisses the telephone story as one that was fed to the press to provide a cover for the villain who had betrayed him.

At 9 a.m. on Wednesday 11 November the end came. John McVicar had just got out of bed to make a cup of tea when armed detectives burst into the flat, shouting at him to come quietly or they would blow his head off. It was not a difficult decision; he went quietly.

After all the ballyhoo and hyperbole of the escape and chase, the press were let down by the recapture. There were armed police on the street and a marksman on a roof, covering McVicar's anticipated bolt-hole from his flat on to the slates, but it was all rather an anti-climax. No shots were fired, there was no blood on the pavement and, worse still, McVicar's landlord and neighbours said what a friendly, normal sort of bloke he was. Some even said he passed the time of day.

Disappointing, too, was his physical appearance. There was no indication of the snarling lips of the police description and he looked different from the photo on the Wanted notice that had stared out of every police station in the land. Now he had more hair, his face was thinner and he looked younger than his thirty years. He looked nothing like a Most Dangerous Man or a Public Enemy Number One should.

During his time on the run McVicar made ends meet by acting as a caretaker of blaggers' equipment, looking after guns, ammunition, stocking masks and pickaxe handles in between jobs. An arsenal of such items was found in the flat above the Blackheath dress shop. These activities led in September 1971 to nine charges of possessing firearms and conspiracy to steal, for which he had three more years added to his existing sentence, making twenty-six years in all.

Sir Carl Aarvold, Recorder at the Old Bailey, told him, 'It is indeed sad to be forced to think that you have been waging your own private war on law and order and on society as a whole. Alas, until now you have given no one any grounds for thinking that you were prepared to consider a truce.

'Offences of this sort, involving being a sort of quartermaster to a unit of armed robbers, would normally call for sentences of between seven and ten years. To add that sort of period to the sentence you are already serving might appear savage, but to overlook these offences altogether might only encourage others.'

The £10,000 reward offered by Security Express was never claimed. McVicar was shopped not for money but in a deal for his betrayer's own licence. Perhaps as well, for if the man had depended on the money he would have been disappointed. The company's head of security, a former Scotland Yard detective, told the press immediately after McVicar's recapture that the information that had led to the arrest was 'worth about £2,000'. The £10,000 offer had been made 'for information leading to the recapture of . . .' but it now looked as though, to claim the full amount, the informer was expected to have personally arrested McVicar and delivered him to Scotland Yard, complete with signed admissions detailing his full activities on the run.

Never again did McVicar try to escape from prison. Since beginning his sentence in 1964 he had done it twice and, as he says, 'both times failed in the endeavour which lights every escaper's tunnel: starting a new life'. The only way to do that would have been to go and live abroad, but when he had the chance he found himself unable to sever his links with his roots and family in London.

John McVicar was released on parole from Leicester Prison in July 1978. Since going back he had spent the intervening years in concentrated study, obtaining a Social Sciences degree. A feature film *McVicar* was made of his escape and time on the run, starring Roger Daltrey of The Who. Today he earns a living as freelance writer and commentator on criminal justice issues. His book *McVicar By Himself*, is one of the classic prison autobiographies. In it he writes of escapes, 'As a means of dealing with a prison sentence they are useless, though this does not diminish their attraction.'

10   TOM McCULLOCH AND
ROBERT MONE

Out of the Asylum

Carstairs State Mental Hospital lies in the remote Lanarkshire countryside, surrounded by high fences, about thirty miles south-east of Glasgow. The Scottish equivalent of Broadmoor, it holds people deemed by the Secretary of State to require treatment under conditions of special security on account of their dangerous, violent or criminal propensities. On 30 November 1976 two patients, Thomas McCulloch and Robert Mone, broke out of Carstairs. In itself that would have been unusual, but not unknown. Over the years the institution had lost its share of inmates and in 1972 two inmates overpowered a nurse, took his keys and departed through a gate to freedom. This time was different – McCulloch and Mone's break-out resulted in a bloodbath hitherto unseen in the history of escapes this century.

Thomas McCulloch was twenty-six. He had been in Carstairs since 1970, when he was detained without limit of time after admitting two charges of attempting to murder a chef and his wife at the West Highways Motel in Clydebank. He had argued with the chef about some sandwiches, before going home and making a tape-recording in which he stated his intention to kill him. Armed with a shotgun and a loaded revolver, he returned to the motel, but the chef had got out of the way. McCulloch fired through a door where he thought the man had barricaded himself, injuring the chef's wife. A commis chef was also shot before the police arrived and McCulloch was disarmed. He was described by a psychiatrist as having a psychopathic personality and ordered to be detained without limit of time.

Robert Mone, twenty-eight, had been sent to Carstairs in 1968, following a murder in Dundee. At the time he was a nineteen-year-old private in the Gordon Highlanders, on leave from Germany. He had joined the army straight from approved school, but did not take to the soldier's life and formed the notion that if he committed a crime he would be discharged. In Dundee he took a shotgun to a needlework class at a secondary school and held a teacher and thirteen pupils hostage for two hours. A nurse who knew him was brought to the scene and she tried to persuade him to release the hostages, to no avail. After sexually assaulting two fourteen-year-olds, Mone shot and killed the teacher before police dogs were unleashed and he was arrested. He was declared insane and unfit to plead and ordered to be detained in the State Hospital, where he obtained three GCEs, completed a correspondence course in playwriting and for a while studied for an Open University course.

McCulloch and Mone became friendly with each other around 1973. Staff were aware of this, but there was not thought to be any cause for alarm. McCulloch had settled well at Carstairs and showed no signs of violent behaviour. Mone, whose argumentative attitude and aggressive behaviour had initially marked him out as a troublemaker, seemed to calm down, although he was still described by a psychiatrist as having a sadistic, schizoid, psychopathic personality.

Both progressed through the hospital system, where good behaviour was rewarded with increased privileges and freedom of movement within the perimeter fence. McCulloch, a time-served painter and decorator, worked in the paint shop and Mone edited the hospital magazine. But despite their good behaviour, neither was considered safe enough for transfer to an ordinary psychiatric hospital and so, in due course, they decided to escape.

Few escapers have gone to the lengths that Tom McCulloch and Robert Mone went to in preparing for their break-out. First of all they set out to acquire the tools and necessary equipment. In a secure institution holding a large number of inmates who were there for the very reason that they were dangerous, this should have been difficult if not impossible, but security at Carstairs was lacking and soon McCulloch and Mone were on their way to gathering everything they needed.

From visitors they obtained a motoring map of the area around the State Hospital, a torch and £25 in cash. In the woodwork department McCulloch constructed a rope ladder from cord, with rungs to fit. He made false identity cards for Mone and himself, complete with photographs taken with Mone's own camera. They even got nurses' caps from the drama group props.

Much more lethal were the various weapons which McCulloch set his hand to making. The original plan was to incapacitate a member or members of staff by squirting ammonia at them. They would then be threatened with weapons and locked in a large wall safe, having been relieved of their keys. But the plan took on a deadly air when McCulloch began to manufacture his armoury in the woodwork shop. As he fashioned and sharpened the weapons, he became possessed by feelings of homicidal intent. These feelings grew and grew. On the surface everything was normal – but inside McCulloch was burning with violence. By the time of the escape he had resolved within himself to kill anyone who stood in his way.

Without arousing any suspicion at all, Tom McCulloch was able to make three knives from steel that was used for sledge runners, manufactured in the woodwork shop. He did a thorough job, worthy of a craftsman, honing the blades to a fine edge on a power buff and making wooden handles, each complete with a metal guard. As if three knives would not be enough, another, used for cutting leather in the occupational therapy department, was stolen and replaced by a dummy from the drama group props. A small axe was then made from a piece of metal and attached to a hammer handle.

The knives were hidden until needed in hollow pieces of wood which were screwed to a bench and appeared to be part of it. The axe was secreted in a space between panels on the side of another bench, or in a box. The box was especially useful to McCulloch, because everyone was so used to seeing it that no one ever thought to search it.

The final item of hardware was a sword which he made from a long metal bar. He sharpened one end to a point on the buff and hid the sword in a hollow piece of wood incorporated into shelving in the paint shop. The sword was not used in the escape and it was so well hidden that it only came to light later after two thorough searches of the workshop. Other items of equipment, which were not used in the escape, were discovered after the event. They included two garottes, one made from a violin string, the other from wire, and wooden replica pistols, again borrowed from stage props.

With an ingenuity that would have been admirable had it not been employed for such a sinister purpose, McCulloch put the finishing touches to his armoury by making sheaths for the knives and a holder for the axe, so that they could be carried on a belt. With material he found in the occupational therapy department, he made the sheaths on a sewing machine that had been allowed into the hospital for him to pursue his hobby of making soft toys.

The only thing he could not obtain was the ammonia with which he and Mone intended to immobilise staff. None was to be found anywhere on the premises. This looked as if it might pose a minor problem but, ever resourceful, McCulloch managed to obtain a satisfactory substitute – Nitromors, a strong, caustic paint-stripper. They poured some into plastic bottles, from which it could be squeezed out in a jet and pointed at the unfortunate victims. The planning was over. It was time to go.

Tuesday 30 November was a cold day. The moorland around Carstairs was frozen over and the roads were slippery with ice. But this was the day Tom McCulloch and Robert Mone had chosen to make their move and the weather, like everything else from this point onwards, was now incidental. They had decided to leave on a Tuesday because Mone had done a study of the volume of traffic that passed along the road by the State Hospital and discovered that it was at its greatest between 6 and 6.30 p.m. on that evening. The time also coincided with a meeting of the drama group in the hospital social club, conveniently situated away from the main wards, and supervised by only one male nurse.

The drama group comprised McCulloch, Mone and another patient, himself a double killer. They spent their time tape-recording books and plays for illiterate patients. That evening Mone was escorted from his ward, carrying a folder, and McCulloch from his with two boxes, but as they had given no one any cause for suspicion, neither of them was searched.

Their escorts left them at the social club and they went inside, getting down to business immediately. McCulloch opened the boxes and put on the belt holding his knives and axe. He and Mone then went to the office where the nurse was talking to the other patient and, without more ado, squirted the paint-stripper in each of their faces. As Mone attacked the powerfully built male nurse, McCulloch stabbed at the patient's head, but he struggled and gained possession of the knife. The nurse ran out of the office into a corridor, to try to raise the alarm, chased by McCulloch, now wielding his axe. The nurse tackled him and managed to gain possession of the weapon, but, in a scene like one from the most blood-thirsty horror movie, McCulloch simply pulled another knife from his belt and began to cut at the nurse with it, recovering his axe in the process.

McCulloch had not told his fellow escaper about the homicidal feelings that had been growing inside him during the long months of planning. When he first stabbed the patient, Mone had been taken by surprise by the violence, and this had enabled the nurse to break away. McCulloch was furious at what he saw as his partner's failure to help him, so much so that, having chased the nurse, felled him and recovered his axe, he now punished Mone with the deadly weapon, striking him a glancing blow to the back of the head – while Mone was fighting with the patient. This seemed to spur Mone on, for he picked up a garden fork that happened to be in the office and repeatedly stabbed the patient with it until he collapsed.

With both nurse and patient overpowered by the relentless savagery they had been subjected to, the next stage of the escape plan began. Mone, though still dazed by the blow from McCulloch's axe, cut the internal and external telephone wires from the social club. This done, McCulloch shoved him outside the club door and told him to keep watch. McCulloch then went back into the club, where the nurse and other patient lay unconscious and covered in blood. There he used his axe to finish off the two men.

Before leaving, he took the nurse's keys and opened the office safe, taking a large fire axe that he knew was kept there. Outside he joined Robert Mone and they put on the nurses' caps they had appropriated from the drama group props and walked across to the perimeter wire. Throwing their rope ladder over the fifteen-foot fence and barbed wire, they were able to easily climb over. It would be almost half an hour before anyone within the hospital discovered they had gone, or that a nurse and a patient had been murdered.

★ ★ ★

159

In darkness the two escapers plunged into the wild countryside. Striding over fields and crossing a railway line, they eventually came upon a road. In the distance they could see the lights of an approaching car. Mone lay down, as McCulloch, now wearing a false beard and spectacles as well as his nurse's cap, signalled to the driver by waving his torch. When he stopped, McCulloch told him that there had been an accident.

The driver got out of his car, but at the same time, by sheer coincidence, a police van happened to pull up. Two officers were in it and one of them got out to check on what was happening. As he shone his torch in McCulloch's face, the escaper responded by slashing at his throat with one of his selection of knives. The driver who had been flagged down did not wait for more – he jumped back into his car and drove straight to Carstairs State Hospital. There he told the gate officer that two of the hospital's male nurses – in uniform – were fighting with policemen along the road. He had a hard job convincing the officer that he was serious.

Back on the roadside both escapers were attacking the two policemen with knife and axe. The unarmed policemen, hopelessly disadvantaged, posed little opposition. As one lay dead in the road and the other seriously injured, McCulloch and Mone got in the police van and set off. McCulloch took the wheel, but conditions were bad and he was a poor driver. Somehow he managed to keep the car on the icy roads for ten miles, before skidding off and crashing down an embankment.

Again a passing vehicle, this time a van carrying two workmen, was flagged down. They were asked for assistance with a prisoner by a man whom they thought was a police officer. Seeing the crashed van with its blue light flashing, they readily obliged. They were rewarded by a vicious assault which left one with axe wounds to the head and the other stab wounds to the back that broke a rib and left him with a deflated lung.

McCulloch and Mone took the workmen's van and sped away. Further along they attempted to reverse off the road, became bogged down in mud and had to abandon the vehicle. Still armed with axe and knife, they waded across a river to a farm, where, after a confrontation on the doorstep with the farmer, they took the keys to his Austin Maxi and made off in it. But while they were arguing with the man, unbeknown to them, his twelve-year-old daughter had slipped into a back room and dialled 999.

By now an hour had elapsed since their escape and the alarm had only just been sounded at Carstairs. The full horror of McCulloch and Mone's murderous trail was known, but the discovery had come about in a strangely haphazard manner. The nurse's body was found first and it was thought that he had been murdered by the other patient who had then escaped. Only when the searchers went further into the social club did they see that the man they thought had escaped had also been savagely murdered.

Amazingly, when police officers went to the gatehouse to make inquiries following the attack on their two colleagues, they were not told of the murders in the social club, even though both bodies had by that time been discovered. Such was the lack of communication at Carstairs that the hospital's Principal Nursing Officer only found out about the night's events when he received a telephone call at home from the Scottish Information Office. They had taken inquiries from a newspaper and the BBC and wished to check whether Carstairs patients had been involved.

After taking the farmer's car, McCulloch and Mone sped south along the A74, in the direction of Carlisle. Now the pursuit was about to begin. So far they had been running free, but the discovery of their victims and the telephone call from the farmer's daughter meant that the police were now on their trail and aware of the car that they were driving. At Beattock Summit they were spotted and a furious chase took them southwards, screaming through Lockerbie and Gretna towards the English border. For mile after mile McCulloch managed to keep the Austin Maxi in front, but then, as they reached the M6, they were forced off the road at the Rosehill interchange and crashed on a roundabout.

They were not about to give up yet, though. A Mini had stopped at the scene and the four young people in it got out to offer assistance. Leaping from the crashed Austin, McCulloch wielding his fire axe and Mone a knife, they ran to the Mini with the intention of a third hi-jack, when police reinforcements arrived. After a violent struggle they were at last overpowered.

It was 9.14 p.m. and Thomas McCulloch and Robert Mone had been at liberty for less than three hours. In that time three men died and three others were seriously injured. The following day, as the two Carstairs patients were appearing in court, charged with murder, Bruce Millan, Secretary of State for Scotland, told the House of Commons that he was making inquiries to ensure that the escape did not disclose any obvious security deficiencies.

★ ★ ★

The Carstairs staff had their own opinions on security deficiencies. Their grief at the loss of a colleague, and sympathy for the other victims, was tinged with anger that the escape and murders had been allowed to happen. In an atmosphere of heightened emotions and uncertainty as to the full facts, the hospital management's failure to heed earlier warnings and proposals by staff was seen as a direct cause of the tragedy. Some staff felt that the hospital regime, in which supervision was progressively relaxed and inmates were allowed freedom of movement within the grounds, was wrong. Others believed that security had been neglected. The withdrawal of nurses from the occupational therapy department and the refusal of the management to appoint a security officer were also condemned. A meeting attended by more than 300 men and women brought a vote of no-confidence in the management of the State Hospital and a demand that four senior members of staff be suspended from duty. Bitterness reached boiling point when the Principal Nursing Officer was prevented from entering the premises by a picket line.

At Edinburgh High Court on 28 February 1977, Thomas McCulloch pleaded guilty to three charges of murder and three of attempted murder. He had accepted full responsibility for his deeds as soon as he was recaptured and now instructed his counsel to offer no mitigation to the court on his behalf. Robert Mone pleaded guilty to the murder of the policeman, but not guilty to the murder of the nursing officer and the patient. His counsel blamed McCulloch for those two and for persuading Mone to escape, saying that Mone had wanted to use the minimum amount of violence, but his co-accused had gone berserk. Mone told police that he and McCulloch had been promised a day out of the hospital, but could not wait. 'It's too easy to get out of that place,' he said. They were both sentenced to life imprisonment, the judge, Lord Dunpark, stating that as far as he was concerned that meant for the rest of their natural lives.

So McCulloch and Mone said goodbye to the asylum and went into the prison system. Yet until their escape and trail of murderous mayhem they were considered suitably insane to be kept at Carstairs without limit of time, both having been regularly assessed by psychiatrists throughout their stay at the hospital. It seems ironic that three people had to die and three more be seriously wounded for the psychiatric profession to form a new opinion – that both killers were sane and fit to plead. The official explanation for this incongruous state of affairs is that they were now both considered to be dangerous psychopaths with untreatable personality disorders. As to how long each had been in this state and why the psychiatrists had not noticed it before, there was no explanation.

Two weeks after the events of Tuesday 30 November, the Secretary of State appointed Robert Reid QC, Sheriff of Glasgow, to report on the circumstances surrounding the escape from Carstairs and on security and other arrangements at the hospital. His inquiry was held in the Memorial Hall at Lanark from 21 March until 15 April 1977 and heard evidence from all relevant parties, including an advocate representing the widow and son of the murdered nursing officer, who was said to have acted 'with great courage and in accordance with the highest traditions of the nursing service'.

On 12 April Robert Reid and his three assessors went to Barlinnie Prison in Glasgow to hear evidence from Thomas McCulloch and Robert Mone in person. Both men cooperated with the inquiry and gave accounts of their respective parts in the escape and murders. They even offered advice on security. According to Reid's report, they 'more than once stated that any means of detention could be subverted and that the best method of maintaining security was to search for the individual who was a security risk and not for breaches of security precautions.' Homicidal madmen McCulloch and Mone might have been, but the Sheriff agreed that there was much truth in what they were saying, although in practice it was not so easy to carry out their suggestions.

Consultant psychiatrists for both killers gave evidence to the inquiry. Of McCulloch it was said that he was considered to have had long-term prospects of becoming 'a reasonably safe member of society'. The doctor expressed surprise that he had prejudiced these chances and that he had escaped. The inquiry was told that Mone was a psychopath and as such a social rather than a medical problem. Only time would lead to maturity and no medication or treatment was likely to help. Hospitals were not the place for psychopaths, according to Mone's psychiatrist. Yet throughout the eight years he had been in Carstairs Mone had been repeatedly assessed as possessing psychopathic traits.

The Reid Report was published in October 1977. It contained many criticisms of security at Carstairs and in all forty-four recommendations were made as to improvements. These related to the management and staffing of the hospital, closer scrutiny of visitors and of gifts to patients and the searching of patients after visits. A central control room was to be established, with all movements of patients under escort reported and recorded. An inner fence was to be erected, plus flood-lights. The woodwork department, where many of the escapers' weapons were made, was singled out for special attention, in particular the need for greater control over work done, materials issued, the disposal of waste and searches of patients carrying boxes in or out.

Reid's proposals received more attention than similar suggestions made earlier by the hospital staff. The government took heed and three months later it was announced that £2million was to be spent on making Carstairs State Hospital more secure, including the erection of a secondary perimeter fence.

Locked up for life he might have been, but the public had not heard the last of Robert Mone. Two years after the Carstairs escape his name was again in the news when his father, also called Robert but known as Sonny, was convicted of the murder of three women in Dundee. Mone senior, aged fifty-four, was alleged to have boasted of his son's deadly deeds, to have told police, 'All I live for is to be in there with him,' and to have often claimed, 'I am going to be more famous than the Carstairs killer.' He was sentenced to life with a mini-mum fifteen-year recommendation, but in January 1983 the aggressor became the victim when Sonny Mone was stabbed to death in Aberdeen Prison by a one-eyed armed robber whom he had referred to as 'Cyclops' and threatened to kill. His assailant got eight years for justifiable homicide of the prisoner he told the court was 'probably the most obnoxious man in the country'.

166

In between his father murdering and being murdered, Robert Mone made the news on his own account when, in 1981, he was transferred to Perth. The jail's location in the heart of housing estates led to an outcry from the public that such a dangerous man was in their midst. The prison Governor assured local residents that there was no need whatsoever to worry, security arrangements at the top-security prison were sufficient to hold Robert Mone.

Only a few days later this claim looked rather weak when Mone bade farewell to a working party, climbed a drainpipe and sat on the laundry roof for eight hours. Long and loud were his protests about being banged-up for twenty-three hours a day at weekends. He came down of his own accord, but it was enough to confirm the local anxiety, to raise questions in the Commons and to make the Scottish Prison Officer's Association express their thoughts on the increasing numbers of mentally disturbed people going into prison.

While on the roof, Mone had declared that Perth was a powder keg waiting to explode. In 1987 the prison did erupt, when a prison officer was taken hostage and a great deal of damage was done to a wing. Mone took no part in the riot, but sued the Secretary of State, alleging that his radio, spectacles and other property had been broken by prisoners who entered his cell. He gave evidence manacled to an officer, but lost his case. Still in Perth Prison in September 1992, Robert Mone spoke at a conference on the need for prisoners to be responsible for their actions and to realise what they had done.

The other Carstairs escaper, Tom McCulloch, maintains a consistently low profile in Peterhead Prison, where he has been held in solitary confinement since 1976. He has no contact at all with other prisoners and much of his time is spent making soft toys, which are sold for local charities. Demonised by the Scottish press, whose accounts of that terrible November night have often been high on sensation and low on insight, he has steadfastly refused all requests and offers from the media to tell his story, believing that to do so would serve little purpose and would only bring further grief to the relatives of the deceased and the other victims.

At the time of writing there are no indications that either man will ever be released. In view of the judge's recommendation when sentencing them to life imprisonment in 1977, such a possibility seems unlikely.

11   BILLY HUGHES

The Pottery Cottage Killer

Escapes by prisoners in transit have occurred with great regularity in recent years. As perimeter and internal security has increased, many inmates have found that their best chance of breaking out is during a journey from prison to court, or while being transferred from one prison to another. Cars have been hi-jacked, their occupants liberated and escort officers attacked. Gun-toting rescuers have suddenly appeared on the pavement between courthouse door and prison vehicle. Men have cut their way out of mini-buses, dived through coach windows. On one occasion a robber on his way to Brixton from the Old Bailey blasted a hole in the roof of the prison van, with explosives that had been smuggled to him inside boiled sweets.

Serious incidents involving dangerous and ruthless men, but the worst escape by a prisoner in transit was that of Billy Hughes in 1977. Despite the horrific consequences, and the many recommendations and proposals that were voiced in the aftermath, it seems that the lessons to be learned from Hughes' escape have long gone unheeded.

★ ★ ★

William Thomas Hughes was a petty criminal with a record for housebreaking and violence. Thirty years old and heavily tattooed, his idol was singer Johnny Cash, famed for such records as 'San Quentin' and 'Folsom Prison Blues'. Hughes had already served five prison sentences before he was charged with rape and grievous bodily harm and committed to Leicester Prison. There, the authorities took no notice of a warning by Derbyshire police that he was likely to escape, was of an extremely violent nature and had suicidal tendencies, nor did they receive his criminal record until the day after he escaped. Had they done so they would have discovered that the man whom they considered to be a run-of-the-mill inmate, who was described by prison staff as 'placid' and 'quite a pleasant prisoner', was not exactly what they thought he was.

They would have learned that he had a reputation for extreme violence that was known the length and breadth of his native Lancashire. Once, after a high-speed car chase in Blackpool, and while under the influence of drugs, Hughes had punched, bitten and kicked six policemen, putting several of them in hospital. Later the same day he head-butted another officer, sending him to hospital too, before going berserk in the cell area at Blackpool police station and ripping out the entire central-heating system. They would have learned that in another incident, after being hit with a plank by a desperate policeman who was trying to arrest him, he fought on regardless until reinforcements arrived – and that he had once killed two police dogs with his bare hands.

Had they taken heed of the warning from the police,

or obtained his record, which included five convictions for assault and grievous bodily harm, the Leicester authorities might have considered it unwise to allow Hughes to work in the prison kitchen – from where he was able to steal a razor-sharp boning knife, seven and a half inches long. They might also have transported him from the prison to Chesterfield for his weekly remand appearances by means other than a taxi, escorted by two middle-aged officers. As it was, the police warning went unheeded and information was not received – with disastrous consequences.

Hughes spent much of his life, when he was not behind bars, in Blackpool, but in 1976 he formed a relationship with a woman older than himself and moved to live with her in Chesterfield, Derbyshire. He found it hard to keep away from his Lancashire home, in particular from his estranged wife, and after only two weeks he returned, to be arrested after beating her up. He managed to avoid a prison sentence this time, but, back in Chesterfield on a hot August night, he came upon a young courting couple, beat up the boy after hitting him with a brick and dragged the girl off to a park, where he raped her at knife-point. His new lover thought the description given out by the police sounded all too familiar, but chose not to contact the police. Someone else did, and within a few days Hughes was in Leicester Prison on remand and his lover wrote to him telling him their relationship was over.

Each week Hughes was taken from the prison to Chesterfield Magistrates' Court for preliminary appearances, before his case was committed to the Crown Court. He spun out these hearings by giving his solicitors contradictory instructions to the extent that, in all, he made ten journeys to and from Chesterfield. On each occasion he was taken in a taxi, escorted by two warders, and the regular trips gave him plenty of opportunity to work out an escape plan.

On Wednesday 12 January 1977, as the blue Morris 1800 private-hire car turned off the M1 motorway at Junction 29, Hughes, sitting in the back of the car, one wrist handcuffed to a warder, suddenly leaned forward and without warning struck the other warder, sitting in the front passenger seat, a heavy blow to the head. The man was jolted forward and Hughes produced a boning knife and slashed at the neck of the warder to whom he was handcuffed, causing a deep wound five inches long. As his colleague in the front turned round, trying to recover himself, Hughes lunged at him with the knife, slashing his hand and exposing his jaw bone in two wild strokes.

He barked at the driver to keep moving, telling him, 'Do as you're told and you'll be all right.' The car passed through Chesterfield and out on to the moors at Stonedge, where Hughes ordered the driver to stop and the officers to unlock his handcuffs. He made the three men give him all the money they had in their pockets, commenting that the warders, who had only £4 between them 'must be poorly paid'. Bundling them out of the taxi on to the side of the road, both warders bleeding profusely from their wounds, he handcuffed all three men together, jumped into the driver's seat and tore off down the road.

It was a freezing day and on icy roads Hughes did not get far. Before he had gone two miles he crashed into a wall at Beeley, near Chatsworth, home of the Duke of

Devonshire, and made off on foot. By this time the prison officers stuck on the roadside had flagged down a passing vehicle and raised the alarm. More than 100 police officers were immediately mobilised as road-blocks were set up over a wide area and motorists were warned not to pick up hitch-hikers. With the discovery of the blood-splattered taxi at Beeley, all workers on the 1,000-acre Chatsworth estate were warned to immobilise their cars and to keep shotguns and ammunition locked up. 'This man is violent and should not be approached,' said a police spokesman. 'He might still have a knife and is likely to use it again.'

For three days, in bleak, snow-bound weather, the police visited houses and searched farms and outbuildings around the Chesterfield area. Manpower was doubled to 200, dogs were brought in and a helicopter swept across the countryside. But even as they searched for Billy Hughes, Derbyshire police were not anticipating success. It was widely believed that he would head for Lancashire to further harm, possibly even carry out his threat to kill, his estranged wife. Nonetheless, his recent lover in Chesterfield was put under police guard, to such an extent that when she went for a drink in the pubs of the normally sleepy town on the Friday night, a plain-clothes policewoman accompanied her and fifteen detectives lurked in the shadows.

But Billy Hughes was looking for neither his wife nor his most recent mistress. He was not running and hiding nor living rough off the frozen land. He was in Pottery Cottage at the small hamlet of Eastmoor, less than a mile from the place where he had last been sighted, two hours after he hi-jacked the taxi. He was only down the road

from the search headquarters set up by police at a local
pub, The Highwayman. To all outward appearances life
was going on as normal at Pottery Cottage – so much so
that the property was not searched, nor even visited by
the police.

Nothing could have been further from the truth.
Hughes arrived at the cottage on the Wednesday, the
same day that he escaped, and took the occupants, an
elderly couple, hostage. As the other members of the
Moran family – a ten-year-old girl, Sarah, her mother,
Gill, and lastly at 6.15 p.m. her father, Richard – arrived
home, they were similarly taken hostage and kept apart
in separate rooms. The same day, Hughes stabbed the
little girl to death in a bedroom and her grandfather in
the lounge, but kept up a pretence that they were still
alive by taking food to the rooms in which their bodies
lay.

Early the following morning, council workmen arrived
at Pottery Cottage to clean the septic tank. They completed their task and Gill Moran signed their worksheet.
Nothing in her demeanour suggested to them that there
was anything amiss inside the cottage. Such was the hold
Hughes had on the family that later in the morning he
instructed her to drive into Chesterfield to fetch cigarettes and a newspaper. She did so alone, returning to
the cottage without doing anything to raise attention to
her family's plight.

At tea-time that day Gill Moran and her husband,
Richard, attempted to drive into Chesterfield again, at
Hughes' behest, as he remained at the cottage, but this
time they were turned back by a blizzard. Later in the
evening Hughes and Gill Moran drove to Sutton-in-
Ashfield, a distance of sixteen miles. When they got

there, he muttered that he needed some papers and ordered Mrs Moran to drive straight back. No sooner had they returned than he made her drive him once again to Sutton, and on arrival this time he left her in the car for several minutes while he got out, saying he was looking for a friend.

On the following morning, Friday, Richard and Gill Moran left the cottage once more and, leaving Hughes in the house, they again drove into Chesterfield. They visited five shops and filled the car up with petrol before returning home. At 5 p.m. Hughes made Richard Moran drive him to the Staveley plastics company where he was sales manager. There he emptied the safe of £200, arriving back at Pottery Cottage at 6.20. Soon afterwards the seventy-year-old grandmother tried to make a break by jumping from an upstairs window. Hughes raced outside the cottage and dragged her back, slitting her throat right there in the garden and covering the body with snow.

Hughes now decided the time had come to leave. Richard and Gill Moran were the only members of the family still alive, although they did not know that. The charade of Hughes taking food to the grandfather and the ten-year-old daughter, Sarah, had fooled them into thinking that they were all right. After tying up the husband, Hughes ordered Gill Moran into the family's Chrysler car, with the intention of leaving the cottage, but the ground was too frozen and the car wheels would not grip. Amazingly, he and his hostage walked along the road to a neighbour's house and asked him if he would tow the Chrysler out of the drive. The neighbour agreed and, with his way now clear, Hughes left his remaining hostage in the car, on the pretext of going back into the cottage to fetch some maps. Once inside, he went to the upstairs landing where Richard Moran lay trussed and bound and repeatedly stabbed him as he lay there, helpless to defend himself.

Unbeknown to Hughes, when they approached the neighbour for a tow, Gill Moran had alerted the man that her husband was being held in the cottage. 'It's the moors man,' she whispered. After towing the Chrysler on to the road, the neighbour telephoned the police. When they arrived at Pottery Cottage the doors were locked, all the lights were on and loud music was coming from an upstairs room. They broke the kitchen window and climbed in – to discover Richard Moran dying on the landing and the full horror of Billy Hughes' three days on the run.

All police vehicles were immediately alerted, with a description of the Chrysler. Hughes had gone only ten miles when the car was spotted by Regional Crime Squad officers in an unmarked Marina, as it approached crossroads heading towards Tideswell. They tried to flag him down and overtake, but Hughes drove straight at them. For more than five miles they stuck with him along the moorland roads. Conditions were so bad that normal radio contact was impossible and at the first pub they passed an officer had to be dropped off to inform the search headquarters by telephone.

To Hughes' great agitation, the Marina stayed right on his tail. Then, after taking a sharp left-hand bend on the main Chapel-en-le-Frith road, he lost control of the Chrysler and hit a wall. The detectives ran to the car, but he whipped out a knife and pressed it to Gill Moran's throat, threatening that if they did not back off he would kill her. At this point the men who had cornered him had no idea of the murders Hughes had already committed, but it was obvious that he was so frenzied that his hostage's life was in grave danger.

For twenty minutes a detective inspector tried to talk him into giving up the knife and releasing Gill Moran, but he would not entertain the idea. Instead, he demanded the unmarked police car and eventually the inspector agreed that he could take it. With his knife still at the hostage's throat, Hughes, minus his shoes, transferred to the Marina and sped away down the road. What he did not know was that, as the detective had been talking to him, a police Range Rover had pulled up 200 yards away. Now the crime squad men piled into that. The chase was still on.

With radio contact resumed, armed police were summoned and road-blocks set up around the area. Meantime the Range Rover stuck right behind Hughes as they sped along narrow, treacherous roads at reckless speeds. All over the Peak District, on a winding trail towards Stockport and Glossop, the pursuit continued, all through the Friday evening, until Hughes eventually crossed the Derbyshire boundary into Cheshire. There, in the small village of Rainow, police had blocked the road by driving a bus across it. Undeterred, Hughes drove headlong towards the bus, then swerved, trying to get round it, crashing the Marina into a wall. Again, as police surrounded him, he held his knife to Gill Moran's throat and also produced an axe that he had brought from Pottery Cottage.

Police marksmen had not yet arrived at Rainow. As a stop-gap measure a shotgun was borrowed from a house close by, but the officer in charge at the scene knew only too well that if it was to be fired in Hughes' direction it would be likely to cause as much harm to his hostage as to him. Once again negotiations were attempted to try to talk him into releasing his hostage and surrendering, but Hughes was in no state to listen to reason. He became more and more desperate and irrational, demanding another car, a pair of shoes – size 8 – and he repeatedly banged the car door open and shut.

Another car, which Hughes had demanded, was driven up to the side of the Marina – but the killer would not be going anywhere in it. It was brought there to divert his attention while the marksmen, who had now arrived, moved into position. Hughes had no reason to think that the police would kill him – no prison escaper in modern times had ever been shot dead by the British police.

But Billy Hughes would go down as the first. After all attempts to negotiate with him failed, what little control he had suddenly went. An outside light at a house across the road came on and he panicked, shouting that the police were trying to trick him. He went berserk, screamed, 'Your time is up,' to his terror-stricken hostage and began attacking her with the axe. The policeman who had been negotiating dived through the open car window and began to struggle with him, receiving several blows to his arm from the axe. As they wrestled, and the hostage Gill Moran lay underneath this melee, a marksman at the front of the Marina fired his Smith & Wesson .38 pistol through the windscreen from twelve feet, hitting Hughes in the head. He shouted, 'Oh bloody hell!' but continued to hit Mrs Moran with the axe. The officer fired another shot, again hitting

Hughes, who opened the car door and was on the point of getting out when a second marksman shot him in the chest from the driver's side, felling him. The four-times killer who boasted to friends that he did not feel pain, that such things were all in the mind, died instantly.

The full extent of Hughes' three-day rampage was now revealed and the murderer himself was dead. It was time to find out how the whole bloody business had arisen. How had a prisoner with Hughes' record of violence been able to steal a seven-and-a-half-inch, razor-sharp boning knife from the Leicester Prison kitchens? How had he got it into the taxi when he was supposedly searched before setting out? Why had members of the Moran family not raised the alarm, especially when it transpired that Richard and Gill Moran had several opportunities to do so? One of the earliest queries to be publicly aired was the question of how Hughes could have stayed so close to the scene of his last sighting, and to the police search headquarters, without being discovered.

Some of the questions were soon answered. As Gill Moran lay in a hospital bed, suffering from the severe shock of hearing the fate of her daughter, husband and parents, besides the injuries Hughes inflicted to her head and neck, a senior police officer said that whatever happened at Pottery Cottage had been done under the fear of the family's lives. 'The activities in the house were governed by this fear and were made to appear as normal as possible.' Blind terror had prevented Gill Moran from raising the alarm, with the fear of what Hughes might do to her daughter uppermost in her mind. 'She did precisely what Hughes told her to do,' the spokesman said. 'She was very concerned for the safety of her family.'

The prison officer who had been handcuffed to Hughes in the back of the taxi – and slashed on the neck by him – explained that because he and his colleague knew nothing of their prisoner's violent record they had given him only a casual frisking, rather than a head-to-toe search. 'We were not told he could be violent and had a bad record,' he said. 'From what I have heard since we should have definitely stripped him and given him a real going-over.'

A few days later Derbyshire's Assistant Chief Constable admitted that Pottery Cottage had not been visited during the manhunt, even though outbuildings at a near-by public house had been searched. He said that the police had been acting on information that Hughes had violent intentions towards his wife in Blackpool and as a result the search was concentrated westwards, away from the cottage, 'We are satisfied on information and intelligence we have had available to us that the most logical search area was westward from the point at which Hughes was last seen.'

Following the escape and the attack on the two warders, 200 prison officers at Leicester began industrial action, demanding an independent inquiry into the affair. It was alleged that, after the boning knife went missing on 3 December, a request by warders for a search of the prison was turned down because the management felt it would have adversely affected morale among prisoners. One warder told pressmen that an independent investigation was important because, 'We feel a prison inquiry will whitewash the real problems.'

But a prison inquiry, conducted by Gordon Fowler, Chief Inspector of the Prison Service, was all they got. In looking at Hughes' escape and subsequent actions, one of Fowler's first priorities was the boning knife with which he had cut the prison officers. It was revealed that this knife had gone missing nearly six weeks before Hughes attacked his escort, yet there were no records at Leicester of any searches made by staff, and standard searching procedures had clearly not been followed. A number of staff to whom Mr Fowler spoke were not even aware that a knife had gone missing until after Hughes assaulted their two colleagues with it on 12 January.

The inquiry report disclosed that Derbyshire Police's warning that Hughes was dangerous was received at Leicester Prison the day after he arrived there, but the information never reached the security department. He was allocated to work in the kitchen on the basis of what he told staff about himself.

Prison staff were criticised for their failure to take the theft of the knife seriously enough. The report called for urgent communication between police and prisons regarding information about prisoners and the charges they faced. Both the police and the courts were condemned for failing to provide up-to-date information on Hughes, which might have made staff at Leicester regard him more seriously than they did.

After studying the Chief Inspector of Prisons' report, the Home Secretary, Merlyn Rees, announced that no disciplinary action would be taken against any officer at Leicester. He told the Commons that seventeen of the report's twenty-five recommendations were to be implemented immediately, that there had been 'errors of judgement', but they were 'failures of the system, rather than of particular individuals'. On the police's failure to visit Pottery Cottage, he explained that from the outside there was nothing to suggest anything was amiss. But, since they were combing the area all around, why had they not visited, if only to warn the occupants that a dangerous prisoner was on the loose?

It was left to two local MPs, one Tory the other Labour, to reflect public opinion in Derbyshire. There was, they both agreed, great anxiety and criticism about the way in which the police operation had been conducted, a view shared by the Shadow Home Secretary, William Whitelaw, who expressed grave concern and called for 'immediate action to ensure that dangerous prisoners cannot escape while being moved from prisons'.

Billy Hughes was, according to the Chesterfield mother-of-four with whom he was living at the time of the rape, a shy person with a Jekyll and Hyde personality, who liked to make matchstick models of gipsy caravans. 'He loved the country, walking and swimming and having a good laugh. But when he had a drink he would change – he would not argue with them, he would just hit them. He never carried knives, he was strong enough by himself,' she said.

Meanwhile, the problem of Hughes' funeral was causing some consternation. Local people were enraged to hear that the killer's body was to be buried in the town cemetery. Speaking on behalf of the protestors – and exhibiting a curiously perverse grasp of folk-lore – a town councillor said, 'People will be walking all over the cemetery to look at this infamous grave. It will be like going to look at the grave of Robin Hood.'

182

On the day that Hughes' funeral was due to go ahead, the gates to Boythorpe Cemetery were mysteriously chained and padlocked, to prevent the hearse from entering. As local women ignored a downpour to fill in the freshly-dug grave, scraping at the earth with their bare hands, a funeral service was being held instead at the near-by crematorium. The priest who took the service told the small gathering of mourners – Hughes' wife and ten or so of his relatives – that it was not for people to judge Hughes' actions, that would be in God's hands. Local people, livid that Hughes' funeral had been allowed to take place at all in their town, and that he had been cremated at the very same place as his victims, did not agree. As the mourners left they were confronted with placards and banners.

If the official inquiry shed some light on Hughes' escape and four murders, it offered no explanation as to why he had gone to such extreme lengths. In possession of a knife, he could have escaped from the taxi by threatening his escort, without having to wound both prison officers as he did. Having taken the Moran family hostage, he held them in separate rooms and could have taken the money and car without doing them any physical harm at all – their compliance posed no threat to him.

So what sparked such a wave of wanton violence? The only explanation put forward came from his brother, who attended the funeral. He said that Hughes hated prison – something he told a number of people who met him – and knew that on the rape charge he was going down for a long time. Even so, if the police had not shot him, the actions he chose were guaranteed to ensure that he would be going inside for longer, if not for ever.

The last word goes to a police spokesman who was asked by reporters if Billy Hughes had a history of psychiatric disorder. 'It appears so recently,' he said.

12   ALAN REEVE

Through the Dragnet

On the general public's panic scale, news of a break-out from a top-security mental institution usually triggers off a more extreme reaction than any escape from prison by a notorious criminal. The villain, by and large, tends to lie low and avoid conflict while the mental patient is invariably less equipped to deal with the outside world and much less likely to have back-up resources. Billy Hughes, a prison rather than mental hospital escaper, does suggest an exception to the rule, but he was no big-time criminal. Of the major villains whose escapes have been detailed so far, none, from Ruby Sparks to John McVicar, Johnny Ramensky to the Great Train Robbers, harmed members of the public either during their break-outs or while on the run. Conversely, and to some extent justifying the public's fear and alarm, John Straffen got out of Broadmoor and killed a young child, Frank Mitchell broke out of Rampton and Broadmoor to instill terror with his axe, besides the more recent triple murders at Carstairs.

In the mid-1930s escapes from Broadmoor averaged five a year – a figure that caused unease among the residents of near-by Crowthorne, but a few years later seemed very moderate when fifty-one inmates escaped in one twelve-month period. The Straffen and Mitchell episodes, which were followed by other less eventful but equally worrying examples of flawed security, at last brought about effective improvements. Albeit as *The Times* protested, 'only under pressure of a public scandal', but for nearly two decades security at Broadmoor was under control. There were no high-profile manhunts linked to attacks on local residents, no questions in Parliament and it seemed that, as successive Ministers of Health had long promised, the perimeter wall could now contain the institution's most dangerous and desperate inmates.

In the summer of 1981 all peace of mind was destroyed when child-killer James Lang climbed the Broadmoor wall. His freedom was short-lived – he lasted only a day after breaking his ankle, but he had got out. Then, before the repercussions of this breach in the defences had died down – before many of the questions that it raised could be answered – another Broadmoor patient went over the wall. This one got away.

Alan Reeve, thirty-two years old, was committed to Broadmoor without limit of time in 1964 at the age of fifteen. He had absconded from Rochester Borstal after his brother was arrested for plotting to free him. The brother was himself sent to a different Borstal and once Reeve got out – supposedly on a day's compassionate leave to see his parents – he decided that the least he could do for his brother was obtain a gun and kill the two people he thought had betrayed him to the police.

Although still a boy, Reeve went about his mission

186

with obsessive purpose, deciding that as well as avenging his brother he must liberate him. Heading for Plymouth, he arranged to buy guns and dynamite via a contact he had made in Borstal. Needing money, he burgled houses, stealing several hundred pounds, and he bought purple hearts and benzedrine pills to keep himself awake. In a disturbed and depressed state he arrived at a Youth Hostel in Colchester, having deposited a shotgun and ammunition, stolen from one of the houses he had burgled, in the bus station left-luggage department.

At the hostel Reeve became friendly with another boy, also fifteen years old, who was on a cycling holiday. The following day, after swallowing handfuls of pills, he showed the boy the shotgun and they began to discuss juvenile crime. To Reeve's dismay the boy did not share his views, going so far as to suggest that crime was wrong. This was bad enough, but when the conversation was steered round to Borstals, the boy made what Reeve considered to be derogatory remarks about the inmates of such places. In a fit of anger, Reeve exploded, telling the boy that his brother was in Borstal and no one was allowed to make nasty comments about him. Raising the shotgun above his head, he brought it down with such force that the butt shattered on the boy's head. He fell to the ground and tried to get away, but Reeve continued to strike him repeatedly with the barrel, then finished him off by stabbing him a number of times with a knife.

In the dead boy's clothing Reeve found three postcards addressed to his parents. As he later told detectives, 'He had written them out so I thought the people would like to have them.' He posted the cards from Southend, where he fled by bus, adding to the family's grief by writing on each one DOA – Dead On Arrival.

★ ★ ★

Three years later Alan Reeve was convicted of murdering a fellow Broadmoor inmate after admitting the killing to staff. The victim, who had been released once from Broadmoor only to murder someone on the outside and be returned, had asked Reeve to kill him as he felt life was no longer worth living. Reeve retracted his confession, which he claimed to have made in a confused mental state, but would not name the man he said was the real murderer. The jury found him guilty. Still only nineteen, he was described by the judge as a merciless killer.

By 1974 Reeve had begun a course of study that would open his mind to a world far beyond the Broadmoor walls and the narrow confines of his previous life. He also formed a group to organise the inmates on a political basis, and embarked on various protests, including one seventy-two-hour stint on the roof. In December, along with two other inmates, he cut through cell bars with a hacksaw blade. Their escape attempt was foiled when, moving across the exercise yard, the three men were met by a warder. They headed for a drainpipe and instead of leaving Broadmoor had to be content with airing their grievances by way of a rooftop demonstration.

Reeve did well at his studies. In 1980 he obtained an Open University honours degree and was looking forward to taking a PhD course. He was looking forward even more to being released from Broadmoor, having spent sixteen years there, but in this he faced continual frustration. The Broadmoor staff had recommended him for conditional discharge since 1977, but the Home Secretary refused. On three separate occasions his hopes were raised, only to be dashed at the top level. In June 1981 he sent telegrams to the Queen, the Prime Minister and the Home Secretary, complaining that he had waited seven months for a decision and that such treatment was inhuman. When the decision did arrive, it recommended that Reeve should leave Broadmoor. He was not, however, to be released, only transferred to another secure mental hospital, Park Lane in Liverpool. Reeve had a better idea. Like others before him he came to the conclusion that if the authorities would not let him out, he would have to let himself out.

On Sunday 9 August 1981, at 1.15 p.m., Alan Reeve escaped from Broadmoor. He set off with an improvised rope and a grappling hook, but found the rope too thin to climb up. Nevertheless he made it – by going over two high walls and a fence, falling twenty feet in the process, breaking bones in his back and foot and ripping his hands to shreds on the barbed wire. He went out to a girlfriend he had met only three months earlier and an outside world he had not known since childhood. A fellow inmate saw him escape, but waited an hour before telling staff – and setting off a full-scale manhunt.

The hospital's siren blasted across the Berkshire countryside, road-blocks, dogs and a helicopter were rushed to the area, but Reeve had slipped the net. Although his doctors considered him no longer dangerous, police warned the public not to approach him, as the local MP called on the Home Secretary to launch an inquiry into how he had got out.

Two days later a Ford Escort car hired by his girlfriend was found at the hovercraft terminal in Dover and, as the search switched to the Continent, Interpol were brought in. Spain, where his girlfriend's parents lived, and Strasbourg, headquarters of the European Commission of Human Rights, were identified as possible destinations. A month earlier Reeve had discussed taking his case to Strasbourg with his solicitor, who now said he might be aiming to create European as well as British publicity for his case.

Reeve's father, a military prison officer, told reporters he was worried that his son's left-wing views would lead him to seek shelter among political activists on the Continent. 'Alan knows the political scene in Europe very well,' he said. 'He studied it for his Open University degree course. He knows about the various left-wing groups and I gather his girlfriend has contacts with political organisations. I am worried that he might get mixed up with some extremist group that will want to make capital out of his plight.'

The assumption that Reeve and his fiancée had slipped out of the country was correct. In a lot of pain from the injuries he sustained on the way out of Broadmoor, Reeve made it to Holland, where he settled quietly as the search for him went on elsewhere.

Three weeks after he went over the wall, a letter addressed to Home Secretary William Whitelaw was reproduced in full in *The Times*. In it, Reeve confirmed that his reason for liberating himself was the continuing refusal of the Home Secretary to release him, contrary to the advice of Home Office psychiatrists. He issued a firm denial of the second killing of which he had been convicted, that of the Broadmoor patient in 1967, asking Mr Whitelaw to examine the case and the 'inadequate and misrepresented forensic evidence which would have cast doubts on the validity of my initial "confession".'

Reeve told the Home Secretary, 'I am a communist, Mr Whitelaw . . . I seek to serve the class from which I come, the working class' and went on to rail against 'this democratic society of yours'. He ended by saying, 'No doubt you will issue statements that I am "mad" or "dangerous", or even "mad and dangerous" but how are you going to ignore the often repeated conclusion of YOUR experts? . . . You have condemned me to a life outside the law – unless, that is, your legal system is replaced by a legal system more conducive to justice. I shall work for such a replacement.'

Another letter, to journalist Lucy Hodges who had visited Reeve in Broadmoor in 1980, was dated, like the one to the Home Secretary, on the day he escaped. Typed, it was posted through her front door in an unfranked envelope some time after 11 August, at which time Reeve had been free for two days. He told Ms Hodges, 'As you receive this I shall be an escaped prisoner, wanted by the police for returning to detention – a circumstance I shall do my utmost to avoid'. He said he intended to continue with his studies and to contribute 'to the political theory and practice to which I am committed'. He said he hoped he got a reasonable press, as the people he left behind would benefit from a little rational comment and that, apart from the illegality of leaving Broadmoor without permission – 'something I feel any self-respecting person would try' – it was not his intention to enter into negotiation with the Home Office or conflict with the law. But in Amsterdam, three days before the first anniversary of his escape, Alan Reeve entered into major conflict with the Dutch law – he shot a policeman.

★ ★ ★

Reeve enjoyed his first year of freedom and planned to celebrate with a party on 9 August, a Monday. On the Friday before, he cycled to an off-licence near to the squat where he was living and stole two bottles of whisky and a bottle of Cointreau, the latter a treat for his fiancée. Outside the shop he was stopped by two police-men, the Cointreau was found in his bag and he was requested to return to the shop with the men.

Not overly worried about being apprehended for shoplifting, of which he thought he could probably talk his way out, Reeve suddenly realised that in his pocket he had a gun. He knew that when the policemen discovered it full checks would be made on him and the game would be up.

He ran – a return to the isolation wards and forced drug treatments of Broadmoor looming large in his mind. As he did so, he turned to shoot at the policemen. They backed off, but as he ran on, one followed. Reeve fired again, hitting a car window. The chase was now on and, as a police car appeared with two men in the front seats, Reeve fired one shot at the windscreen and another at the driver. There was an exchange of fire and a desperate gun battle flared before Reeve hi-jacked a car at gun-point, forcing the driver to drive on.

He later claimed that he had bought the gun a month earlier to kill himself if cornered and faced with arrest, but when the time came he did not want to give up. If this explanation was true, it did not explain why he needed so much ammunition. Reeve tried to make it to his flat, weaving through the Amsterdam streets. He had crossed a canal and was tiring fast when once again he found himself trapped by police. He had only two bullets left as the police began firing, hitting him in the foot and back. Attempting to take a hostage, he grabbed a woman passer-by, but police had crept up behind him. In a swift movement he was overpowered and thrown into the back of a van. Before being taken to the police headquarters there was a short stop-off at a hospital, where he had a bullet removed from his foot. Reeve's were not the only wounds – two policemen had been hit by his bullets and one had died.

In September 1982, a month after his recapture, Alan Reeve married his girlfriend in a Utrecht prison. In December, for the third time in his life, he faced a murder charge, the Dutch prosecutor asking for a twenty-year sentence. Reeve took the opportunity to make allegations about political control and maltreatment in British psychiatric hospitals, to let the world know his own political commitment and to show his contempt for the Dutch court. The three-man bench accepted that he had shot the two policemen intentionally, but did not find him guilty of murder, giving him fifteen years for manslaughter and attempted manslaughter. Reeve showed no emotion as he heard the sentence. In a signed statement issued afterwards he said, 'Whatever happens to me the struggle will go on.' Later he condemned the sentence as 'savage'.

His sentence did not pass uneventfully. He resumed his studies and became a doctor of political psychology. Later he qualified as a lawyer and impressed his keepers so much that a prison Governor said, 'He is amazing. We have never had such an intelligent prisoner in our legal system.' In February 1985, he was one of five convicts who tried to escape from Scheveningen Prison. Transferred to the jail's high-security wing he embarked on the longest-ever hunger strike by any prisoner in Holland. When, after fifty-two days, his body could no longer take fluids and he vomited a litre of bile, it was expected that Reeve would become the first prisoner in the country to die on hunger strike. But he did not die – against all expectations he began to take food and made a recovery.

In early 1992, the British authorities heard that Alan Reeve was being considered for parole in Holland. A psychiatrist, despatched to Scheveningen Prison to examine him, formed the opinion that he was psychopathic and should be returned to Broadmoor. An extradition hearing was fixed, but before it came up the Dutch Ministry of Justice advised British officials to withdraw their extradition application. They wished to seek permission from a judge to keep Reeve in jail until he could be deported back to Britain. When that case came up, the judge did not comply. Expressing irritation that the Dutch and British authorities had 'colluded', he freed Reeve in October 1992.

Reactions to the freeing of the triple killer, still 'unlawfully at large' in Britain, varied. A spokesman for Amsterdam police, two of whose officers Reeve had shot, one fatally, said, 'We are no longer concerned with Alan Reeve. He has served his sentence and is now free to go.' In London, the Shadow Home Secretary, Tony Blair, described the situation as worrying and a matter of deep concern to everyone. 'Psychiatrists say he is still a danger, yet a man who has killed three times has his liberty again.' The relatives of Reeve's victims were astounded. The mother of the fifteen-year-old boy he had murdered twenty-eight years earlier expressed great shock when told the news, while an uncle of the Dutch policeman he killed said, 'This is dreadful – but that's the way it goes in Holland. We are sometimes very lenient in these cases.'

Twelve months later Reeve was at the centre of further outrage when he got a job as an advisor with the Dutch prison reform group, Coornhert Liga. A member of the organisation replied to criticism of the appointment by saying, 'Mr Reeve is a nice man who is a real expert on prisons. We know his job has created a lot of fuss but we are not worried.'

Reeve had gone to ground since his release and was believed to be living in a village in Eastern Holland as the British considered a renewed extradition application. Back home, one Tory MP said, 'It's appalling. The families of his victims in Britain and Holland must think the world has turned upside down.' Another asked the inevitable question, 'How can a man who has killed three people have views on law and order that can be respected?'

13   GERARD TUITE, JIMMY MOODY AND STAN THOMPSON

The Bomber, the Blagger and the Innocent Man

Brixton was never a showpiece jail. Overcrowded, insanitary and prone to industrial action by militant warders, it was described by the Deputy Director of the Prison Service in 1981 as 'one of the worst examples of the inadequacies of the prison estate'. Few inmates would have argued with him, although from their point of view Brixton did have a positive side – it was possible to escape. In 1978 a warder got eighteen months for taking bribes in an escape conspiracy and in all, during the 70s, twenty-three men broke out of Brixton. Yet this was the prison where the most infamous criminals in the country were held on remand, awaiting trial at the Old Bailey.

These men – the gangsters, the terrorists, the spies, the serial rapists and murderers – were all Category A. They were housed separately from the other prisoners on D Wing, in a twelve-cell maximum-security unit considered to be one of the most impregnable in any British prison. Official visitors to the jail were told 'confidentially' that a team of soldiers had tested the wing and been unable to escape from it. Perhaps the soldiers' motivation was not as strong as that of prisoners, perhaps they did not have sufficient time – always an advantage in planning a major break-out – but where the British Army failed, the London underworld, in association with the IRA, succeeded.

Gerard Tuite was arrested by the Metropolitan Police Anti-Terrorist Squad in December 1979 during a raid on a flat in Holland Park, London. A member of an IRA bombing team which had caused havoc in the capital for over a year, he headed the police's Most Wanted list following bomb attacks on a swimming pool and a YMCA hostel, and attempts to blow up a gas works in Greenwich and an oil depot on Canvey Island. Tuite, twenty-four years old and described as 'a dangerous and dedicated terrorist', was a prized capture for the police. Ironically, considering what was to happen twelve months after his arrest, he was caught while plotting to spring another IRA man, Brian Keenan, from Brixton by air-lifting him off the exercise yard in a hired helicopter.

That plot failed. Instead of liberating Keenan from Brixton, Tuite joined him behind the walls – and from the day he arrived he began to work out how he could himself escape. Although he had conspired to help another prisoner escape and was Category A, Gerard Tuite was not considered an exceptional escape risk by the Brixton authorities. Consequently his task was made much easier than it might have been, because he did not have a light burning in his cell through the night, nor any of the other severe restrictions imposed on escape list prisoners – including a special uniform of yellow patches.

No sooner had Tuite arrived at Brixton – initially not

in the maximum-security unit – than he started to bore a hole in the wall of his cell, using makeshift tools. The hole was covered with a punk-rock poster, but the plan had to be abandoned when he hit steel mesh and granite beneath the plaster. This early effort was nearly his undoing – while he still occupied the cell the hole was discovered, fortunately for Tuite by a warder with whom he had managed to successfully ingratiate himself. The matter was not reported – had it been he would have been placed on the escape list.

In due course, but not as a result of this episode, Tuite was moved to maximum security on D Wing. With him went three hacksaw blades, hidden in the lid of his art box and carried by a warder. When he arrived at the new wing he underwent a full search – but no one thought to look in the art box because a warder was holding it.

Gerard Tuite was put in a cell on the bottom landing. He studied the escape possibilities and decided that he needed to move to the end cell on the first floor. At the time this cell was occupied by Henry Mackenny, on remand for a series of contract murders in London. Mackenny, known as 'Big H', was later sentenced to life imprisonment, principally on the evidence of his co-accused who turned Queen's Evidence. He was not, however, interested in escaping, so Tuite set about persuading him to change cells. 'The thing was to work on him,' he later told a journalist. 'To work on him or kill him.'

Mackenny was unpopular on the wing, both with warders and with other prisoners. Tuite cultivated him in a big way and soon Mackenny was approaching staff with a request for a cell change downstairs, on the basis that no one would talk to him. He was told that there were no vacant cells on the ground floor – until Tuite offered to swap with him, thus seeming to do everyone a favour.

The IRA man was now in the end cell. To one side was a cell occupied by an alleged armed robber, Stanley Thompson, to the other an outside wall bordering a roof. If Tuite could get through that he would be well on his way to freedom.

Two doors away, in the next cell to Thompson, was an East London villain, James Moody, a man with contacts on the outside and his own reasons to escape. Thirty-nine years old and with a fearsome reputation for violence, Moody was awaiting trial at the Old Bailey. He was a member of the Thursday Mob, a gang of robbers who picked up over £2million in the late 1970s from payroll raids on security vans. Moody was a pioneer of an original approach to armed robbery – he cut through the sides of security vans with a chainsaw. He had not been an easy man to catch either – five other members of the team were already serving sentences of up to twenty-one years before Moody was scooped up in a thirty-handed Flying Squad raid in Peckham.

It is doubtful that Gerard Tuite would have escaped from Brixton without Jimmy Moody's involvement. Later speculation suggested Moody was actually paid £10,000 by the IRA for springing Tuite, who was important to them, not least for the propaganda value of his escape. Whether or not this was true, it was Moody's brother who smuggled masonry bits, screwdrivers and glue into the prison. He carried them through the metal scanner hidden in his socks, figuring correctly that the scanner was not passed over the lower part of visitors' legs.

Tuite the bomber and Moody the blagger made a lethal partnership. The plan was for Moody to bore through the wall of his cell, into Thompson's and onward into Tuite's. They would then go through the outside wall and depart across the roof. As the man in the middle of these two desperadoes, Stan Thompson was included, whether he liked it or not.

With masonry bits to hand, all they needed now was a drill to get through the walls, each fifteen inches thick. Before long Tuite found a pencil sharpener with a broken handle in the wing office and on the pretext of taking it away to sharpen his pencil, he removed it to his cell. The staff never noticed that the sharpener was not returned and, by fitting a metal coat hanger as a handle and forcing the masonry bit into the part that revolved, he now had an improvised drill.

They set to work with a fervour known only to men striving for their freedom. The wall between Tuite and Thompson was the first job and for two weeks they turned and turned their drilling contraption, but all they had to show was a space one and a half inches square with nine thin holes drilled in it. Heavier equipment was required, urgently. Moody spotted a tubular bar attached to a prison table and decided that would do the trick. The only difficulty was that the table was not allowed in cells, but he got round this restriction by taking up jigsaw puzzles with a sudden and all-consuming enthusiasm. His particular favourite was one extremely large jigsaw – and when it became bigger than the table-top, he asked if he could move the larger table into his cell. To the plotters' quiet delight, his request was agreed to, and with the bar removed from the table, they could now make much faster progress on the holes.

Soon the hole between Tuite and Thompson was finished, concealed by a cabinet on Thompson's side. Tuite then went to work on the outside wall, covering his efforts with a piece of cardboard the same colour as the wall and placing his paintings and cabinet in front of that. He got the cardboard the exact colour by mixing emulsion paint with ink, supplied by other prisoners. Moody's hole was the last one to be drilled and again this was hidden by his cell cabinet.

While all this industry was taking place, other prisoners kept watch, giving warning whenever staff approached. Any escape that depends on other prisoners' cooperation is always vulnerable to betrayal, but such were Tuite and Moody's reputations that no one would have dared to grass them. One newcomer to the wing was assaulted because Tuite suspected he was a plant – he lit a cigarette with a lighter, and prisoners were not allowed to have lighters in their possession. The man was taken away and did not return. But whatever the reason for his short-lived presence, it had not come about through the authorities getting wind of the escape. Throughout the weeks of digging and boring, on a maximum-security wing fitted out with closed-circuit television, electronic locks and supposedly ever-vigilant, keen-eyed staff, the officers never had a clue what was going on.

By the night of Sunday 14 December 1980 Tuite, Moody and Thompson were ready for the off. Transport was laid on and waiting outside the prison as Jimmy Moody broke through the last layer of plaster into Stan Thompson's cell and Thompson broke through into Tuite's cell. But all was not well – the first hole, from Moody to

Thompson, was not wide enough. The armed robber was not called Big Jim for nothing – no matter how hard he pushed and shoved, he could not squeeze his six-foot-three, seventeen-stone frame through the gap.

There was no alternative – the mission had to be aborted. The hole in Tuite's cell was covered with a pillow, made to look as if it had fallen off the bed, and the hole in Thompson's cell covered by a bedspread which hung from the table. The next night, after frantic activity to widen the hole, they tried again. This time Moody got through the first hole, and the second, in the wall between Thompson and Tuite, but when it came to the final one, on the outside wall, he took one look and knew it was too small.

Moody told the others to go through first, in case he got stuck, which in the circumstances was inevitable. He tried to follow, but became utterly wedged within the fifteen-inch-thick wall, unable to move forward or backward. Urging the others to go without him, he said he would give them an hour, or as long as he could bear the discomfort, before calling for help, but neither Tuite nor Thompson would hear of it. They had worked together too long to let a too-small hole stop them all getting out together. Grabbing the big man's arms, they forced his huge body through the narrow gap, leaving chunks of flesh and muscle stuck to the side of the hole.

Once outside the wing and on the flat roof, they were within the range of closed-circuit television cameras. This had not slipped their notice in the careful planning stage. As they got on to the roof another prisoner on D Wing switched on his cell light and one of the cameras automatically swivelled to focus on his window. By the time it reverted to its normal scan, the escapers were well out of view.

It was 3.15 a.m. They had evaded cameras and dodged dog patrols. The only obstacle that remained in their path was the perimeter wall. At the point they chose to go over it was fifteen feet high, but although adjoining walls were topped with barbed wire, this one was not. Using scaffolding equipment left lying about by workmen, they climbed to a wire fence, threw over a blanket they had brought with them and went up the scaffolding poles to the top of the wall. From there they dropped down into Lyham Road. They were free.

There was no car waiting. When the escape had been aborted the previous night the outside back-up retired from the scene, fearing the plot was rumbled. Once on the street the three men – who as unconvicted prisoners wore their own clothes – walked half a mile before hailing a mini-cab. As soon as they got clear of the area they split up and went their separate ways.

Not until 5 a.m. was the break-out discovered. The news was greeted with astonishment – how three Category A prisoners could have tunnelled their way out of a maximum-security prison-within-a-prison, under the supposed constant watch of warders, was beyond the comprehension of press and public. 'THE INCREDIBLE JAILBREAK' ran the *New Standard* headline. 'WOODEN HORSE ESCAPE FROM BRIXTON' said *The Times*.

Of the three prisoners, the loss of Gerard Tuite attracted most attention. Scotland Yard, incredulous and angry that their work in putting such a high-profile terrorist behind bars should be neutralised by lax prison security, issued an urgent appeal to help them once again find Gerard Tuite. At the same time they announced a special police operation to cover London against bomb attacks. Two photos of Tuite – one clean-shaven, the other bearded – were issued on a poster headed 'TERRORIST ALERT. THIS MAN MUST BE CAUGHT'.

By the following day, 16,500 posters were printed and distributed. Commander Peter Duffy, head of the Anti-Terrorist Squad, said he believed Tuite was hiding in London and he asked hotel-keepers and landladies to memorise his features. This was not as simple as it might have sounded. Because Tuite was said to be a master of disguise, nine different photo-fit pictures, showing him in a range of possible appearances, were published. In a variety of combinations he had a beard, moustache, spectacles, sun-glasses, long hair and short hair. In one picture he bore a strong resemblance to the singer Bob Dylan, in another to footballer George Best. The Commander was asking a lot of the public.

At the time of the escape, prison officers in Brixton were engaged in industrial action and were working to rule. The Prison Officers' Association strongly denied that this situation could have assisted Tuite, Moody and Thompson, and the Home Office supported their view. One man who disagreed was former Public Enemy Number One, John McVicar. He knew Moody and Thompson, but declined to discuss them when approached by the *Sunday Times*. He did have an opinion on the circumstances of the escape, though, saying, 'They had three walls to go through, which would have taken a lot of work – a month perhaps – and I don't think it's just coincidence that they got out during the warder's dispute. Security must have been lax.'

John McVicar's words, in particular a comment that a warder might have supplied the escapers with the tools they used, incurred the wrath of the Birmingham branch of the Prison Officers' Association, who made a complaint to the Press Council. They claimed that McVicar should not have been quoted because of his 'prejudiced views' of prison staff. The Press Council rejected the complaint, saying that it was precisely because of his antecedents that McVicar's views were worthwhile.

In February 1981 the Home Secretary, William Whitelaw, revealed to the House of Commons the results of an inquiry into the Brixton escape. He said it was not appropriate for the report to be published because of pending criminal proceedings. The main conclusion of the inquiry was that the escape was made possible by human error, specifically by serious weaknesses at all levels within the prison, in the application of existing security procedures for Category A prisoners. There was no evidence to suggest any conspiracy or collusion in the escape by prison staff and although Brixton was one of the worst examples of the many worn-out and antiquated prisons, the physical fabric was not in itself a principal factor in the escape.

The Home Secretary said it had to be acknowledged that 'when we contain high-risk prisoners in far from ideal, though not insecure, conditions, we increase the weight of responsibility on the staff concerned.' The inquiry had reported that with one senior officer and seven officers responsible for supervising fifteen Category A prisoners in the maximum-security wing, and with one officer responsible for surveillance at night, the staffing level was adequate.

How then had Messrs Tuite, Moody and Thompson been able to escape? The buildings and walls of Brixton were said to have not been a factor – yet, two years before the escape, the Home Office had been warned about the jail's security shortcomings by prison department chiefs. Furthermore, although there had not been a major escape for some years, there had been plenty of lesser ones – twenty in the previous decade – and only a few weeks earlier a prisoner had been caught climbing back into the prison after going out for a night's drinking!

One man took the overall rap for the escape – the Brixton Governor, Michael Selby. 'In the circumstances the Governor, Mr Selby, must accept, and very properly does accept, the principal responsibility,' said the Home Secretary. He added that the responsibility was not entirely the Governor's, and that the weaknesses and errors attributed to other members of staff had been brought home to them. He said the Governor's record, and that of his staff, had previously been one of real achievement in difficult circumstances.

The Brixton Governor had been considered a rising star within the prison service. The escape of Tuite, Moody and Thompson changed all that – now he was moved into an administrative post, his job taken by the Governor of Gartree.

As for the three escapers, their separate fates could not have been more diverse. Stanley Thompson, the man who occupied the cell between Moody and Tuite, was due to appear in St Albans Crown Court later in the morning that he escaped. He faced six charges of armed robbery, conspiracy to rob and seven firearms charges.

The case went on in his absence – and the jury acquitted him of everything!

Thompson was on the run from charges of which he was innocent. The only crime he had committed was to escape from custody, regardless of whether he should have been there in the first place or not. That same evening his girlfriend made a television appeal to him to give himself up. Soon afterwards he walked into Brixton Police Station with his solicitor, but any hopes that he would be able to lead the police to Tuite were misplaced. He had parted from the Irishman without having any idea at all of his intentions.

Thompson was now back in custody for escaping from custody. Had the escape been delayed just one more night he would have walked from St Albans Crown Court a free man, but once he had vacated his cell, the holes would very likely have come to light and Tuite and Moody would not have got away. He had spent seventeen months on remand and told police that he escaped because he was innocent and he feared a miscarriage of justice. He went back inside for another six months before going to court in June when he was given a suspended sentence for escaping.

At the same court James Moody's brother was charged with smuggling the escape tools into Brixton. He had passed them over on visits, when the warders' attention was diverted. He told the police that he would not have assisted his brother if he had known that the IRA man was involved. He got eighteen months for his trouble.

The fugitive life was no new experience for Jimmy Moody. Prior to his arrest for the Thursday Mob robberies, he had been on the run from the police for two years.

Such was his status as a top-league criminal even then, that only a few days before he was captured a nationwide publicity campaign was being considered, with Moody described as 'a most dangerous wanted man'. But in the aftermath of the Brixton escape, all attention was on Gerard Tuite. By comparison, the hunt for Moody was a very low-key affair.

In April 1981, three months after the break-out, the police issued a statement saying that Moody might be hiding on the south coast in a chalet or caravan. He was known to have spent time in the area earlier and was a keen scuba diver. A poster was circulated, describing him as six feet one inch tall – with a tattoo of an eagle on his left forearm and a geisha girl on his right. In a new development in the history of man-hunts, adverts were placed in camping and sub-aqua publications. All trails led nowhere, the search came to nothing.

For thirteen years Jimmy Moody remained one of the very few major escapers to stay at large. According to one rumour he was enjoying life in Spain on the profits of his blagging days, others said he was dead. All the time he was still in London, having strayed no further than Hackney, where he lived in a grimy first-floor council flat on Wadeson Street.

On Tuesday 1 June 1993, Moody's life on the run – indeed, his life – came to an end. He was sitting alone in the Royal Hotel, half a mile from his home, when he was shot four times in the chest with a Webley .38 revolver. It was a classic gangland hit – the killer walked to the bar, bought a pint of lager which he paid for but did not touch, then turned, sauntered past Moody and pulled the trigger. As the long-sought fugitive lay dying, his killer swore at him then left the pub and was driven away in a stolen Ford Fiesta XR2.

What had James Moody been up to in the past thirteen years? Why had he been killed? Those who might have known were not saying. There was speculation that, after escaping from Brixton, he had worked as a contract killer for the IRA, but his murder was more likely a reprisal for deeds committed closer to home. After his death Moody's name was linked with several gangland killings, notably the shooting of David Brindle at The Bell public house in Walworth Road. Moody's flat turned up no clues whatsoever as to his activities over the years, apart from a few rolls of wallpaper. A spot of DIY decorating was the only evidence of his activities during thirteen years on the run.

It is remarkable that a man so well known in the London underworld, an avid womaniser and one whose face stared for so long from police station notice boards, could remain at liberty for so long. It is even more remarkable, given that he was not a man who was accustomed to living the quiet life. 'Never MENSA material, he made up for it by growling at everybody,' wrote John McVicar in *FHM* magazine. 'He was the sort of person who could be walking down the middle of the Sahara desert and still be at odds to cause a row – even if it was with himself.'

Gerard Tuite, the man they were most keen to find, turned up nine months after the escape – but only on the radio. A political correspondent in Northern Ireland, Eamon Maillie, was invited to interview the wanted man. He took up the offer, was collected in a car by people he had never seen before and was driven into the Republic in darkness. There, in an unidentifiable location, he tape-recorded a two-hour interview with Tuite, which was broadcast on Belfast's independent Downtown Radio.

Tuite gave his account of the planning and execution of the escape – and revealed insights into the shortcomings of prison security that should have caused embarrassment to the British authorities. Asked how he and his fellow escapers were able to spend eighteen weeks tunnelling through walls in the maximum-security block, his explanation was simple. Although the corridors between the cells were scanned by television cameras, 'the screws left it to the people with the cameras and the people on the cameras left it up to the screws in the wing'. Look-outs warned of approaching warders and, while the other prisoners in the wing knew that an escape was afoot, no one dared to speak out. 'I think the police did me a favour,' Tuite told the radio man, 'because they gave me so much bad publicity that the other prisoners really feared me.' He omitted to mention the part played by James Moody, whose own reputation for instilling fear was not diminished by a previous conviction for smashing a man's head in, nor by his close association with leading London gangsters.

The radio interview attracted great interest at Scotland Yard. Detectives there studied Gerard Tuite's words and the circumstances in which they had been uttered, but there were no clues as to where he might be found. But six months later, at 11 a.m. on a cold March morning, Tuite's luck ran out. Irish police raided a house in Drogheda and there he was. No shots were fired, he went without a struggle, to be held under the Offences Against The State Act. Since it had become known that

Tuite was in the Republic, his case had been a source of embarrassment to the Irish Government, focusing as it did on the controversy of the problems involved in extraditing alleged IRA activists back to the mainland.

The outcome in this case made Irish legal history. To the dismay of the British Government, the IRA man could not be extradited to face the terrorism charges that he had escaped from in London. Instead, on 4 July 1982 at the Special Criminal Court in Dublin, Gerard Tuite was convicted of possessing gelignite and other bomb-making equipment in Greenwich, London. He smiled as he was sentenced to ten years' imprisonment. It was the first time an Irish citizen had been tried in the Republic for offences committed in Britain.

14   CRUMLIN ROAD MASS ESCAPE

The A Team

Escape is the prime aim of Irish Republicans held in Her Majesty's Prisons. In keeping with the prisoner-of-war mentality, it is every prisoner's duty to break out. Escapes liberate men to return to active service, raise morale among other prisoners in their defiance of British justice and cause disruption to the authorities. Most of all, a successful escape, like that of Gerard Tuite, generates valuable propaganda – a commodity with which the IRA have long been familiar.

The IRA prisoner has an advantage over most others when it comes to escaping. He has an organisation behind him to plan, to provide and assist in whatever ways are necessary. His own role, as actual escaper, is often but a small part in an operation that has been worked out to the finest detail by an escape committee inside the jail and then agreed by the Army Council, the highest IRA authority on the outside.

The first escape from a British jail by Irish Republican prisoners was that of four men who got out of Usk, in South Wales, in 1918. The following year Eamon de Valera, at the time President of Sinn Fein and later

Prime Minister of Eire, broke out of Lincoln and travelled to America to enlist support for the Republic. Throughout the civil war years of the 1920s, and onwards, a steady stream of IRA men escaped from British prisons. But it was the troubles which erupted following the arrival of troops in Northern Ireland in 1969, and the internment of suspected terrorists, that brought a new phenomenon of jailbreaks to the province.

In Irish escape-lore, legendary exploits abound and the past quarter of a century has brought many. Republicans under armed guard in hospital have been rescued by men disguised as doctors and carrying sawn-off shotguns; they have slipped away dressed as priests in dog collars and long black robes; they have run off in their bare feet and hidden in the back of dustbin lorries, while one Long Kesh internee cut and crawled his way through five sets of barbed wire, dodged warders, soldiers and dogs and then had to avoid the Secretary of State as he arrived for an official visit.

Best of all, the IRA likes to organise mass break-outs. They are guaranteed to grab the headlines and news bulletins. The first mass escape occurred at Crumlin Road Jail in Belfast in November 1971 when nine men, all on remand for firearms and explosives offences, abandoned their game of football to climb up two rope ladders which were thrown over the perimeter wall. In football shirts, shorts and boots they were picked up by three waiting cars and whisked off. The event was celebrated in song by a best-selling record in Ireland, 'The Crumlin Kangaroos'.

The following year seven men escaped from a ship that

had been converted into an internment centre and moored in Belfast Lough. Covering their bodies in butter and oil, they dived under the barbed wire surrounding the vessel and swam across the freezing sea to the shore, where they hi-jacked a bus. They were dubbed 'The Magnificent Seven'.

In making it three in a row, the IRA went for their most spectacular escape to date. This time it was not the British who were annoyed, but the Irish Government in Dublin. A helicopter was hi-jacked and the pilot directed to Mountjoy Prison, where he landed on the exercise yard – and took off again with the three most important IRA men in the jail. Seamus Twomey, chief of staff of the Provisionals, had flown to London a year earlier to negotiate with the British Government; Kevin Mallon was commanding officer of border units in West Ulster and J.B.O'Hagan, a veteran campaigner, had played a part in a recent attempt to smuggle arms into Ireland on a German coaster.

This break-out was a massive propaganda boost, the first escape by helicopter from any prison in Britain or Ireland. The three heroes became known as 'The Whirly Birdies' and in Belfast bonfires were lit as celebrations went on for days.

Long Kesh internment camp, eight miles out of Belfast, was the scene of continuous activity in the escape department. Built on the site of an old airfield, with its watchtowers, barbed wire, searchlights and patrolling soldiers, it resembled a prisoner-of-war camp – which to its inmates, of course, it was.

Tunnelling through the sandy soil was the favoured method of escape from Long Kesh and in 1974 it was

estimated that 200 tunnels undermined the camp, origi-
nating from both the Republican and the Loyalist com-
pounds. Some were only holes, others stretched up to
100 feet, some even headed in the wrong direction –
further into the camp. One, shored up with bed-boards,
collapsed under the feet of a soldier just before sixty men
were due to crawl down it in 1972.

Two years later, thirty-three men wormed their way
along a sixty-five-yard underground passageway that had
been dug with spoons and improvised tools. This was to
be the mass break-out of all time. They emerged just
beyond the perimeter wire, but then their problems
began. Thirteen were picked up on a deserted airstrip
next to the camp and in an extensive helicopter, police
and army search all but three of the thirty-three men
were recaptured within two hours. The rest did not last
much longer. A sequel to this foiled attempt came at
Newry Courthouse when the men were charged with
escaping from Long Kesh – twelve of them got out
through a toilet window and ten made it to freedom.

The most successful mass escape from Long Kesh took
place in 1976 when twelve men of the Irish Republican
Socialist party, a splinter group of the IRA, went down a
trapdoor in a compound hut and along a forty-foot
tunnel, negotiating five old tunnels and seams of concrete that had been poured down some of them. They
were expecting to surface in the free world, but found
they were faced with a high wire fence and beyond that
an army watchtower, floodlights and a twenty-foot wall.
The tunnel was too short.

Amazingly, they were equipped to deal with such
obstacles. They went through the fence with bolt-cutters,
climbed the wall with the aid of a grappling hook and

nine got away. Let down by their back-up people, they had to walk to the M1 motorway and it was not until two were picked up by the RUC, eight miles from the camp, that the authorities found out that anyone had escaped. By then the other seven had got away and were able to slip across the border into the Republic.

Crumlin Road Jail in North Belfast was, by the beginning of the 1980s, one of the most secure prisons in Europe. Its individual cells, courtyards and high walls were a far cry from the Long Kesh internment camp, which had housed many of the earlier suspected terrorists. At Crumlin Road, remand prisoners did not even have to go out of the prison gate when they went to court – an underground tunnel connected the jail to the courthouse on the other side of the main road.

The official tunnel was the only one to lead out of Crumlin Road. Underground escape routes were a nonstarter here, but that did not stop inmates scheming a variety of other possibilities. One resulted in an alert in 1977 which caused the cancellation of all visits and food parcels after ten pounds of gelignite and twenty detonators were found in butter packets inside the prison.

Since the escape of The Crumlin Kangaroos in 1971, security in the prison had been progressively upgraded, to the extent that the focus of IRA escapes switched elsewhere. On Wednesday 10 June 1981, swiftly and suddenly, it moved back to Crumlin Road.

The background and timing to the events of that day lie in the IRA's failure to force the British Government's hand, first through the 'dirty protests' in the Maze, then by hunger strikes. The Republicans' commanding officer in the prison, Bobby Sands, died on hunger strike, under the glare of attention from the world's media. Neither the Pope's envoy who travelled to the Maze from Rome, nor the expressed concern of President Ronald Reagan had any effect and Sands' death was quickly followed by those of three more hunger strikers. The IRA realised that new tactics were urgently required to raise flagging morale within the movement.

At the time, Crumlin Road held a group of remand prisoners known as the M60 Squad. They got their name from the American M60 machine gun used in three attacks on security forces in 1980, including the ambush of a British Army patrol that left a SAS captain dead. One of the M60 Squad, Joseph Doherty, was a member of the jail's six-man escape committee which, for almost a year, had been gathering and analysing intelligence with the intention of staging a mass escape. Throughout the jail all aspects of security were monitored: the timing of staff change-overs, the position of remote-control cameras, the memorising of codes used by prison officers in locking and unlocking doors and all other snippets of information, gleaned and collated by inmates assigned to the task.

The trial of the M60 Squad took place in April and May, before Lord Justice Hutton. After hearing all the evidence, the judge adjourned to deliberate. When IRA intelligence picked up that he intended to deliver his verdict on 12 June, it became imperative to stage the long-planned escape before that date, because once Doherty and his co-accused were convicted they would be moved from Crumlin Road to the Maze.

Doherty's escape committee had worked on a plan for up to fourteen prisoners to get out, but the word came back from outside that only eight were to go – and there was a stipulation that certain names should be included. They were selected for their publicity value as escapers and for their recognised capabilities in dealing with the gunfight situation that would undoubtedly arise – outside the jail if not inside. The final escape list comprised all four members of the M60 Squad on trial for the murder of the SAS captain: Joe Doherty, Robert Campbell, Angelo Fusco and Paul Patrick Magee; plus three of their co-accused – Michael McKee, Anthony Sloan and Gerard Sloan. The eighth man was Michael Ryan, accused of a 1979 murder in Omagh.

At 4 p.m. on 10 June, all eight men were in the visits area, where for the past hour they had been in discussion with their solicitors in three separate groups. The visits had been coordinated so that all the men chosen to go would be in the same place at the same time. Another eight men, who would not be going, but whose presence would help add to the confusion, were also taking visits.

Prior to going on their visits the men had been searched, but as they left the interview cubicles Paul Magee whipped out a small .25 revolver and held it to his escort's head. The officer tried to call Magee's bluff, but it was no bluff, as he realised when the gun pressed tighter to his temple and he saw Joe Doherty pointing a similar gun at one of his colleagues. The escape was now under way.

The prison officers present were in no position to put up a fight. One, Richard Kennedy, made a brave effort, even with a gun sticking in his back. He managed to draw his baton and strike a prisoner, Robert Campbell, two blows to the head, not knowing that others had weapons. Kennedy was felled from behind and repeatedly punched and kicked, his wounds requiring thirty-eight stitches. He later recalled one of his attackers telling the others not to shoot him or they would not get out.

At gunpoint, ten prison officers and the three solicitors were bundled into a room, one of the solicitors protesting loudly that he wanted nothing to do with whatever was about to happen. The officers were ordered to remove their uniforms, which some of the escapers then put on, as others took the solicitors' clothes and briefcases. So far everything was going to plan. No one was in a position to raise the alarm, but the real test – getting through the two gates, electronically sealed with a secure area in between – was still to come.

Using the keys they had taken from the officers, the eight men left the visits block and crossed the prison yard. To get through the gates they had to convince the staff on duty that they were prison officers and solicitors. As they approached the first gate, one of the staff on duty recognised Joseph Doherty and Anthony Sloan as inmates, but, seeing so many prison uniforms, he assumed that the men were simply under escort. Reaching the gate, Sloan tried to push past the officer who suddenly felt a gun sticking in his back. At the same time a threatening voice told the man quite calmly that if he did not keep the gate open he would be 'blown away'.

The men were now in the sealed area and needed only to overcome the guard on duty at the main gate, fifteen feet away. But he was suspicious, his attention drawn by the sight of a prison officer wearing a regulation navy blue tunic – with brown trousers. As he looked up and recognised the 'officer' as a prisoner, Doherty, he instantly moved to seal the gates, but the men fell on him and he was knocked to the ground.

They were out. They were beyond the prison gates, but the alarm had been raised and there was now a fifty-yard dash across Crumlin Road to a car park. Here they were to rendezvous with their back-up unit and pick up the stolen getaway cars that had been left for them. As they ran out of the jail, a policeman on duty at the courthouse across the road heard the alarm go off and set off in pursuit. He reached the car park to be confronted by two men crouched behind cars. Calling on them to halt, he was answered by a round of gunfire. He fired back and then realised that other shots were coming from behind him and he was caught in the middle. Three off-duty policemen who happened to be passing the jail had seen the escapers run along the road and chased them in their car. They got out and began firing, over and round the police officer from the courthouse. Another car, carrying three detectives, drew up, but they initially thought that it was merely an incident involving genuine prison officers and only began shooting when one of them was shot at by an escaper in warder's clothing.

The car park was now surrounded by RUC men and an estimated fifty shots in all were fired. Still the eight escapers and their back-up unit, who had been heavily involved in the shooting, all got away, only one, Michael McKee, suffering a gunshot wound. At a crucial point in the firing, Joe Doherty, in prison officer's uniform, stood up and shouted, 'Police. Police. Don't fire.' The confused police hesitated – long enough for some of the escapers and their back-up to jump into the cars and drive off. As they went, the police, realising that they had been fooled, opened fire, riddling the cars with bullet holes but amazingly not hitting any of the men.

Only three of the escapers got away in cars, the others made it on foot. Their path took them directly through the Shankhill estate, one of the most staunchly Loyalist areas in the whole of Northern Ireland. It was not the sort of place at all where five fugitive IRA men could expect to find shelter, but some of them got into a house. Discarding their warder and solicitor clothes, they re-emerged to hi-jack a car at gunpoint, driving to the Falls Road, territory in which a Republican could feel more at home.

Back in Crumlin Road Jail, the three solicitors who had been visiting the escapers were arrested under the Prevention of Terrorism Act. They were taken to Castlereagh Detention Centre and questioned for two days before being released without charge. In Belfast legal circles this unprecedented action was greeted with astonishment and outrage.

On the streets traffic was held up for long periods as the security forces closed down side-roads and questioned people at checkpoints. The photos of the eight escapers soon adorned 20,000 Wanted posters, distributed throughout the city. The IRA responded by circulating their own poster with the pictures of the wanted men replaced by photos of RUC policemen. In a propaganda war that would span the Atlantic Ocean, these were merely early skirmishes.

True to tradition the break-out was given a title – 'The Great Escape'. After the failed 'dirty protests' and the tactical miscalculation of the hunger strikes, Republicans at last had something to celebrate. While the revelries went on the eight escapers – now known as 'The A Team' – hid in safe houses, making no contact with their families or known friends. Plans were under way for them to be moved across the border, once the heat had died down.

An immediate inquiry was launched by the Chief Inspector of Prisons. In the Commons, dismay was expressed on both sides of the house, with an Official Ulster Unionist MP claiming that one of the three arrested solicitors was a former Republican internee who had qualified in law while in the Maze. Ian Paisley, the Democratic Unionist MP for Antrim North, followed this up by saying that the solicitor had been interned not once but twice and that his brother-in-law was a known bomber who had been shot dead by the RUC. Furthermore, said Paisley, the solicitor's own brother was election agent for the Irish Prime Minister, Charles Haughey, and had been appearing on television with him 'night after night'. He did not think there would be much cooperation given to the government from that quarter, he said. The Secretary of State for Northern Ireland, Humphrey Atkins, replied that he hoped and believed that if the escaped prisoners were in the South the authorities would assist in their return.

To no one's great surprise, the inquiry into the escape failed to discover how the guns used by the escapers had found their way into the jail. It was announced in September 1981, only three months after the break-out, that the report of the inquiry would not be published for security reasons, but in future all solicitors and other professional visitors would have to undergo strict searches. Three weeks later two prisoners in A Wing produced handguns, fired a shot and held six warders hostage for two hours before they were overpowered.

As had been predicted by the IRA's intelligence network, Lord Justice Hutton returned to Belfast Crown Court on 12 June to pass sentence in the M60 case. Only one man had been left behind to face him in the dock, the other seven were sentenced in their absence. Joseph Doherty, Robert Campbell and Angelo Fusco were each given life imprisonment with recommendations that they serve a minimum of thirty years. Paul Magee got life with a minimum twenty-five years. Anthony Sloan got a straight twenty years as did Michael McKee, while Gerard Sloan got eighteen years.

The first of The A Team to surface was Paul Magee, eight days later at Bodenstown, County Clare, in the Republic. He signed autographs at the graveside of Wolfe Tone, the eighteenth-century revolutionary, during an annual Provisional tribute. Arrested the next year, Magee was sentenced to ten years in the Republic and on release in 1989 he fought extradition to the North and was bailed. He took advantage of this to disappear and the next time he made the news was in 1992 when he murdered an unarmed special policeman following a routine road check in North Yorkshire. Magee was again jailed for life.

Other members of the Crumlin Road escape gang were caught and imprisoned in the Republic. The first to fall were Robert Campbell and Michael Ryan. They also became the first defendants to be convicted under the new Anglo-Irish law that allowed terrorists on the run to be tried wherever they were arrested. In Dublin on 23 December they got ten years for their part in the escape, but were acquitted of attempted murder of a policeman.

Their case preceded that of Gerard Tuite, the first man to be convicted in Southern Ireland of offences committed on the British mainland.

Shortly before Campbell and Ryan were sentenced, Michael McKee, who had been hit in the gunfire on Crumlin Road, was picked up. His wounds had never been life-threatening, but he had needed medical treatment and a doctor sympathetic to the IRA had attended to him later on the day of the escape. Now he was in the custody of the Garda, as a result of a dawn raid on a council house in Dundalk. The following month Anthony Sloan surrendered when armed police surrounded the house in Cork where he was living with his wife and child, and soon Angelo Fusco and Gerard Sloan joined the others behind bars in Southern jails.

Angelo Fusco got ten years for firearms offences. In 1986 he tried to escape from Portlaoise Jail and another three years were added on. He was released in 1991 and taken before a Dublin court which ordered his extradition back to the North. There he had three life sentences waiting for him, imposed after the Crumlin Road escape. Fusco was not sent back, instead he was given bail pending appeal. He remains free to attend Republican rallies and celebrations, where he is hailed as a hero, and to spend his days salmon fishing in County Kerry, where the *Sunday Times* found him in early 1993.

Fusco claimed to no longer play an active role in IRA matters. Of the SAS captain he killed, he said, 'I don't find it easy to talk about killing somebody and I do not pride myself. I do not think he would have lost a night's sleep if he had killed me, and he would have killed me.' An Ulster Unionist MP, John Taylor, expressed concern about the Irish Government's attitude to extradition. He said, 'It's all sweet words saying "we are out to catch the terrorists and we will extradite them". But these words are never turned into practice.' So far Angelo Fusco has not served a day of his three life sentences.

The last of the eight escapers to come to notice was Joseph Doherty. Belfast born and bred, he was the man believed to have fired the M60 that killed the SAS officer, Captain Herbert Westmacott. 'That's my baby,' he said of the gun as he was arrested at the scene. Doherty had lived and breathed Republicanism from his earliest years. At fifteen he joined Na Fianna, the junior branch of the Provisional IRA. He was interned the day after his seventeenth birthday – first on the Maidstone ship and then in Long Kesh – and gradually he moved up the ranks of the organisation. Highly regarded by his superiors, Doherty received special arms training with the M60 gun – and once he had mastered its every function he was unleashed in the murky, underground world of guerilla warfare. Not long afterwards he was captured at the scene of the murder of Captain Westmacott.

After The Great Escape, Joseph Doherty moved from safe house to safe house in the Republic but, as the other men were picked up one by one around Christmas time 1981, it became clear that he had to get away from Ireland if he was to remain free for long. In February 1982 Doherty flew from Shannon to New York on a false passport bearing the name Henry J. O'Reilly. He was welcomed by IRA sympathisers, provided with accommodation, obtained a work permit and soon found employment with a construction company. Doherty's mistake was to take a job in Clancy's Bar in Manhattan, a known hang-out for IRA sympathisers. There he came to the attention of the FBI, fingered by an informant who thought the newly arrived Henry J. O'Reilly looked interesting and might not be exactly who he claimed to be.

Early one June morning in 1983, two undercover FBI agents, disguised as construction workers, walked into Clancy's Bar. They ordered drinks and moved in to arrest Doherty on a warrant which stated that he had illegally entered the United States. The British Government immediately sought extradition, but Doherty of course resisted. So began a legal tussle that would elevate Joseph Doherty from being just another prison escaper on the run into a well-known personality of the American media.

One reason for the high profile attached to Doherty's case was the personal interest taken in him by the Prime Minister, Margaret Thatcher. A vigorous opponent of terrorism in general and the IRA in particular, she was determined to get him back to Britain to serve his life sentences. A stumbling block lay in the Supplementary Extradition Treaty between the UK and the USA, which denies political asylum for terrorist crimes, but was not applicable in the case because it had been signed after Doherty's recapture. When a large body of influential Irish-American supporters emerged to laud Doherty as a 'prisoner of conscience' it began to look as if victory would be his and the British Government could be thwarted.

Such was the convicted killer's popularity that rallies were organised for him, concerts were staged to raise funds for his legal fees and a cottage industry in badges, brooches, trinkets and books did thriving business. He was made honorary Grand Marshal of St Patrick's Day parades and 'Free Joe Doherty' murals adorned walls in New York and Belfast. New York City Council went so far as to name an intersection 'Joe Doherty Corner'. A hundred and thirty-two congressmen and senators signed a 'friend of the court' brief on his behalf and even the United Nations High Commissioner for Refugees criticised the US Government for denying him asylum.

Doherty became a regular face on US television, interviewed in the visitors' room at the Metropolitan Correctional Centre where he was held in custody. He wrote a column – 'Letter From The Cell Block' – for the IRA's weekly US newspaper the *Irish People* and, when the editors sacked him for daring to criticise the bombing of a children's hospital, his supporters made sure that he was quickly reinstated and the editors rebuked.

Nine years passed before Doherty's case finally wound its way through the US legal system. In all that time Margaret Thatcher never let up the pressure on first the Reagan and then the Bush administration. In 1986 she obtained the leverage she was seeking – she allowed American warplanes, on a mission to attempt to kill Libyan leader, Colonel Gaddafi, to take off from British airfields. Mrs Thatcher was heavily criticised at home and in Europe, but her decision meant that the US Government owed her a favour. She was determined that favour would be the return of Joseph Doherty.

For the fugitive, repeated applications for bail were made, but none succeeded. The US legal system was willing, but every time a court was minded to free him pending an immigration hearing, a higher authority blocked the decision. He stayed in custody throughout, the longest residency that the Correctional Centre had ever known. Eventually the US State Department declared that not to deport him would impede the fight against international terrorism and 'could damage the relationship of the US with the United Kingdom'. All Doherty's hopes were pinned on one last appeal to the Supreme Court and when that failed there was only one outcome.

On 19 February 1992 Joseph Doherty was flown back to Northern Ireland aboard a US Air Force jet. The thirty-six-year-old plumber-cum-terrorist's days of media celebrity were over. He went to the Maze Prison, near Belfast, to begin the life sentence with a recommended thirty years that had been passed on him in his absence two days after the escape from Crumlin Road nearly eleven years earlier. In August 1993 Doherty appealed to the High Court in Belfast to allow the time he spent in American custody to be counted against his sentence. He lost his case, which Lord Justice Murray told him was 'wholly without merit', saying that he had no one to blame but himself that he now faced the whole term imposed as long ago as 1981. If the thirty-year minimum recommendation is upheld, Joseph Doherty will be at least sixty-seven years old before he is released from prison.

15   ARTHUR HUTCHINSON
The Murderous Fox

The press love to dub fugitives with headline-grabbing nicknames. The Yorkshire Ripper and The Black Panther are but two British examples of criminal identities that were established in the public imagination long before the men were caught and their real names known. Arthur Hutchinson, petty-criminal turned triple-killer was known as The Fox. To a man impatient for notoriety, this was a badge to be worn with pride. On the run from the police, Hutchinson signed himself 'A.Fox' in a guesthouse visitors' book. To one of his victims he boasted that he had evaded the police helicopter searching for him by living in fox holes. But The Fox was eventually 'out-foxed' by police misinformation. And when he ran to ground his pursuers moved in on him.

Born in the North-east, Hutchinson had the misfortune to be the only illegitimate child in a family of eight. He appeared in court at the age of twelve for indecent assault, and went to prison for the first time at twenty-two for having sex with an under-age girl. He had a variety of short-lived jobs, working as a dairy hand, a coal miner and a labourer on farms. Here he picked up a knowledge of the countryside that would later enable him to survive on the run by living rough.

Hutchinson was a man who could not hold on to anything for long. Married twice, he had a history of broken relationships with women, frequently ending in violence, and was well known to court officials for a string of unpaid maintenance orders on several illegitimate children. His half-brother, whom he had threatened to kill, described him as 'a violent man and a coward'. His seventy-eight-year-old mother said he was a 'gentle lad, he would always do things for me' – seemingly forgetting the time he had knocked her out of the chair she sat in. He had a crucifixion scene tattooed on his chest, and decorated the rest of his body with other designs, including the Stars and Stripes and Top Cat. In a nondescript, sordid life of predatory sex and petty crime, Arthur Hutchinson's only claim to fame before he escaped from custody was that he had once worked in a circus, boxing kangaroos.

On 28 September 1983, Arthur Hutchinson left Armley Prison, Leeds and was taken by car to Selby Magistrates' Court, in North Yorkshire, to face charges of burglary and rape. When he and his two-man escort arrived at the police station situated in the same building as the court, the only police officer on duty was dealing with a couple of juveniles who had absconded from a children's home. The constable, only two weeks away from retirement, pressed a button that opened an automatic door and Hutchinson, handcuffed to a warder, walked into the station's interview room with his escort.

As the policeman counted out £120 in cash that

Hutchinson had brought with him, the prisoner said to the warders, 'I want a slash.' They removed his handcuffs and he was allowed to walk into the cell next door, where there was a toilet. Neither of the warders followed him or kept an eye on him. They were still watching the policeman write his signature on a form accepting responsibility for Hutchinson when they heard him running up the steps that led to the magistrates' court on the floor above. The paperwork was in order but the prisoner had gone.

Thinking that he would run through the court and try to get out by the public entrance on the other side of the building, the police constable and the warders dashed round and waited for him to show. They were disappointed. Hutchinson had studied the lie of the courthouse and had been able to make a detailed sketch of it after four previous remand appearances. He was so sure that he could carry out his plan that on the journey from Leeds he told the warders that he intended to escape. They thought he was joking.

To Hutchinson's great advantage, the internal doors in the court building were all unlocked because decorators were at work. Thus, when he raced up the stairs from the police side of the building, he went through a door that led him straight into the dock in an empty court. There, a decorator who was painting the walls was startled to see him jump over the rail of the dock, leap on to the press bench and, without a second's hesitation, dive headlong through a closed window, sending glass flying in all directions.

He only fell six feet, on to the wire netting that covered the police station's tiny exercise yard below. From there he dropped on to the roof of a parked van, crossed the schoolyard next door and vanished into the streets of Selby.

There was no major search for Hutchinson. To the police he became just another of the many prisoners who escape each year, causing detectives and uniformed officers who have sought and arrested them to shake their heads in wonderment at the lax security arrangements in so many jails. This time, though, the prisoner had escaped from a police station – one that had repeatedly been declared 'the worst in North Yorkshire' and 'top priority' to be replaced over the previous seven years.

Arthur Hutchinson, forty-two years old, was described as five feet, eight or nine inches tall, slim, with light brown hair, blue eyes and a ruddy complexion. He was, said the police, 'dangerous and violent', but they had no indication of how dangerous and violent. There were no indicators in his previous record to suggest that he was capable of the motiveless murder of three people in cold blood.

In his first days on the run Hutchinson had a problem. As he crashed through the courtroom window on to the barbed wire below, he gashed his left leg. The wound was now infected and needed medical attention. Four days after he escaped, he went to the Royal Infirmary in Doncaster, giving his name as Patrick O'Reardon and his address as Londonderry, Northern Ireland. The four-inch cut was dressed and he was told to return in two days' time. When he did so, he was given a course of antibiotics. The knowledge of this wound, not serious in itself, would prove to be of great tactical advantage to the senior policeman who masterminded the murder hunt that would later be launched for Hutchinson.

From Doncaster, where he stayed for a few days, Hutchinson travelled to Cudworth, near Barnsley, where he visited a man with whom he had once shared a cell in prison. He hung around South Yorkshire for the next three weeks, eventually booking into a Sheffield bed-and-breakfast guesthouse where he shared a room with two other men. He had been at liberty for nearly a month without coming to any sort of attention whatsoever.

Why Arthur Hutchinson chose to visit Sheffield is a mystery. He had no known contacts in the city and the only explanation seems to be that he was less likely to be recognised and was seeking new hunting grounds for his criminal activities. Whatever his reasons, in the early hours of 24 October he made his way to the home of a local solicitor and his family at Dore, a residential suburb well off the beaten track. In the grounds of the house stood a marquee where, earlier that day, the family had celebrated the wedding of their eldest daughter. Hutchinson, armed with a Bowie knife, broke into the house and in a brief few minutes of frenzied murder he stabbed to death the fifty-nine-year-old solicitor, his wife and their twenty-eight-year-old son.

There was one other member of the family in the house that night, the solicitor's youngest daughter, aged eighteen. She awoke to find an intruder moving about in her room and then heard screams and shouts on the landing outside, followed by the choking sounds of her father's dying moments. Still not really knowing whether she was awake or in the throes of a nightmare, the girl heard her mother shouting to Hutchinson, 'Take the money. Take everything and go and leave us alone.' This was followed by her mother's screams as Hutchinson set about her with the Bowie knife.

Terror-stricken in her darkened room, the girl lay there as Hutchinson put the knife to her throat and told her that if she screamed he would kill her. He took her out of her bedroom, saying, 'You'd better keep your eyes closed because your Dad's there.' As he pushed her through the house, he told how he had killed her 'boyfriend' – in fact it was her brother. In the marquee, outside, he took a pair of handcuffs from his pocket and put them on the girl's wrists. He then raped her on the ground, before taking her back into the house and raping her again, as he boasted of how he had killed her parents and brother, at the same time telling her to be careful not to knock his injured knee.

The eighteen-year-old girl, the only survivor of Hutchinson's carnage-ridden visit, was found the next morning at 8 a.m. by two workmen, as they arrived to take down the marquee. Hutchinson had gone, taking with him cash and a gold and diamond watch valued at £3,000.

A massive murder hunt swung into operation and, unusually in such a case, the police knew the identity of the man they were seeking. Arthur Hutchinson's name came into the frame at an early stage when his finger- and palm-prints were found on a champagne bottle in the marquee. With the help of the surviving victim, a local newspaper artist compiled a sketch bearing a remarkable likeness of the wanted man and, as the public were alerted that he was somewhere in their midst, hundreds of police officers from nine forces began their manhunt.

After leaving the house at Dore in the early hours of

Monday morning, Hutchinson made his way into Sheffield and returned to the guesthouse where he had booked in over a week earlier. He sat down to a cooked breakfast and afterwards gave the landlady a £20 note to pay for the previous three nights – although he had not been in the guesthouse since the Friday. Another guest later told police that as he was shaving, Hutchinson, whom he knew as Patrick O'Reardon, came up behind him, picking his teeth with a long-bladed knife.

Hutchinson's movements for the weekend that preceded his arrival at Dore were never established, but he ordered a taxi and left the Sheffield guesthouse at 11 a.m. on the Monday, saying he was heading for Woodhouse, about seven miles away. He travelled further – to Worksop, where at lunch time he booked into another guesthouse, signing in as Mr A. Fox and giving a false Manchester address. The following morning he asked the landlady for an early morning call and tried to persuade her to go jogging with him. She declined and he went alone, returning with a newspaper which detailed the murders. Hutchinson showed the landlady the reports, asking her if she wanted to read the paper.

He was still keen to discuss the murders after breakfast and began to talk about them to the landlady's son as he sat watching television. He asked him, 'Who could have done such a terrible thing as these killings? Why did he spare the girl? It must have been because she was a woman so young.' Later he informed another guest that he was a supporter of the Prime Minister, Margaret Thatcher, and again brought up the murders, saying that the girl's boyfriend must have done the murders 'or she would have been killed'.

The following day Hutchinson left Worksop and went

to Scarborough on the east coast, where he had his hair cut. From then on he took to living in the open air, making only occasional visits to public places. On 3 October, a week after the murders, he called at a pub near Doncaster, his dishevelled state attracting the attention of the landlord. A day earlier he had called the *Yorkshire Post* office in Leeds, telling a reporter who taped his call that he was following the press coverage of the manhunt, but making no reference to the Dore killings.

By this time the police search had been stepped up, with fears that Hutchinson might be carrying a gun and could take a hostage. In his native North-east, twenty people who were thought to be at risk from him, including his ex-wives and members of his family, were put under police guard. More than a thousand 'sightings' had been reported and in these early days of computer-assisted police hunts, a Stockport company came up with £70,000 worth of equipment to help South Yorkshire Police collate the mass of information.

During the first week in November the chase continued, with the police no nearer to their man, although some interesting side issues arose. A paperback James Bond book which Hutchinson had in his possession prior to his escape from Selby was found, and inside it was a sketch of a farmhouse. It was assumed that this was a target for burglary, but the location was never discovered. Hutchinson then followed up his telephone call to the *Yorkshire Post* with a letter, saying the police were searching for him, 'like boy scouts'. He wrote, 'Shoot me if you must – but get on with the job,' leading police to believe that he was looking to go out in a major confrontation. The same day his sister gave a press conference, telling reporters that all the publicity was going to Hutchinson's head and that he would not allow himself to be caught.

Hutchinson had now travelled homewards to the North-east, believing that there was less chance of the police shooting him there than in South Yorkshire. He was staying at the Arcadia Hotel in Darlington under the name John Smith, telling the landlord that he always paid in advance because of his name. On Thursday 3 November, he telephoned his seventy-eight-year-old mother from a call box, speaking of the charges that had led him to Selby Magistrates' Court, but not of the Dore murders. The following night he called a girlfriend in Hartlepool and his mother again. As the police listened in, he told her his leg was causing him pain and he was ready to give himself up.

His injured leg provided his police pursuers with a ray of hope. In press conferences the man leading the hunt, Assistant Chief Constable Bob Goslin, put great play on the fugitive's wound, saying, 'If it's as bad as we think it is, living rough would make it far worse than it is.' Hutchinson was led by press reports to believe that he needed urgent treatment, that gangrene was a possibility and that there was a strong likelihood of his losing his leg. In fact the wound was relatively minor and he was in no danger at all, but he fell for the bait and convinced himself that what the police were saying was true.

On 5 November, 300 police swamped a ten-square-mile area outside Hartlepool, sensing that at last they were closing in on their target. They combed fields and farm buildings, looking for anywhere that a man could hide on the land. Just before darkness fell, the pilot of a police spotter-plane noticed a figure hobbling across fields close to the village of Dalton Piercey. He reported the sighting and all available men rushed to the scene. As they closed in on him, dogs were unleashed and Hutchinson pulled out a knife, wrapping his jumper around his arm to protect himself as he tried to ward them off. It was to no avail – he knew he was cornered and in a last pathetic gesture before he fell he made to stab himself in the chest. But Hutchinson was better at hurting others than hurting himself and he caused only a superficial wound.

At Durham Crown Court in September 1984, Arthur Hutchinson denied all knowledge of the Dore murders. When, on the sixth day, he took the witness stand, the evidence he asked the court to believe was the most bizarre to be heard in a murder trial for many a long year.

He told the jury that he had been at the Dore house at the invitation of the eighteen-year-old girl, and that sex had taken place with her agreement after they had drunk champagne and danced to taped music. As he left the house, he was chased by three men on foot, and other men in a car, across gardens and fields – although he had no idea why they were chasing him. He turned back and saw a man whom he knew as 'Jim or Jimmy' and when he returned to the house he was punched by someone holding a kitchen knife, who turned out to be the girl.

At this point in his evidence Hutchinson pointed to a *Sunday Mirror* reporter in the press gallery and accused him of being one of two men responsible for the killings and the rape of the girl. 'That's your murderer,' he said, recounting how, on the Friday evening prior to the murders, he had been in The Lion pub in one of the less salubrious areas of Sheffield. The girl was in the pub, talking with the reporter, Michael Barron, who told her to approach Hutchinson and ask him what his name was and where he was staying. Hutchinson said that Michael Barron was with another man named Barron and two of the girl's friends, also called Barron – Gail and Sharon. Imaginative claims from the witness box are not unusual, but Hutchinson's performance was in a class of its own.

These people – 'the Barrons' – had, according to the accused, forced the girl to invite him to her family's house at Dore. As if that was not too much to ask the jury to believe, he went on to claim that he had also seen the girl's mother, father and brother – the three deceased – in the run-down, city centre pub. He said he had not caused the scenes of carnage at the house and, when showed pictures of one of his victims, said he could not stand the sight of blood.

Hutchinson did make one admission. He agreed that during his time on remand in Leeds Prison, he had sent a letter to the Director of Public Prosecutions. The letter had claimed that 'the Barrons' were planning to murder the family at Dore and 'put the murder of the Jews on my back'.

After Hutchinson had left the witness box, having smiled and waved to the public gallery, the *Sunday Mirror* man, Michael Barron was called. He covered the North-east area and had visited Hutchinson's mother in respect of his job – and because he felt sorry for her. He denied Hutchinson's allegation – that he had threatened to kill Mrs Hutchinson and, asked if he had anything to do with the murders, he replied, 'It is preposterous. I cannot deny that vigorously enough.'

★ ★ ★

The Durham jury took four hours to find Arthur Hutchinson guilty on three counts of murder and one of rape. Mr Justice McNeill told him, 'You are rational and well orientated. You show no evidence of thought disorder, hallucination or mental delusion suggestive of mental illness.' The judge went on to describe him as arrogant, manipulative and self-centred, with a severe personality disorder not amenable to any kind of treatment. He sentenced him to life imprisonment on each count of murder with eight years for the rape and five for aggravated burglary, recommending that he serve a minimum of eighteen years in prison. The sentence was condemned as one of 'pathetic leniency' by Tory MP Peter Bruinvals, who said it 'would not scare a rabbit'.

Hutchinson never gave any indication as to why he had killed three mild-mannered and harmless pillars of the Sheffield Jewish community. The only explanation appears to be that he broke into the house with burglary in mind and panicked when he was disturbed. His treatment of the eighteen-year-old girl was no surprise to those who knew him – as one said, he always put more effort into his sex life than he ever did into earning an honest living. Even in the witness box he boasted of his attractiveness to women. 'I haven't had many complaints,' he told the jury.

The nobody who thought that he had become a somebody by killing innocent people was unabashed when recaptured. Not the most intelligent of men, Hutchinson had believed the press coverage about the seriousness of his leg wound and thought he might have to have the leg amputated. Relieved of that concern, he did not seem overly worried about being charged with three murders. 'He was a bit deflated but still cocky,' said one of the police officers who questioned him. 'He made references to himself as The Fox and did not seem bothered about being caught. It was as if he was aware of the notoriety he had achieved and he liked it.'

16   MAZE MASS ESCAPE

The Big One

The 'A Team' break-out from Crumlin Road might have been labelled The Great Escape in Irish Republican circles, but the greatest-ever escape was yet to come. Like Crumlin Road, this one was planned and perpetrated by the IRA. On Sunday, 25 September 1983 thirty-eight men got out of the Maze, supposedly one of the most secure prisons in the world. It was the biggest jailbreak anywhere in Europe since the Second World War and a bitter blow to the Thatcher Government's war against terrorism. The political and legal ramifications would go on for years.

The Maze Prison was built in the mid-1970s beside the Long Kesh internment camp. Eight hundred and fifty prisoners were housed in eight H Blocks, so-called because of their shape. The arm of each block contained twenty-five single cells and in the centre rectangle of the block, known as the Circle, were classrooms, offices and stores. With its workshops, hospital and dental surgery, range of sports activities and educational and vocational classes, the Maze was claimed by the authorities to be the most luxurious prison in Europe.

Security at the new prison was intense. A precast concrete wall, eighteen feet high and two miles long, contained the site. Armed soldiers were posted in sentry boxes every 200 yards and all gates were solid steel and electronically operated. Surrounding the wall was a razor-wire fence. Within the walls the prison was sectioned off by more walls and fences, with television monitors and alarms at every turn. A thousand prison officers manned the jail, a ratio of more than one to every inmate. But nearly half the workforce had less than four years' experience – a reflection of the rapid increase in recruitment brought about by the upsurge in terrorism in the 1970s.

To the IRA, the Maze posed the supreme challenge. Demoralised by 'on the blanket' protests that had seen men refuse to wash for five years, while smearing their cell walls with excrement, by the 1981 hunger strikes that had led to ten deaths and by the recent betrayals by supergrasses, the escape committee knew only too well that a break-out from the Maze would lift spirits both inside and out.

Larry Marley was head of the escape committee in the Maze. A veteran of many break-out plots, he was one of ten men who got away through the toilet window at Newry Courthouse in 1975, while awaiting trial for tunnelling out of Long Kesh. In jail he organised classes in escape preparation and procedure, but his plans for the Big One did not include himself. No one with less than twelve years to serve would go out; Marley had only two years left to do.

Marley collated information from all sources within the Maze. At the same time, other leading IRA men manoeuvred themselves on to H Block 7, the one from which it was decided the escape would be staged. Those who would play leading roles on the day managed to get jobs as orderlies, a role that also gave them licence to roam around the block – very useful with an escape plan in progress.

After years of grief, the summer of 1983 brought an unusual peace between inmates and staff on H Block 7. The normal intransigence was temporarily put on hold. Efforts were made to be friendly to warders, who were only too happy to respond and help create a better atmosphere. What they did not know was that it was all part of the plan.

The afternoon of Sunday 25 September seemed to the staff on duty on H Block 7 just like any other Sunday. At 2 p.m. the 125 men were unlocked after lunch, to engage in recreational activities and to move about the four wings as they wished. Sunday afternoon was a relaxed time in the H Blocks – so much so that some officers left their posts and went home before their replacements arrived. The prisoners were not allowed to leave the block and little harm could be done – or so it was thought. Later, tea would be served, the meal arriving by a kitchen lorry which toured round the prison, delivering at each block. The kitchen lorry was the vital link in Larry Marley's escape plan.

Shortly after 2.30 p.m., five prisoners congregated in the Circle – the central rectangular section of the H – and positioned themselves in close proximity to warders who could have reached alarm buttons. All five of the men were armed with handguns, so far hidden. At a signal, one prisoner, Brendan McFarlane, produced his gun,

247

the other four did likewise and throughout the block the prisoners rose to overpower the staff. One officer was shot in the head, another was stabbed in the left shoulder. In the midst of the chaos the block medical officer walked out of his room in the Circle, up to that point completely overlooked by the escapers. He was ordered to treat the wounded prison officers.

The prisoners had control of the block within twenty minutes, without any alarm being raised, and the captured staff were bundled into two games rooms where they were stripped of their uniforms. One was moved to the communications room in the Circle and instructed at gun point to answer all radio and telephone calls as if everything was normal.

At 3.25 p.m., nearly an hour after the take-over had begun, the kitchen lorry, driven by an officer, accompanied by an orderly, arrived at H Block 7. It had been expected at 3 p.m. and the twenty-five-minute hold-up was to prove problematic when the escapers got as far as the main gate. The driver and orderly were hastily grabbed and the driver ordered to take the lorry back along the route to the main gate. To ensure he concentrated on the task, his left foot was tied to the vehicle's clutch, his door lock was jammed and he was told that a cord beneath his seat was attached to a hand grenade – though in reality it was tied to the frame of the seat.

As prisoner Gerry Kelly lay on the floor of the cab with his gun trained on the driver, thirty-seven others climbed into the back of the lorry. The shutter was lowered and the driver set off for the gate. Back in H Block 7 a rearguard party of prisoners, armed with chisels and screwdrivers from the block workshops, were left to make sure staff did not raise the alarm until the escapers had got away.

When the lorry reached the first gate, the driver and orderly were recognised by the officer on duty and allowed through without question. At the next gate the same thing happened. There was now only the main gate left to negotiate – and that was where difficulties created by the twenty-five-minute delay were going to happen.

The escape had been timed to get the men to the gate when there would only be five prison officers on duty in the lodge. Now it was all happening at the same time as staff changed shifts and instead of there being just five staff there were many more, coming off and arriving for duty. But a lorry load of prisoners all intent on escape was not going to turn back now – nine prisoners dressed in officers' uniforms jumped out of the lorry and held up the five staff on duty in the lodge. As others checked in their passes, they too were taken captive by the armed prisoners.

Confusion and chaos reigned as prison officers were held up by what appeared to be other prison officers wielding guns. At first some thought it was an exercise by the army, until the reality of the situation dawned. One officer managed to reach an alarm, which brought a telephone check from the emergency control room to the lodge. Disaster for the jailbreakers was averted when another officer with a gun pointed at his head took the call and reported that alarm had been pressed by mistake and all was in order. He tried to hint that this was not really so, but the hint was not picked up.

As the number of officers arriving at the lodge from their afternoon break increased, it was becoming more difficult for the prisoners to maintain control. Suddenly an officer, James Ferris, ran out of the building, shouting to a colleague to raise the alarm. He was chased by a prisoner and stabbed in the chest. The forty-three-year-old officer died soon afterwards.

In what was fast developing into a full-scale melee, one of the captive officers managed to contact the emergency control room and tell what was happening. It would later emerge that staff there had just received a call from a soldier in a watchtower, who reported seeing what he thought was prison officers fighting. He had been told that everything was all right. This time the control room took the call seriously and the alarm was raised. It was 4.12 p.m. and, in the midst of the fighting and confusion at the lodge, an officer with a gun pointed at his head had just opened the gate.

Prison officers ran for the gate as the escapers raced for freedom, a freedom that many could not legally have expected to see this side of the twenty-first century. There was shouting, screaming and swearing – and as dogs barked, bullets flew and warders fought with prisoners, three more officers fell with stab wounds, allegedly caused by the man who had killed James Ferris.

Outside the main gate the men had to negotiate the perimeter wire, stretched out in rolls across the ground. Some became caught up in it and were quickly recaptured. Others got clear and took to their heels. It had been hoped to drive the lorry right out of the prison, but this part of the plan had been aborted in the confusion at the gate and the vehicle had been abandoned. A prison officer's car was taken but soon crashed and the men inside ran across neighbouring fields, chased by officers and soldiers. One officer was shot in the thigh and the

Alan Reeve, still wanted after escaping from Broadmoor in 1981. (*Press Association*)

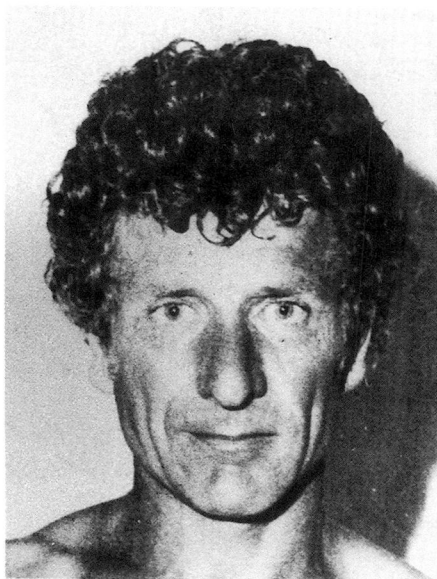

Arthur Hutchinson – killed three members of a Sheffield family after escaping from police custody. (*Sheffield Newspapers*)

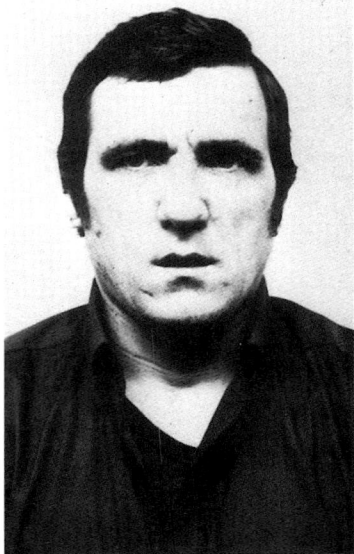

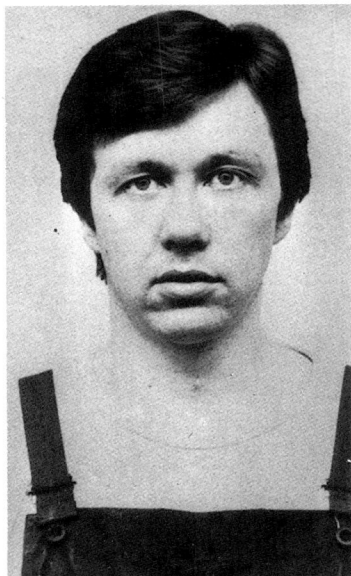

Gerald Tuite (above left), Jimmy Moody (above) and Stanley Thompson (left). (*Press Association*)

PAUL MAGEE   MICHAEL A. McKEE   ANTHONY GERARD SLOAN

JOSEPH DOCHERTY   ANGELO FUSCO

The 'M60 Squad' who escaped from Crumlin Road Jail, Belfast 1981. (*Press Association*)

Joseph Doherty – Crumlin Road escaper who became a media celebrity in New York. (*Pacemaker Press International*)

The Maze Prison: an aerial view of the H-Blocks. (*Pacemaker Press International*)

Larry Marley, 'brains' behind the Maze mass escape – but he stayed behind. (*Pacemaker Press International*)

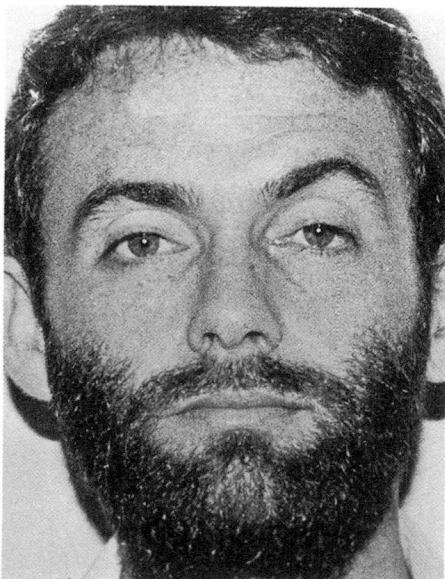

Brendan McFarlane leader of the mass escape from the Maze in 1983. (*Pacemaker Press International*)

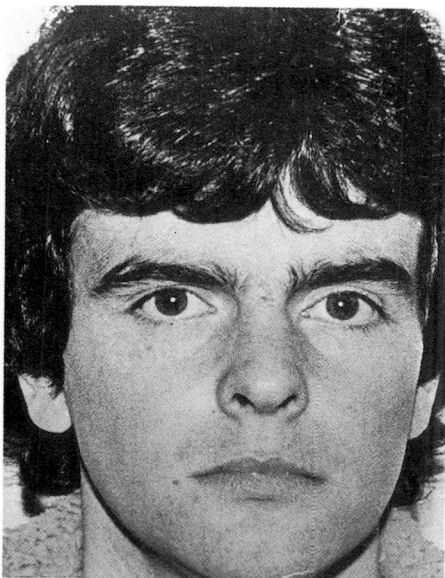

Seamus McElwaine – shot dead by the S.A.S. while on the run. (*Pacemaker Press International*)

Four faces of Nikolaus Chrastny, master of disguise. (*Press Association*)

John Kendall – serving 8 years when he escaped by helicopter from Gartree in 1987. Recaptured, he was sentenced to 35 years. (*Press Association*)

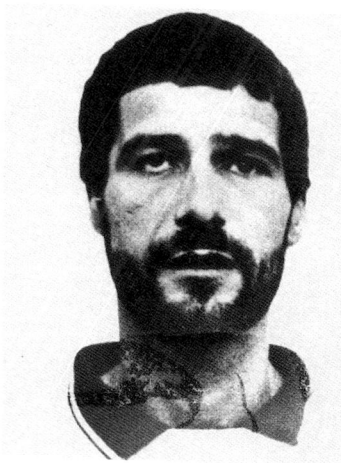

Sydney Draper, the lifer who accompanied Kendall. (*Press Association*)

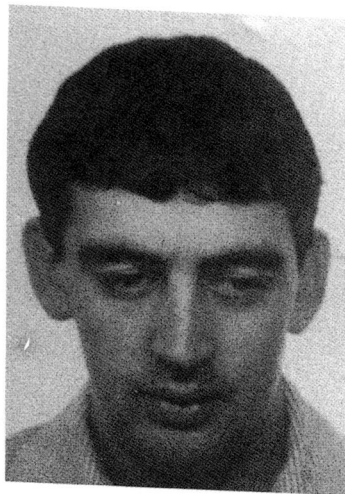

Pearse McAuley and Nessan Quinlivan. IRA men who shot their way out of Brixton Prison, 1992. (*Press Association*)

Joseph Steele, superglued to the railings at Buckingham Palace, 1993. (*Scottish Daily Record*)

Patrick McKearney, 29, fourteen years for possession of a loaded sten-gun;

Dermot Finucane, 22, eighteen years for possessing firearms and ammunition;

Patrick McIntyre, 25, fifteen years for attempted murder of a UDR man;

James Smyth, 28, twenty years for the attempted murder of a prison officer;

Anthony Kelly, 22, detained at the Secretary of State's pleasure for the murder of a reserve constable;

James Clarke, 27, eighteen years for attempted murder;

Terence Kirby, 27, life for murder of a garage owner;

Anthony McAllister, 25, life for murder of a soldier;

Gerard McDonnell, 32, sixteen years for possession of bomb-making equipment;

Seamus Clarke, 27, life for murder of five people in a Shankhill Road bar.

Of the ones who got away, most hi-jacked cars. Eleven men piled into an old banger they stumbled upon in a farmyard, driving it until better transport presented itself further along the way. Two took a Volkswagen van and eight, including Brendan McFarlane and Seamus McElwaine, commandeered a blue Mercedes. They knew the car would easily be spotted by a helicopter and, with no clear idea about the direction they should head in, they decided that the best ploy was to hide the car and take over a house.

Brendan – known as 'Bik' – McFarlane, was the IRA's commanding officer in the Maze at the time of the hunger strikes. McFarlane was widely credited in the media, by those unaware of Larry Marley's role, as having masterminded the Maze escape; now he and seven of his men burst into the home of a quantity surveyor, his wife and three children at Dromore, only four miles from the prison.

The family were also called McFarlane, a coincidence that the IRA leader pointed out. He made them swear on a Bible that they would tell no one of their ordeal and threatened what would happen if they did. Telephone wires were ripped out and the men took clothes and other items from the family, making out an inventory which Brendan McFarlane signed, telling them they could use it to claim compensation. The couple and their three children were ordered to go to bed in one bedroom at 10 p.m. When they came down on the Monday morning, the men had gone. The hi-jacked Mercedes was still hidden in the garage.

The family were in a predicament. They had been held hostage in their own home by the IRA and, as staunch Presbyterians, they were hardly supporters of the Republican cause. On the other hand they had sworn an oath on the Bible and felt responsible for that. They sought the advice of their minister and he told them the oath must be obeyed. It was not until the agreed seventy-two hours had passed that the family called the RUC. By that time the eight escapers, led by Seamus McElwaine, a specialist in guerilla warfare in open country, were on their way to the safety of South Armagh, on foot. The journey took them four days, walking by night and hiding by day, eating crab apples and drinking water from cattle troughs.

★ ★ ★

In County Down, Hugh Corey, the former commanding officer of the Provisional IRA in South Londonderry, and Patrick McIntyre, a Donegal man, were holed up in a lonely farmhouse near Newcastle. Their freedom lasted only a day. Surrounded by armed RUC officers and soldiers of the UDR, they gave themselves up on the Monday. Eight spent two weeks under the floorboards of a safe house, sweating and stinking in a space barely high enough to roll over in. The only time they emerged was to go to the toilet.

Now there were nineteen men on the run, exactly half the number that had got out of the prison. That would be the situation for the next eight months. Gradually the road-blocks and searches of late September were scaled down and the nineteen fugitives enjoyed their new-found freedom.

For those who had tried but failed, the nineteen who were recaptured and returned to the Maze, life was doubly unpleasant. Not only were they back inside, but they had to bear the brunt of warders' anger at the escape – and at the death of one colleague and the wounding of others. In late October detectives from the RUC were drafted into the prison to investigate allegations made by solicitors, priests and prison visitors that officers set dogs on prisoners and assaulted them after the escape. The men left behind in H Block 7 were said to have been forced to run a gauntlet of warders wielding batons and dogs biting at them, as they were moved from the block to H8. Thirteen of the men who were picked up immediately after the break-out were alleged to have been stripped on their return and then assaulted.

The issue of brutality towards prisoners after the

escape arose again, six years later, when two of the Maze men, Dermot Finucane and James Clarke, were saved from extradition by sympathetic judges in the Irish Supreme Court. The judges stated that the escapers were likely to be assaulted if they were returned to the North. Finucane, who was identified in the official report into the break-out as having been involved in the killing of prison officer James Ferris – although the officer's death was subsequently attributed to a heart attack – would be, said the Irish Chief Justice, 'a probable target for ill-treatment'.

This decision, condemned as 'offensive and insulting' by Downing Street, led to a new breach in Anglo-Irish relations. It was based on earlier court cases in which Maze prisoners had been successful in claiming damages. In November 1988 a prisoner who did not escape was awarded £3,000 by the Ulster Lord Chief Justice, after claiming he had been kicked and punched and bitten by a guard dog. This was followed in January 1990 by awards totalling £35,000 to nineteen other prisoners arising from similar assaults. No officers were charged in connection with any of these matters.

The inquiry into the break-out began on the very next day, Monday 26 September, under Sir James Hennessey, Chief Inspector of Prisons in the United Kingdom. His brief was to concentrate on how knives and guns had been smuggled in, whether prison officers had cooperated, and on the vetting procedures for people entering the prison complex.

As Hennessey and his thirteen-strong team set about their task, anonymous sources from within the prison officers' ranks were quoted in the press, providing grass-roots opinion on where the blame lay. One 'Senior Maze officer' told reporters that a catalogue of security lapses throughout the prison allowed the terrorists to escape. He claimed there was speculation inside the prison that warders were bribed to smuggle guns in and the prisoners were able to flee because doors and gates were left open.

Morale of the staff had been low and security was lax, he said, with only 196 instead of 350 prison officers on duty on the day, and only 12, instead of more than 20, working on an H Block containing 127 men. He said that in three of the wings there was only one officer on duty, which made it easy for prisoners armed with guns, knives and chair legs with nails through the end, to take control. If the officer in the H Block 7 control room had been locked in, as he should have been, he could have raised the alarm, but instead he was having tea with other officers. Some of these criticisms would ultimately be validated by the official report.

Sir James Hennessey's inquiry into the Maze mass escape was completed within three months. By mid-January 1984, when publication of his report was known to be imminent, the government took precautions. The Spearhead Battalion of the British Army – a trouble-shooting contingent of 650 men from a rota of regiments, on permanent alert to cover emergencies anywhere in the world – was put on stand-by to move to Northern Ireland at short notice.

Tension was mounting by the day, with speculation in the media that the Governor and at least ten of his staff were to face serious disciplinary charges. The Governor, Ernest Whittington, who was due to retire later in the year, had already attempted to resign, but the Northern Ireland Office refused to accept his resignation. The great fear was that the publication of the inquiry's findings would precipitate action by prison staff and trouble among prisoners.

Sure enough, when the *Report of an Inquiry by HM Chief Inspector of Prisons into the security arrangements at HM Prison Maze* did appear, in the last week of January, it proved to be a scathing indictment of the jail and its staff. Hennessey pulled no punches in outlining the findings of his thirteen-strong team. He made it plain that the Governor must be held accountable for a major failure in security and he suggested disciplinary action against other senior officers, with the transfer of some, including the Assistant Governor in charge of the security department. He recommended a new post of professional Head of the Prison Service, an extension of the closed-circuit television system and the formation of an emergency quick-reaction force within the prison.

Hennessey's report outlined the events of the Sunday afternoon, pointing out the ways in which failure to adhere to security procedures – at times inadequate in themselves – had brought about the circumstances whereby thirty-eight men could escape. As he reported, nineteen were still at liberty.

The deployment of staff in the blocks was designed to ensure that even if officers were attacked by prisoners, it should have been possible for the alarm to be raised before all were seized. But, said Hennessey, 'In H7 on the day of the escape only nine of the sixteen officers detailed for duty on the four wings were actually at their posts at 2.40 p.m. Of the remainder, four were in the staff tea-room and three were in the staff lavatories . . . Thus there were three wings with only two officers in each. This would have made it comparatively easy for the prisoners to overcome the staff in the wings without the alarm being raised.'

The escape could have been averted by the officer in the communications room raising the alarm – if he had kept the steel door locked in accordance with orders. That had not happened because a lack of ventilation made conditions in the room barely tolerable, and it had become customary for the door to be left open.

'To complete this sorry tale,' wrote Hennessey, 'it is necessary to mention that there were no calls from the Emergency Control Room to H7 throughout the ninety minutes that the prisoners remained in control, because there was no system of routine checks within the blocks. This was yet another flaw in the security arrangements of the prison. These various weaknesses in security must be remedied if a similar takeover is to be avoided in the future. Some immediate action is necessary.'

As usual in the reports of inquiries into escapes, the big question – how five guns had been smuggled into the prison – was not answered. The route by which they had got in could not be established, said the report, recommending a greater thoroughness in the searching of supplies, vehicles, visitors and staff entering the prison. Highly critical of the lax attitude towards visiting, Hennessey said, 'We cannot discount the possibility that a member of the prison staff carried the guns in.'

There were, he said, serious deficiencies in the supervision of visits, in particular domestic visits, when it had become practice for staff to patrol so infrequently that on occasions sexual intercourse could have taken place. Said the report, 'We are satisfied that the supervision was sufficiently lax to have allowed this to occur,' adding the comment that in such circumstances it would have also been easy for a visitor to remove a weapon from its hiding place and to transfer it to a prisoner. In the two months preceding the escape, thirty-seven prisoners from H Block 7 had been allowed fifty-two such visits.

Amazingly, in view of the nature of the prisoners in the Maze, procedures for searching men after visits had not been followed. 'Rub-down searches were perfunctory and no metal detector was being used in the visiting areas.' Random strip searches were recommended, not only for inmates, but for all professional visitors.

Even the vetting of staff was found to be flawed. One man who had been recruited was found to have a criminal record; another, a probation officer seconded to the prison, had, a month before the escape, admitted having been a member of the Provisional IRA in the early 1970s.

The Hennessey Report conceded that the Maze, holding the largest concentration of terrorists in Western Europe, presented unique difficulties for management and staff at all levels: 'In no other prison that we have seen have the problems faced by the authorities been so great.' Staff were in conflict with prisoners 'almost every day of the week' and what was an already dangerous task had been made harder by the government's determination not to give in to the terrorists' political demands. Furthermore, the task of maintaining security had not been made any easier by the Northern Ireland Prison

Officers' Association calling upon its members to leave the prison in support of a claim for travelling time allowance, placing the responsibility of manning the jail on the police.

Since the troubles in Northern Ireland began, twenty-two members of the prison service had been killed and many more had been threatened and their families intimidated. It was important, said Hennessey, to take into account the pressure staff came under from terrorist organisations. 'It should not need to be stated that each prison officer was in much closer contact with terrorists, in circumstances in which he personally might incur their animosity, than soldiers, policemen and politicians.' Prison staff would not be human if they did not fear invoking aggression and reprisals, he said, adding, 'Certainly we believe that the tendency for staff to turn a blind eye to activities which threaten security is, in part, a direct consequence of terrorist pressures.'

Having said that, he lambasted the prison staff – from the top to the bottom. He said he met staff in all grades and branches at the Maze who were conscientious and professional in their outlook and not prepared to give less than their best in their everyday work. 'But the Maze also harbours officers who show too little concern for their duty . . . Then there were the complacent staff, ripe for manipulation by inmates . . . The restoration of a sense of professionalism must therefore be an immediate objective if security is to be improved.'

He singled out the Security Principal Officer, as not having 'a proper grasp of security procedures' and the Governor, 'who carries the ultimate responsibility for the state of the prison and the general malaise that was apparent.' That malaise was evident in the Sunday afternoon practice of staff leaving early. On 25 September a large number had not been at their posts, having either left before relief officers arrived, or handed over to officers with other duties to perform.

Previous Maze chiefs were not absolved. Of the many weaknesses in security at the prison, deficiencies in physical security at the main gate, and in the communications room, had been long standing. 'Successive Governors failed to effect the improvements they could have made,' said the report, making a point that would seem ironic when the identity of the next Governor was revealed.

As soon as the Hennessey Report was published, the Governor of the Maze, Ernest Whittington, resigned. Many people thought James Prior, Secretary of State for Northern Ireland, and Nicholas Scott, the junior minister, should join him, but Prior stood firm. Fighting off demands from both sides of the House of Commons, James Prior said, 'I do not believe that in any policy decision there was negligence by myself or Mr Scott. I see on this occasion no need for my resignation.'

Of the seventy-three recommendations made by Hennessey, the Secretary of State told MPs that twenty-one had already been carried out, thirty-eight would be carried out as soon as possible, and fourteen were under urgent review. The Assistant Governor in charge of security had been transferred and was to face a disciplinary investigation, along with about a dozen prison officers. The probation officer formerly a member of the IRA had been dismissed. The report, said Hennessey, marked, 'The blackest day in the troubled history of the Northern Ireland prison service.'

James Prior's refusal to be accountable for the security deficiencies that led to the Maze escape riled Unionist politicians in Ulster. 'In days gone by,' said one, 'ministers accepted responsibility for this sort of thing and would have resigned.' Another declared the Governor's resignation to be 'like firing the stoker when the ship had gone on the rocks'. The Reverend Ian Paisley accused the government of trying to get itself off the hook by pinning the blame on prison officers, while Seamus Mallon of the Social Democratic and Labour Party said the report showed the prison service in the Maze to be 'very inefficient and decadent'.

The new Governor was named as Stanley Hilditch, aged fifty-four, a former estate agent and Baptist minister. He had been in charge of every major prison in Ulster, including a previous spell at the Maze, leaving at the time of the hunger strikes in 1981. He could thus be assumed to be one of the previous Governors who had been criticised by Hennessey for failing to introduce necessary security improvements.

Following the report, the Northern Ireland Prison Officers' Association issued three press statements in quick succession, blaming political pressures for the circumstances leading to the escape and claiming the Governor had been made a scapegoat. The real blame, it was maintained, could be traced back to a deal done by Lord Gowrie, then Ulster prisons minister, with the Provisional IRA, in ending the 1981 hunger strike.

An anonymous 'senior prison officer' told the Press Association that the British Government was 'so anxious to end the hunger strike two years ago that senior officers were "ordered" to relax security'. He said that

IRA prisoners were allowed to force Loyalist prisoners out of certain H Blocks, with the result that 'our intelligence-gathering operations were virtually wiped out'. During the 1981 protests IRA prisoners had refused to work, but afterwards the government issued instructions for work to be found as quickly as possible. Now, with a mass break-out planned, this suited the IRA men, as it enabled them to get hold of equipment and tools.

In the aftermath of the Hennessey Report, Northern Ireland's 3,000 prison officers refused to cooperate with the disciplinary inquiries that were ordered. Of much more pressing concern to them was the need for new measures to break the hold that the paramilitary had on the running of prisons. They expressed anger at the criticisms of their complacency and alleged negligence and demanded increases of twenty-five per cent more men in the Maze.

By mid-February a new row had broken out between Maze officers and the Northern Ireland Office when it was announced that copies of the Hennessey Report had been made available for prisoners to read. This, it was alleged, was 'all part of the bungling and mishandling which had done so much to destroy the morale of the prison service'. The report was obviously of interest and use to the IRA, but even if it had not been allowed in the prison, it could be purchased by anyone outside as an HMSO publication. The real point was whether or not the inquiry's findings should have been published at all.

William McConnell, the Deputy Governor at the Maze, went a step further than anonymous quotes to the press. Bitterly resentful of Hennessey's criticism of himself and his colleagues, he appeared on television to express his opinions. McConnell had been the officer responsible for allocating work at the time Brendan McFarlane was made an orderly. He knew that by speaking out publicly he was putting his life in danger.

He was indeed. On a March morning as he kissed his wife and three-year-old daughter goodbye outside his home, William McConnell was shot dead by gunmen who had occupied a house across the street. He left a letter, written in apparent anticipation of his demise, which was read out at his funeral. To howls of outrage from the Northern Ireland Office, the Reverend Ian Paisley alleged that one interpretation of the letter could be that British Intelligence was involved in the killing. 'They would have an interest in silencing a person who would be a grave embarrassment,' he said.

Twelve months later a retired civil servant and wartime RAF officer who had flown thirty bombing missions over Germany – before becoming a spy for the IRA – was jailed for life for the murder. His wife got five years and his daughter, a typist with the DHSS, a suspended sentence.

The rows and controversies, the recriminations, allegations and counter-allegations would rage on and on. Security in the Maze was tightened, with searches of cells and prisoners creating increasing conflict between staff and inmates. Then in August 1984, amidst all these tensions with Republican prisoners, two Loyalists, both serving life for murder, attempted to escape from the Maze compound section. Their quest for freedom coincided with a wave of rioting and petrol-bombing throughout Loyalist areas of Ulster, in commemoration of the thirteenth anniversary of internment.

Escape attempts by Loyalist prisoners were rare; this one ended in tragic failure. The pair, Benny Redfern and Edward Pollock, hid in a bin prior to a refuse collection and were wheeled to the lorry, lifted hydraulically and tipped into the back among the refuse. Many years earlier, the same method had been successful for another escaper, Brendan Hughes. But refuse lorries had become more sophisticated and as the waste-compressing machinery got to work before the lorry had even left the prison, both prisoners were severely mangled. One died later in hospital.

After Hugh Corey and Patrick McIntyre were picked up the day after the break-out, it would be another eight months before the next Maze escaper surfaced. Nineteen men were still at liberty. In May 1984 Irish gardai and special branch detectives raided a house on the Ballymun estate in Dublin. Inside was Robert 'Goose' Russell. He was served with an extradition warrant and a warrant in relation to the alleged murder of prison officer James Ferris.

After six months in custody, while his lawyers fought the extradition warrant, Robert Russell attempted another escape, this time from Portlaoise Jail in the Republic. Twelve men were involved as a gun, duplicate keys and explosives were used to try to blast open a steel door. Unfortunately for the men, the door buckled under the blast and the escape was foiled. In 1988 Russell lost his legal battle and was taken back to the North, a move that sparked off riots as his supporters showed their disapproval.

Russell's story was not over yet. In early 1991 his

conviction for attempted murder of a police superintendent was overturned and he walked free from his twenty-year sentence. In May he was arrested by immigration officials at Toronto airport as he arrived there, hoping to start a new life.

More months passed until December 1984 brought a flurry of activity. A Saturday night border shoot-out between an IRA unit and the Army left one terrorist and one SAS corporal dead. James Clarke was picked up south of the border. He had been doing eighteen years in the North for five attempted murders at the time of the Maze escape, now he got eighteen years in the Republic for possession of a weapon. Nevertheless, efforts were made to extradite him – his was one of the cases that the Irish Supreme Court later refused to allow on the grounds of likely ill-treatment.

Another Maze escaper was involved in the shoot-out, but got away, only to drown as he tried to cross a river. Shortly before Christmas, Kieran Fleming's body was dragged from the river, in County Fermanagh. At his funeral in Londonderry, mourners hurled bricks, bottles and paving stones at RUC officers. They replied by firing plastic bullets.

Scotland was the scene of the next recapture. Gerry McDonnell had a Browning automatic pistol, £5,000 in cash and a document that police described as 'a bombing calendar' on his person when he was arrested, along with two other terrorists, Peter Sherry and Patrick Magee, in a swoop on a Glasgow flat in late June 1985. The arrests spoiled IRA plans to bomb an hotel close to Buckingham Palace and to conduct a bombing campaign in seaside resorts around England that summer. McDonnell, doing sixteen years in the Maze at the time of the escape, was sentenced to life for conspiracy to cause explosions. This time he remained in a mainland prison.

Brendan 'Bik' McFarlane had the highest media profile of all the Maze escapers. Besides being credited with masterminding the Maze escape, during his time on the run his name was linked with two kidnappings: the supermarket executive, Don Tidey and the Derby-winning racehorse, Shergar. In January 1986, McFarlane and fellow escaper, Gerry Kelly turned up in Amsterdam, on an arms-buying mission. Asleep in a flat in a quiet suburb to the south of the city, they were seized in a dawn raid when twenty armed police burst through the windows throwing stun grenades.

The Dutch authorities were tipped off by British police, who had followed the movements of McFarlane and Kelly. Inside the flat they found a pistol, false passports and £1,000 sterling. In a cargo container, destined for Ulster and the struggle, Dutch police discovered fourteen semi-automatic rifles, a Kalashnikov, automatic pistols, hand grenades, ammunition and four drums of nitrobenzene, used in bomb-making.

Extradition battles followed, with one Dutch court saying that Kelly could not be returned to Northern Ireland, but McFarlane could. The Dutch Supreme Court then decided both should go and after an appeal to the European Court of Human Rights had been rejected, the Dutch Parliament had the final say. By December 1986 Brendan McFarlane and Gerry Kelly were back in the Maze Prison. Kelly was released from his double life plus twenty years sentence in 1989, after serving sixteen years. In November 1993 he was alleged to be one of the IRA hardliners behind a wave of IRA bombings and killings.

For Seamus McElwaine and Patrick McKearney, liberation from the Maze meant a return to action. McElwaine operated around the border country, where, in a field in County Fermanagh, he was shot dead by the SAS as he went to detonate a mine at dawn on Sunday 26 April 1986. It was said at his funeral, 'In prison yards all over Britain and Ireland, they remember him . . . His name will live for ever.'

McKearney met a similar fate in an abortive attempt to blow up a police station at Loughgall, a village in County Tyrone. Three IRA men aboard a mechanical digger – with a 200-pound bomb in the bucket – drove straight into a joint SAS-RUC ambush. Five other men were following in a car. All eight were shot dead.

Before much longer, several escapers were picked up in the Republic. Dermot Finucane was taken in County Longford, to begin what would be a successful appeal against extradition. Anthony Kelly and Seamus Clarke followed suit in Dublin. James Smyth, arrested in San Francisco in 1991, was later granted bail. In 1993 when his extradition case was heard, British MP Ken Livingstone appeared as a witness for him, in respect of Smyth's claim that he would be shot by the British security forces if he was returned to Northern Ireland.

Kevin Barry Artt was also arrested in the USA, as was Paul Brennan, who came to light in 1993 in Berkeley, California when he applied for a new passport in the name of Morgan. By then several others had been released on either parole or bail. At the time of writing, two of the nineteen men who got away are still unaccounted for.

Larry Marley, the man who schemed and planned the escape, but took no part in it himself, was released from the Maze in November 1985, having served eight years. On 2 April 1987 he was shot dead by Loyalist gunmen at his home in the Ardoyne district of Belfast. His funeral had to be postponed twice because of violent clashes between Republican mourners and the RUC. Marley's role as the real mastermind behind the Maze escape was only publicly revealed after his death, by Irish journalist Derek Dunne in his book *Out of the Maze*.

The charges relating to the Maze escape did not reach Belfast Crown Court until April 1988, four and a half years after the event. Sixteen of the accused were found not guilty of the murder of James Ferris, the prison officer stabbed during the break-out. The Lord Chief Justice of Northern Ireland, Lord Lowry, said he could not be satisfied that the stabbing was the cause of death, following a pathologist's report which revealed that the deceased had a heart complaint.

The alleged leaders of the escape, Brendan McFarlane and Gerry Kelly, were each sentenced to five years for imprisoning a prison officer. They were not charged with escaping because of the terms under which they had been extradited from Holland. Bobby Storey, one of those immediately recaptured, got seven years and Harry Murray, whose charges included one of shooting a prison officer in the leg, got eight to add to the indefinite detention at the pleasure of the Secretary of State that he was already serving. Others were sentenced to between three and seven years on charges which included escape, attempted escape, imprisoning officers, wounding, assault and riotous behaviour.

Lord Lowry was highly critical of evidence given by prison officers. He said the escape had been a humiliating experience which they would rather forget, but the possibility that some were not carrying out their duties properly could have given them a motive for 'misdescribing' the events, so as to conceal their own misdemeanours. Dismissing their evidence, he said 'They may have a motive to exaggerate the number of prisoners and the weapons used to overpower them.' He said that many of the officers had contradicted each other and the verbal statements they had given to the police had in many instances contradicted written evidence.

The judge's words were a damning indictment on the Maze authorities. Four years earlier, after the similarly scathing Hennessey Report, it had been announced that a total of 700 charges were to be brought against the thirty-eight who escaped, including murder and attempted murder. Now no one was convicted on either of those charges, despite one officer being killed and another lucky to survive after being shot in the head. For those who had hoped to see stiff sentences imposed, what had come in like a lion had gone out like a lamb.

17 NIKOLAUS CHRASTNY

Who Sprung Chrastny?

When Nikolaus Chrastny was arrested on the pavement outside his London flat in June 1987, Scotland Yard and customs officers had every reason to be pleased with themselves. An international drug smuggler, Chrastny was straight out of the top drawer, a leading player in a multi-million-pound operation that moved cocaine between Columbia, the United States and Britain. When the forty-four-year-old German began dropping names and a haul of cocaine worth an estimated £14million was found at a neighbouring Harley Street flat, detectives and customs men were delighted. But delight turned to discomfort when Chrastny named his partner in crime.

The man Chrastny said was his partner in the drug smuggling business was Roy Garner, a Londoner who had greatly profited from a dual life as a villain and a police informer over many years. Old Bill found he had more on his plate than he had bargained for. Because, as Chrastny explained to his captors, Garner had a friend, a very useful friend. That friend, he said, was Detective Superintendent Tony Lundy himself of Scotland Yard.

Roy Garner was arrested, to eventually get twenty-two years, reduced to sixteen on appeal. Tony Lundy was suspended from duty, but allowed to retire on health grounds with a pension and a medal. Chrastny, having struck a deal in which his admission and information on others would enable his wife to avoid prosecution, was remanded to the custody of customs officers, who, wanting to get him out of London because of the corruption he had alleged, handed him over to the safekeeping of South Yorkshire police. He was held in supposed strict secrecy at Rotherham police station and interviewed at length by a South Yorkshire team which was already investigating allegations made against Lundy and his informant, Garner, in a 'World In Action' television programme.

When Chrastny arrived at Rotherham, customs officers wanted him kept in a residential annexe, next door to the police station. This was in the full knowledge that he was a high-risk prisoner who was suspected of murder as well as drug offences, moreover one whose life was said to be in danger from people who did not want him to give evidence against them. The superintendent in charge of prisoners refused the customs request and housed Chrastny in the normal cell block. There, it quickly became apparent that he was becoming over-friendly with the police officers guarding him and, as he ingratiated himself further and further, a complacent attitude quickly developed among them.

The superintendent decided this constituted a danger. He was right. After only nineteen days at Rotherham, Chrastny was transferred to the custody of the West Yorkshire force and a cell in Dewsbury police station

which, only a few years earlier, had held the Yorkshire
Ripper.

At Dewsbury, Chrastny's stay was subject to special
orders, code-named Operation December. It was made
clear to those who came into contact with him that his
presence must remain top-secret and that he must be
held securely as he was there to protect his life. Customs
officers who wished to interrogate him were to be given
access at all times. He was placed in a cell in a section of
the custody area normally used for women prisoners.
The cell had a barred gate on the outside of its door and
opened into a hallway. Chrastny settled in for a long
stay.

Every effort was made to keep Nikolaus Chrastny
sweet. He was treated, as the chairman of the local
police authority said later, 'as a guest, he wasn't a
prisoner in the normal sense'. For a master of charm and
manipulation, it was an ideal situation. Chrastny had no
difficulty winning over the West Yorkshire officers and
in no time at all was allowed to have a television set and
a stereo. This was more than a desire for home comforts;
his cell had no power socket, thus a lead had to be run
from the doctor's room across the corridor. That meant
his cell door had to be left open.

If it seems incredible that Chrastny was allowed such
privileges, given the reasoning behind his sudden transfer from Rotherham to Dewsbury, it was only the
beginning of thirteen weeks in which Chrastny 'charmed
those police officers like birdies off a tree', as a barrister
later told the Old Bailey. Chrastny's wife, Charlotte,
who, prior to meeting her husband had been a policewoman in Germany, was allowed to visit him frequently,

sometimes to share a meal with him. Since they spoke in German, their conversations could not be understood by officers. Staff soon got to know her – and did not always bother to search her. When they did, and found rolls of banknotes containing as much as £500 in her possession, they allowed her to take the cash in to Chrastny. No one questioned what a man confined to a cell, with everything provided, was likely to do with £500.

And everything was certainly provided for Nikolaus Chrastny. As well as the television set, which his wife had been allowed to bring in, he had a stereo system, hand-exercisers, bottles of beer, cigars, jars of his favourite chutney and forty-one books. It would later be alleged that his wife had brought him one of these books, the Sherlock Holmes mystery *The Hound of the Baskervilles* – with two files concealed in the spine.

Besides these items that eased his incarceration, Chrastny was provided with model-making equipment to while away the long hours in between interviews by customs officers. His captors, apparently ignorant of the use that such materials had been put to by several well-known prison escapers in the past, allowed him Plasticine, paint, glue and Blu-tack. Whether Chrastny made any models or not, he did put the materials to good use. Left unsupervised in his cell for long, long periods, the door open and unlocked, he sawed away at the bars of the outer gate and filled in the cuts with Plasticine.

How such a high-risk prisoner was able to saw through bars three quarters of an inch thick on a cell gate which opened on to one of the main thoroughfares within the cell block, while supposedly being under the closest watch, was a real poser later for investigators. He was able to do it because no one ever checked the bars and he worked late at night and into the small hours, covering the noise he made by playing his television or stereo at top volume. In early October Chrastny was told he would soon be leaving Dewsbury. He set about his sawing with a greater urgency and by the early morning of 5 October, the day before he was due to appear in a London magistrates' court, the task was completed.

Once the bars were out of the way, Chrastny's escape route was relatively simple. He knew that the medical room across the hallway had an unbarred window – he had managed to wheedle his way in there to check it out several times, on the pretext of weighing himself. The cable from his television ran into the room, which meant that the door could not be locked and so, within the space of a few yards, he was able to climb through the window and out into the police station yard. From there he climbed a gate and it is believed he was picked up in a waiting car and driven away. A couple of days earlier he had asked one of his guards where Dewsbury lay in relation to the M1.

The next morning at 11.30 a.m. police officers called upon Chrastny as usual to bring him his breakfast and newspaper. When there was no answer, they went away again, assuming that he was sleeping in, as he was wont to do. There were no clues that he had departed – after removing the gate bars Chrastny had replaced them with Plasticine so that everything looked normal. Twenty minutes later the guards returned. This time an inspector accidentally caught his foot in the gate, whereupon a bar fell to the floor. The 10 foot by 8 foot cell was empty and on the bed was a note which read, 'Gentlemen, I have not taken this step lightly. I have been planning it for several weeks. The tools have been in my wash-kit for several years in preparation for such an occasion.' It was signed, 'Greetings, Nick'. Later the same day, ever the gentleman, he telephoned Dewsbury police station and told an astonished officer, 'I apologise for any inconvenience caused.' That was the last to be heard of Nikolaus Chrastny.

A row of monumental proportions erupted with the disclosure of Chrastny's escape. For reasons that were never explained, the news was withheld for two days. On the Monday that he was found to have gone there were no searches or road-blocks around the town, nor any indications that a major criminal had escaped. This was considered surprising in some quarters, especially as Chrastny was considered so dangerous that when he was arrested four customs officers pressed him to the pavement with guns pointed at his head.

Neither police nor customs officers were accepting responsibility for his disappearance; each blamed the other. Customs claimed that security at Dewsbury police station was the responsibility of the police, while the police insisted he was in the custody of customs and that they had not followed the usual procedure of half-hour inspections of the prisoner. The West Yorkshire branch of the Police Federation went so far as to issue a statement saying that none of their members had been guilty of negligence.

The dispute was to rage for a long time to come. Eighteen months later the superintendent in charge at Dewsbury police station at the time of the escape would say at the Old Bailey that he was amazed when customs officers relaxed the rules under which Chrastny was being held – after a precise operational warning had been given that he would escape if given the slightest opportunity. He said he did not believe the customs officers were as professional as his own and that he did not believe they were conversant with the detention of prisoners, criticising their decision to allow Chrastny to telephone his wife and to receive visits from her.

At the same hearing a customs officer was asked whether the strict orders governing Chrastny's custody had been ignored, especially regarding the telephone calls. He said, 'I didn't see fit to query them. I was led to believe by senior officers in the West Yorkshire force that they were well-qualified to deal with high-risk prisoners.' The situation was not made any better when it was revealed that three prisoners had previously escaped from the cell block at Dewsbury police station.

Chrastny's capture had been a triumph for the police, now he had slipped through their fingers after starting to name people whose arrest would seriously damage the cocaine trade in Britain. A senior detective said, 'We are devastated because we believed Mr Chrastny could have opened doors that have been closed to us for a decade. What we fear is that we have let escape the net the one man who could expose an international drugs network.'

At the time of his arrest, Chrastny was on the run from the police in West Germany, where he had been wanted since 1973 for an armed robbery in Munich in which he got away with jewellery worth a million Deutschmarks. Born in Czechoslovakia, he had acquired West German citizenship and was known to have passports from Austria and the United States, the latter obtained in Florida in 1984 in the name of Charles Flynn. Tubby, short and bald, he was fluent in five languages and an expert marksman who, during fourteen years on the run, had changed his appearance by plastic surgery several times. 'He is known as The Man Of Many Faces,' said a spokesman for the Federal Criminal Office in Wiesbaden, West Germany.

West Yorkshire Police took the rap for Chrastny's escape from Dewsbury. An inquiry was conducted by the Chief Constable of Northumbria, Sir Stanley Bailey, who decried police officers for giving Chrastny his model-making equipment and made harsh comments about inefficiency, lack of clarity of orders and confusion over who was actually responsible for the prisoner's custody. In order to investigate allegations of corruption that had been made, immunity had been given to junior police officers regarding minor disciplinary matters, but no evidence of collusion between Chrastny and either police or customs officers came to light. It was pointed out that when the supergrass was passed on to Dewsbury police, written instructions stated that customs men should be in constant attendance. No one was now saying why they had not been there during the prolonged period when Chrastny was sawing through – and going through – his bars. The only outcome of the inquiry was a recognition that Dewsbury was unsuitable for a prisoner requiring such a high level of security, a formal warning for two senior police officers and 'counselling' for another.

Nikolaus Chrastny was thought to have been smuggled out of Britain within twenty-four hours of his escape from Dewsbury – but who had sprung him? Had his criminal associates, of whom there were many on at least three continents? Had corrupt Scotland Yard detectives, keen to prevent him giving evidence against their colleague Tony Lundy? Had his wife, Charlotte Chrastny, who had visited him only hours before he escaped?

Said investigative journalists Jennings, Lashmar and Simpson in their book *Scotland Yard's Cocaine Connection*, 'Chrastny's escape was good news for everybody named in his confession.' When Charlotte Chrastny appeared at the Old Bailey in April 1989, charged with aiding and abetting her husband to escape, her counsel claimed that Scotland Yard detectives could have helped the supergrass escape, so as to prevent him revealing details of alleged corruption by Metropolitan officers. He said, 'A number of people had a motive for helping Chrastny escape – Scotland Yard, Mr Garner and other members of the drug conspiracy.' Charlotte Chrastny was acquitted of the escape charge, but convicted of conspiracy to import and distribute cocaine. Despite her counsel's eloquent and persuasive pleas that 'her husband had fooled her in the same way that he fooled his guards', she was given seven years.

Martin Short, the author of books on such topics as the iniquities of Freemasonry, the U.S. Mafia and an earlier dark episode involving systematic corruption at Scotland Yard, published, in 1991, a biography of the by-now retired Chief Superintendent. In *Lundy – The Destruction of Scotland Yard's Finest Detective*, he expressed the opinion 'it is worse than perverse to blame Scotland Yard for Chrastny's escape'.

Short pointed out that Chrastny's whereabouts had been kept a closely-guarded secret. If Mrs Chrastny had leaked the information, he said, she would surely have also betrayed any police officers with whom she was in league, in order to receive a lighter sentence than seven years. Another view might be that a sentence of seven years for conspiracy to import and distribute cocaine was already much less than it might have been and certainly not one to complain about. Many people convicted of similar charges involving lesser amounts – £2.6million had been seized by customs officers – would be pleased with only seven years.

Short went on to say that it would have been almost impossible for Scotland Yard detectives to know where Chrastny was, and as for Tony Lundy, he was suspended at home with his phone 'almost certainly' tapped. Whether or not Chrastny's whereabouts could have been discovered, or whether a suspended detective could use a telephone other than the one in his home, the location of any prisoner is not usually too difficult to ascertain, less so in a case like Chrastny's where his wife was visiting him. When, in 1991, Roy Garner was temporarily transferred under conditions of great secrecy from Full Sutton Prison to Attercliffe police station in Sheffield, for further interviews with South Yorkshire Police regarding his dealings with Tony Lundy, the move soon made the front page of the local paper.

In March 1992, the Home Office issued guidelines to every police force in the country regarding the accommodation and handling of 'resident informers', better known as supergrasses. Said to have been heavily influenced by the Chrastny case five years earlier, the guidelines stipulate that the informer must be held in a special suite away from other cells and that he must be protected by three officers on a twenty-four-hour basis. The officers must be uniformed and unconnected with the case. Prisoners on remand were to be allowed visits of fifteen minutes' duration from family and friends, with no conjugal visits or alcohol allowed.

As for Nikolaus Chrastny, he was last heard of in Costa Rica, far away from the clutches of various law-enforcement agencies who would like to discuss outstanding matters with him. No doubt his liberty has been extended by further plastic surgery and yet another identity. Life on the run is inevitably expensive, but Chrastny should be able to afford it: before he and his cohorts were captured they had already distributed 340 kilos of cocaine, worth an estimated £100million.

18   JOHN KENDALL AND SYDNEY DRAPER

Up, Up and Away

It had to happen. Sooner or later someone was bound to escape from a British prison by helicopter. Of all the means of escape, the air-lift has to be the quickest and the surprise is that no one managed it until 1987. After all, Ronnie Biggs considered using a helicopter to get him out of Wandsworth back in 1965 and Gerard Tuite, at the time of his arrest in 1979, was planning to use one to spring fellow IRA man Brian Keenan out of Brixton. Seven years later, three Israelis remanded to Norwich Prison on £5million drug charges might have become the first helicopter escapers, had an accomplice in America not offered the wrong man $35,000. Instead of getting a pilot he got a FBI agent.

Elsewhere in the world, helicopter escapes became increasingly popular. In 1971 it took only ten seconds to lift an American drug-runner off the yard at a Mexican jail, with the CIA, the Mafia and Cuban agents all rumoured to be responsible. Two years later, the IRA showed the way on this side of the Atlantic by getting Seamus Twomey and two others out of Mountjoy Prison in Dublin.

In 1981 Gerard Dupré became the first helicopter escaper in France, followed by gangster Michel Vanjour, lifted from a Paris jail in 1986. The same year, a Red Cross helicopter was hi-jacked in Rome and two inmates flown to a near-by football pitch and a waiting car. In Brazil, an attempted air-lift met with stiffer opposition – as the helicopter landed on the roof of a Rio jail and two convicts tried to board it, guards opened fire, killing both men and the pilot.

In Britain, the possibility of an air-lift from a prison first occurred to Home Office officials in 1966 when a rooftop protest at Leicester by one of the Great Train Robbers brought a press helicopter to the scene. It was acknowledged that in different hands and in such close proximity the helicopter could have been used for an escape, but no special precautions were introduced. A helicopter escape in Britain was not regarded seriously until a 1981 study, carried out by a senior Scotland Yard officer, emphasised the risk and the likelihood of such an eventuality. His report suggested that helicopters and short-take-off aircraft could be prevented from landing by stretching wires or netting between prison search-lights. The suggestion was adopted, but little action taken; by the end of 1987 only two out of eight dispersal prisons – Full Sutton and Parkhurst – had any sort of defence barriers in place.

Gartree Prison had no wires, netting or other devices to prevent aerial interference. It did have a contingency plan, code-named Operation Rogue Elephant, whereby Harrier jump jets could be scrambled from near-by RAF Wittering, but from an aerial angle the jail had no security at all. Situated in the Leicestershire countryside, well away from high buildings or other hazards, the jail had a large football field in one corner of its grounds. For a prisoner with the right outside connections, Gartree was an ideal jail to be sprung from by air.

John Kendall, as events would show, was a prisoner with the right outside connections. A thirty-six-year-old Cockney, Kendall was a member of the celebrated Hole In The Wall Gang – so called because they used lorries to ram warehouses and steal the contents. In November 1984, while serving eight years for these activities, he and another prisoner were under escort in a van taking them from Maidstone to Parkhurst. At Reigate in Surrey the van was forced to a halt by a BMW pulling in front, as another car rammed it from behind. The van's windscreen was smashed by men wearing balaclavas and wielding pick-axe handles and Kendall and the other prisoner escaped.

He was free for almost two years and on recapture faced charges of attempted murder, robbery and various firearms offences, as well as escaping from custody. He arrived at Gartree in October 1987, but before he could be sentenced on his outstanding charges, Kendall escaped again. This time, together with the prisoner who went with him, he made history.

The Gartree 'Sky-jack', as might be expected for such an ambitious project, was planned to the finest detail. Eight days before the event proper the outside rescue party staged a dummy run. A man giving the name Andrew Downes and purporting to be from a security company, hired a helicopter and pilot to fly him and an associate to Market Harborough, a town close to Gartree Prison.

There the pair were put down at a golf course. They went into the clubhouse where a member who overheard them asking for a taxi gave them a lift into the town centre.

The two men attracted some attention because one of them was carrying a radio frequency scanner, portable equipment which can be used to monitor police signals. In the town they paid a visit to the local library, where they asked to look at Ordnance Survey maps of the area. They wanted to photocopy them, but were refused because they were not members of the library and declined to join. Returning to the golf club, they flew off in the helicopter, back to its base in the south-east.

On Thursday 10 December 1987 Mr Downes again hired a helicopter and a pilot. At Stansted Airport he paid £678.50 in cash and asked to be flown to Leicestershire, saying he represented a security firm and wanted to check possible hi-jack points on the ground below. He was given a receipt in a brown envelope, which was later found in the helicopter, bearing his finger- and thumbprints. The helicopter flew north for forty minutes until, as it reached Leicestershire, Mr Downes, whose real name was Andrew Russell, pulled a gun, held it at the pilot's head and ordered him to fly to Gartree, telling him they were going to pick up two prisoners.

As the Bell 206 Longranger flew in over the jail, John Kendall and Sydney Draper, a lifer, were out on the football field, ostensibly enjoying the afternoon exercise period during a break from the workshops. At 3.17 p.m. the helicopter touched down in the centre circle of the football pitch and Kendall and Draper, waving towels to identify themselves, ran to it as other prisoners formed a human barrier to prevent warders getting to them.

Tempers flared as prison officers tried to force a way through, but the shoulders and elbows of the protective chain held firm. It all happened so quickly and unexpectedly that staff could only stand and watch as, twenty-one seconds after it landed, the helicopter took off again, heading towards Market Harborough. All they were left with was a video tape, filmed by the prison's security cameras.

Operation Rogue Elephant, the air-defence contingency plan, proved useless. When Gartree staff phoned RAF West Drayton, the air-control centre that was supposed to scramble a fighter plane, the reaction to their call was, 'Rogue what? Where's Gartree?' The RAF suggested the prison call the police.

Even if the contingency plan had worked efficiently there would not have been time to track the hi-jacked helicopter. The escapers were not in the air long enough – within minutes of leaving Gartree they landed at a near-by industrial estate. Handcuffing the pilot to his aircraft, they commandeered a delivery van by threatening the driver with CS gas. This was a digression from the original plan – swirling mist prevented the pilot finding the golf course, where a second accomplice was waiting with a car.

Once on the ground, the two escapers split up. Syd Draper went off alone while John Kendall and the hi-jacker, Andrew Russell, sped off in the van. Twenty minutes later they forced a Fiat Uno off the road and left its driver, a woman, with the delivery van. They headed for Corby and there, in a multi-storey car park they kidnapped a sixty-three-year-old man. He was tied up in the back of his yellow Mini Metro as they drove out of Corby, north up the M1. Later that evening the man was found by a taxi driver in a Sheffield back street, eighty miles away. He was trussed up with string and seat belts, in the back of his car. Before they left him, his kidnappers shoved £40 in his pocket saying, 'That's for your trouble. Remember – you've not seen us.' All routes out of the city were sealed, but the fugitives had vanished into the night.

Across Britain, police forces were put on alert as six Midlands forces began a manhunt. Kendall was described as five feet seven inches tall with blue eyes and thinning hair. Draper, a convicted murderer, was said to be five feet ten inches, of medium build with brown hair and a close-cropped beard. Both were described as 'armed and highly dangerous'.

In a dawn operation two days later, dozens of uniformed and CID officers descended on a council housing estate at Dronfield, on the outskirts of Sheffield. Everything came to a standstill in the neighbourhood as vehicles were stopped and searched and gun-wielding police forced their way into three homes, smashing windows and doors in their search for the fugitives. It was believed that they were being sheltered by relatives of a man Kendall had met in jail. The police were out of luck. The startled occupants of the smashed-up houses knew nothing of John Kendall, other than what they had read in the newspapers.

Back at Gartree, where remaining Category A inmates included Donald Neilson 'The Black Panther', Reg Kray and twenty IRA men, the inevitable inquiry was swinging into action. The Home Secretary, Douglas Hurd, appointed the Deputy Director of the Prison Service, Gordon Lakes, who also happened to be a former

Gartree Governor, telling the press that the escape was 'very bad news'. He revealed that the government had been aware of the likelihood of such an event since the Paris prison break-out of Michel Vanjour the previous year.

The Home Secretary said there were three areas to study – the extension of physical barriers, manning and escorts, and instructions to prison officers. He would not elaborate on any of these, but there was speculation that the government had considered gun and rocket defences at prisons. They had been rejected because it was likely that the pilot of any aircraft used in an escape would have been hi-jacked and his life should not be further endangered. The most probable solution was thought to be barrage balloons or nets across open spaces within the prison walls.

The head of the inquiry team told reporters, 'We have always been conscious of the possibility of an aerial-assisted escape and the risk that represents in a prison situation. Contingency plans already exist . . . but in this case they failed and we will now have to look for ways of improving them.'

The Gartree branch secretary of the Prison Officers' Association said morale had been affected by the escape, although there was no action prison officers could have taken to prevent it. He said that the level of security at the prison had long been a worry and he was sure that the Prison Officers' Association's feelings had been passed on to the prison department.

Individual warders were more forthcoming, telling the *Sunday Times* that they expected someone to try to escape by helicopter and that there had been a number of false alarms involving passing airships and hot-air balloons. One said, 'It's been done in France and Ireland so it was bound to happen here.' The Home Office had been warned of the danger and at least part of the blame lay with a shortage of staff, while efficiency took precedence over security and the regular routine meant that recreation was taken at the same time every day.

It transpired that nineteen years earlier the Home Office had been given clear warning of the threat of aerial assault on top-security jails. This warning had come from no less an authority on security than the Special Air Services. In 1968 the then Governor of Parkhurst, along with two of his staff, was flown in low-level runs over the jail before going on to SAS headquarters. Now, that same Governor, Alistair Miller, said, 'We wanted a bird's eye view of the nick to see the places most vulnerable for an aerial escape. I can't remember why we chose then to challenge our security by helicopter but we were always trying to stay ahead of the game . . . I remember thinking a lift in a helicopter was the easiest way for anyone to escape from Parkhurst.' He was right, although when the lift came it was not at Parkhurst but Gartree.

Speculation was hot in press circles as to where Kendall and Draper might be. The boldness of their break-out led to fears that they would not be recaptured without blood being spilled. No one had been hurt so far, but this did not stop one paper, which described them as 'crazed', saying that police believed 'they will want to take as many of their number with them as possible'. The escapers were, it was said, 'preparing for a shoot-out', though since nobody had a clue where they were, such intentions could only be wild speculation.

The usual 'underworld associates' came forward with instant quotes. Educated opinion decreed that the organisation for the break-out was down to John Kendall, with Sydney Draper being included because Kendall needed an ally in the rush for the helicopter. Of Kendall, one 'associate' told *The Times*, 'He's got plenty of nerve. He's been round the block before,' while 'an east London villain' said the operation was 'down to the old pal's act'. Kendall, he said, was well-connected and his friends were determined to get him out.

John McVicar, by now a much-sought-after consultant on prison escapes, was quoted in the same paper, 'The two men will not find it easy. There is no escapees' benevolent society, just a few hand-outs from one or two friends and then you are on your own.' He added, 'The people I feel sympathy for are the top-security prisoners still in jail who are certain to face even tougher regimes after this escape.'

A month after the escape, the film shot from a Gartree security camera was shown on the BBC *Crimewatch* programme. It showed Kendall and Draper in T-shirts and shorts running to the helicopter – initially to the wrong side – as other prisoners kept staff at bay. The showing prompted more than seventy people to contact the police, but no leads were forthcoming.

For John Kendall, Christmas 1987 was the last Christmas he would spend at liberty for a long time. As the New Year came in, so did the hunters who pursued him. All his known associates were put under surveillance and attention focused on a one-room flat in the King's Road, Chelsea. At 3 a.m. on 31 January a forty-strong team of Flying Squad, Metropolitan PT17 firearms officers and

Leicestershire detectives moved in, armed with an arsenal of weapons. Searchlights flooded the area as they clambered over the roofs and balconies of the three-storey flats, while a man on the ground shouted, 'Armed Police!' through a megaphone. Such was the furore and confusion that residents in other flats began telephoning 999, fearing that some innocent neighbour was being attacked by violent criminals.

The wanted man was asleep in bed when the raiding party went in, smashing the door of the flat down. A bonus for the police was the discovery of another man – Andrew Russell, the man who had hi-jacked the helicopter. Kendall and Russell were led away into the cold night, wearing only their underpants, together with a woman who was also in the flat. Detectives at the scene said they were not totally sure they had got the right man until they actually seized him. The strong word in the underworld had been that Kendall was abroad, that he had slipped out of the country soon after the escape. Not so, like many escapers he made the mistake of returning to his home turf, or at least close to it. Few who do that survive for long.

John Kendall and Andrew Russell were interrogated first in London and then in Leicestershire. When Kendall appeared in court to face charges relating to the escape – five days after his recapture – a major commotion occurred. Leicester Magistrates' Court was told by police that he was 'far too violent' to be brought up into the dock and it was decided that the magistrate, lawyers and officials would have to go down to the cell area and hold the remand hearing there. They arrived to find Kendall in a position that did little for the dignity of the court – pinned to the floor by six policemen, with his

294

head trapped on its side by a large boot. He could not move but, despite the boot on his head, he was shouting to be taken into the courtroom, as was his right, to state his case.

The magistrate felt Kendall had a point and agreed to his demand. Handcuffed to a policeman at either side, with four others around him, he was taken upstairs to the court, where the charges were outlined. He was expecting five, and when a further eleven were read out he exploded with anger. He protested to the magistrate about the way he had been handled by the police, saying that before he left the cells he was handcuffed, supposedly to come to court. He pointed at his head and said, 'Suddenly fifteen officers jumped on me and held me on the floor. Then a man in a white coat pulled out what looked like a pair of pliers and started yanking at my head. No one told me why they were doing it – from my understanding of the Police and Criminal Evidence Act I should have been told why they were taking hair samples.'

Kendall's liberator, Andrew Russell, faced twenty-three charges. He too had an uncomfortable ride through the system, at one stage going on hunger strike in protest at the way he was being treated by the police. When he appeared in court in early April in a weakened state, having gone without food for twenty-six days, a doctor had to examine him to establish whether he was fit to sit through the hearing.

All this time the other prisoner who had flown out of Gartree in the helicopter was still free. Sydney Draper, the man who many thought would stand little chance of surviving on the run, proved otherwise. Draper was twelve years into a life sentence with a recommended twenty-five year minimum at the time of the escape. He had long protested his innocence of the murder of a night-watchman, killed during a wages robbery in Glasgow in December 1973. But, unlike some escapers who have conducted campaigns to air their grievances while on the run, Draper went to ground. Not a word was heard from him and, to the surprise of sceptics within the criminal world, he stayed free for over fourteen months. Eventually tracked down to a house in Enfield after a lengthy surveillance operation, he was recaptured in February 1989. He had a gun in his possession when armed police burst into the house, but no shots were fired.

In June 1989 John Kendall, Sydney Draper and Andrew Russell went on trial at Leicester Crown Court on charges which included hi-jacking a helicopter, taking a van and two cars, possessing firearms and kidnapping the Metro driver in Corby. Nine days later they were sentenced. Draper got four years, concurrent to his life sentence; Kendall, seven consecutive to the eight he was serving at the time he escaped. Russell, who hi-jacked the helicopter, was given ten years.

If John Kendall gave a wry smile as he left the dock, it was because seven years was merely the tip of the iceberg for him. To anyone not aware of his full circumstances, the lengths he went to in escaping must have seemed strange for a man nearing the end of an eight-year sentence. In fact at the time of the air-lift, Kendall was still waiting to be dealt with for his escape from the Maidstone-Parkhurst van, three years earlier. He also faced charges of attempted murder, robbery and firearms offences relating to his long spell on the run from that escape.

Eight months after his recapture on the Gartree break-out, Kendall went to court to receive twenty-one years for the van escape and the robberies, to run concurrently with the original eight, meaning that he began the twenty-one in 1988. The seven he got for Gartree took him up to twenty-eight years and the following year he was in court yet again, sentenced to a further seven years for robberies committed while at large from Gartree. At the age of forty he found himself looking at thirty-five years to serve – more than the Great Train Robbers, more than the recommended life sentences for many terrorist murderers. He did get his overall sentence reduced by seven years on appeal in 1992, but twenty-eight years is still a long, long time.

The inquiry ordered by the Home Secretary was completed in six weeks and Douglas Hurd was able to describe to the Commons a range of measures that he said would prevent a helicopter escape ever happening again. He informed MPs that Kendall and Draper's escape had succeeded because there had been no physical barrier to stop the helicopter landing and went on, 'The attempt was made easier because those planning it had been able confidently to predict the time and place at which the escapers would be taking their outdoor exercise that day.'

These findings, as with so many inquiries into prison escapes, were hardly revelational. No one needed a six-week inquiry to tell them that the helicopter had been able to land because there was nothing in its way to prevent it landing. Of more interest were the Home

Secretary's plans for the future. These included the installation of wire barriers across exercise yards and other open areas at all eight dispersal prisons, with observation towers built, high enough to spot an approaching aircraft. Top-security prisoners were to be exercised at irregular times, he announced, with guard dogs always in attendance. Later in 1988 he announced an urgent reappraisal of Category A prisoners, to identify the 'exceptional escape risks' among them. His most contentious proposal was a plan to halve the number of jails in the dispersal system – to concentrate resources and save on the cost of electronic surveillance equipment. Within three years this would have come to fruition.

The already small world of the convicted top-security prisoner was diminishing still further. The price for John Kendall and Sydney Draper's audacious escape was a high one. Back inside and with little hope of release until the twenty-first century, no one knew that better than they did.

19   PEARSE McAULEY AND NESSAN QUINLIVAN

Did Special Branch Know?

By the early 1990s, security in the dispersal prisons was tighter than ever before. Convicted Category A men were marked out as requiring extreme vigilance at all times, and the post-Gartree crackdown meant that the last apparent loophole was firmly closed. The only chance, albeit slim, that a top-security prisoner had of getting away was in transit between jails, or if taken to an outside hospital or court. Even then it had become customary in such situations for the prisoner to be escorted by armed police.

However, if the prison authorities thought that headline-hitting escapes were in the past, they were wrong. While convicted Category A prisoners were held in jails fitted with all the latest technological equipment, for those awaiting trial or sentence it was a different story. The local remand prisons like Leeds, Hull, Winson Green, Strangeways – before it erupted in April 1990 – and Brixton were still overcrowded, their buildings patched and mended as they had been repeatedly for well over a century. Such a situation, as had been seen many times, could lead to lapses in security. Lapses in security lead to escapes. And when the escapers are alleged IRA terrorists, the resultant uproar is loud and long.

The 1991 escape of Pearse McAuley and Nessan Quinlivan from Brixton – a 173-year-old jail built for 730 prisoners but holding more than 1,100 – provoked the greatest and most lasting wave of comment on mainland prison security since the mid-1960s. Intrigue as to what had really happened, whether the authorities had ignored a warning, whether the escapers had been assisted from within and whether the Home Secretary should resign, went on for months.

McAuley and Quinlivan were arrested in October 1990 and charged with conspiring to kill Sir Charles Tidbury, a brewery tycoon and Tory supporter. Unbeknown to the pair, he was placed under police protection after his name had been found on an IRA hit list. They were remanded to Brixton as Category A prisoners and were considered to be so dangerous that every time they travelled to Bow Street Magistrates' Court for their preliminary hearings they were surrounded by a 'ring of steel', with marksmen from Scotland Yard's PT17 Firearms Branch positioned on rooftops along the route.

The two Irishmen had been in Brixton for nine uneventful months when, on the morning of Sunday 8 July, they attended the normal service in the prison chapel. At 9.40 p.m. as they were returning to the security block escorted by three officers, McAuley suddenly bent down, reached to one of his shoes and produced a small calibre automatic pistol. He fired three shots and held the gun to the head of one of the officers, forcing him to give up his keys.

With access to the prison yard now theirs, and the staff held at bay by the gun, McAuley and Quinlivan were able to unlock gates and get out of the building. Once in the yard they headed straight for the perimeter wall. When the warders followed they were fired at and one was hit in the leg. Reaching the wall, and with warders watching every move but unable to do anything to stop them, the two escapers grabbed a wheelbarrow left by workmen, put it on top of a dog kennel and clambered up the wall. Crossing the double-coiled razor wire along the top, they dropped, cut and bloodied into the outside world below.

In Jebb Avenue, alongside the prison, they forced a prison officer out of his car and took it. But they had only gone a few yards before another warder, realising what was happening, drove his car into their path, blocking them in.

On their toes now, they ran the few yards to Brixton Hill, flagging down a passing Vauxhall Cavalier. When the driver, a Canadian tourist, tried to argue and prevent them commandeering his car, he was shot in the upper thigh, dragged out and left bleeding on the pavement. One of the escapers jumped behind the wheel and began to drive off with the female passenger still in the car. She was pushed out as the other man got in, and the Cavalier roared off down Brixton Hill.

Outside Lambeth Town Hall they abandoned the car and, taking with them a suitcase of clothes from inside it, they hailed a black cab and asked the driver to take them to Baker Street tube station. There they paid the fare with a £20 note stolen from the couple left behind on Brixton Hill. As police were throwing a cordon around the area, all off-duty warders were recalled to the jail and a helicopter was summoned to scan the streets from above, Pearse McAuley and Nessan Quinlivan disappeared into the tube station.

Immediate, widespread reaction to the escape was one of amazement that it could have happened, considering the high degree of risk that the two prisoners were known to present. Quinlivan, from County Limerick and suspected of crimes in the Irish Republic, was a known cohort of Patrick Sheehy, the discovery of whose bomb factory and hit list had led indirectly to the Brixton pair's arrest. Sheehy had meanwhile retired from the terrorist fray, shooting himself in a telephone kiosk in the Republic, six months before the escape. Pearse McAuley, like Quinlivan in his mid-twenties, had gone missing from his home in Strabane, County Tyrone a year before his arrest.

Security sources in the Republic said that the pair were 'deadly cunning and ruthless' and 'two of the Provisional IRA's top operators', while George Churchill-Coleman, head of the Anti-Terrorist Squad, described them as committed, dangerous individuals and urged everyone to take the utmost caution. As police were still searching in the vicinity of the jail, the press were pointing out that the Brixton authorities had been warned a year earlier about weaknesses in the prison's security, in a report by Judge Stephen Tumim, Chief Inspector of Prisons. He had pointedly questioned whether Brixton was secure enough to hold Category A prisoners, but still McAuley and Quinlivan – along with forty-nine others at the time of their escape – had been remanded there.

The big question was: how had the gun got into a

prison where all visitors were supposedly searched and where all Category A men had to be escorted by at least two guards every time they left their cells? Had the IRA men collected the gun from the confessional box in the chapel, as they asked the priest to forgive their sins? Had one of the hundreds of civilian workers taken it into the jail and hidden it there? The confessional box was just about the only place where a Category A man could go without being spied upon by an officer.

Explanations were required for more than the gun: why were the two men – co-accused – allowed to be together and not kept apart in separate prisons? How did the wheelbarrow come to be in the yard? Why was a dog kennel situated against the perimeter wall, where it provided an easy step-up for the escapers? Why were two Category A prisoners allowed to wear civilian clothes, which meant that once they were over the wall they could pass unnoticed among the general public?

A few days later an explanation as to how the gun got into the jail was offered: it had been posted to one of the escapers in a parcel, hidden in a cavity cut out of the sole of a training shoe. The parcel was said to have been posted in Ireland and its contents taken at face value on a cursory check because no metal detector was available. This was now the official line. The press were allowed to photograph a shoe showing how it had been done. Nothing more was heard of the confessional box theory.

The Director-General of the prison service told pressmen that the escape was 'an enormous blow' but said, 'We are satisfied Brixton provides an adequate degree of security to enable us to keep top-security prisoners.' He would not comment on Judge Tumim's findings of the previous year. While this was going on Tumim was appointed to conduct an inquiry by the Home Secretary, Kenneth Baker, who told the Commons that he was 'deeply disturbed by this grave lapse of security and by the associated risk to members of the public.' He said that all Category A men in Brixton would immediately be dispersed to other top-security prisons until the secure remand unit at Belmarsh, the new jail/court complex, could take prisoners in the autumn.

His words did nothing to placate angry Opposition MPs who called for his resignation. Roy Hattersley, the Shadow Home Secretary, said that Baker was not accepting 'a jot of responsibility'. He claimed that a gate had been left open because its security lock had not been repaired. Kenneth Baker denied these allegations, saying all visits were screened by a metal detector, visitors' identities were verified by police and prisoners were rub-searched before visits and strip-searched afterwards. This statement contrasted with allegations that Brixton did not have a metal detector, or that it did but it was so faulty that it regularly failed to detect – and with comments by Prison Officers' Association chairman, John Bartell, who told the press, 'We were horrified to find that routine searching had been abandoned a long time ago.'

As Anti-Terrorist Squad detectives raided suspected safe houses, security forces were reported to be furious about the break-out. Said a spokesman, 'It took us long enough to catch them in the first place and it's appalling that this has happened.' One Tory MP said of the escape, 'Someone's head has got to roll for this,' and suggested all prison visits should be stopped. Another was critical of the decision to put two top-security prisoners in a city jail where they could easily disappear once they had got over the wall. The *Sun* reminded its readers that another IRA man, Gerard Tuite, had escaped from the same jail ten years earlier, 'We were assured it could not happen again. No doubt we shall hear the same assurances after the inquiry into this latest escape.'

Judge Tumim's inquiry was completed in record time. The report arrived so quickly that the Home Secretary had to cut short his holiday to read it. On 5 August Kenneth Baker revealed to the Commons that Tumim had found 'a number of causes, of acts or omissions, without all of which the escape would not have taken place'. The report stated that in February, five months before the escape occurred, prison officials were told by the police that they had received information not only that McAuley and Quinlivan were planning to escape – but also that the Sunday chapel service was fixed as the most suitable time. It was even known the pair were actively seeking to acquire a gun. Incredibly, this information had not been passed on from prison officials to appropriate members of staff.

Tumim reported that little heed had been taken of his earlier warning about Brixton's security shortcomings. His report of the previous year had been one of the most scathing ever written on any prison; he had suggested that at that time there were up to sixty high-risk inmates at Brixton who had the ability and resources to mount escape bids.

This time he exposed more specific weaknesses: the failure to search parcels, prisoners, visitors or the prison premises to locate the gun, and a failure to escort

Category A men. He made twelve main recommendations, principally involving improvements in communication and searching, as well as the necessity to hold top-security inmates in jails other than Brixton.

Only certain parts of Tumim's report were made public, the remainder being suppressed for the usual 'security reasons'. One thing he did make clear was his opinion that operational failures were responsible for the escape and that this should not lead to any drastic changes in policy. Concerned that reforms recommended by Lord Justice Woolf in his earlier report on the Strangeways riot should not be undermined, Tumim did not want to see the introduction of a new, hard-line regime. The need, he said, was for a stepping-up of searches and of surveillance and a proper screening of visitors and outside contractors – with high-risk inmates concentrated in prisons that could adequately provide the necessary measures.

A hint of the 'security reasons' that had caused parts of Tumim's report to be kept secret emerged four days after its publication, in an article in the *Observer*. It was disclosed that a special department at the Home Office was responsible for gathering intelligence on Category A prisoners who were thought to be likely to escape – and that a prison officer in Brixton, working with Special Branch, had warned of Quinlivan and McAuley's plans. Now, Scotland Yard was saying that if this had been the case then the information was not passed on to the Anti-Terrorist squad, but other opinions leaned towards the notion that MI5 had let the escape plan develop in the optimistic hope that it could lead to the discovery of IRA safe houses and other details of the organisation's mainland operations.

This sensation was greeted by predictable outrage, with renewed calls for Kenneth Baker to resign. Former Labour Home Secretary Merlyn Rees found Baker's earlier denials of responsibility 'incredible', with one tabloid dubbing the affair 'Bakergate'. The *Observer* quoted a senior member of the Association of Chief Police Officers, who said of Baker, 'He has shown he is not a safe pair of hands. This whole business has been a fiasco.' Shadow Home Secretary Roy Hattersley had already demanded a public inquiry, claiming that the differing versions of the warning about the escape needed clarification; now he asked Kenneth Baker to answer the questions posed about the continuance of Category A men in Brixton after Judge Tumim's first report. Of the questions, Hattersley said, 'Silence on any or all of these would be an admission of responsibility for the many mistakes.' But the Home Secretary was not going to be drawn; a man with a history of extricating himself from tricky situations, he simply went back to France to resume his holiday.

Someone had to take the blame and, as so often happened in these situations, the prison Governor, Reg Withers, resigned. It was said that both he and the head of the Directorate of Custody at the Prison Department were leaving their posts 'as a consequence of the escape on July 7'. The Governor went three days before the report of the inquiry was announced and was immediately replaced at Brixton by the Governor of Peterhead Prison in Scotland.

Withers was seen as a scapegoat by many, including the Prison Governors' Association, who said, ominously in view of what would soon emerge, 'We are extremely concerned that he should not be held accountable for

307

any matters which are neither his responsibility nor within a Governor's remit.' The Prison Officers' Association added their voice in support of the departed Governor, at the same time stating that, rather than the information of the previous February coming into the prison and getting lost, it had originated when a prison officer was threatened that if he did not assist in an escape plot, his family would suffer. He had reported this to the Governor and a request was made to the Prison Department that the prisoners be moved to another jail.

On and on the controversy rumbled, with no news as to what had become of the men who began it all. Neither Pearse McAuley nor Nessan Quinlivan had been sighted since they vanished into Baker Street tube station. By the middle of August the IRA were claiming the pair were back in Ireland. They had travelled, it was said, by a 'tried and tested' route unknown to the security forces. A security source in London was sceptical of this information, saying, 'It could be the Republicans are telling a lie, maybe because their boys are under intense pressure here and they hope this might take the spotlight off them. Or they could be back in Ireland, waiting for us to say what a load of rubbish – and then produce them.'

A few days later the Irish police's Anti-Terrorist Squad in Dublin dismissed the IRA account, 'The story was designed to put British police off their scent. We are certain Quinlivan and McAuley never came to Ireland.' The word was now that the men were on the Continent, possibly at one of the IRA's safe houses in Amsterdam or The Hague. They were said to have slipped out of Britain in disguise, soon after the escape, using fake passports to travel with holidaymakers on a cross-Channel ferry.

In October, doubts were raised as to whether any lessons had been learned from the escape or the subsequent inquiry. An investigation by the *Guardian* brought forth the revelation that a man on bail for serious firearms charges had that same month been given a job installing sanitation in cells at Brixton. On bail on a five-figure surety, the man, who claimed he had not been security vetted, could be seen arriving and leaving work by a contractors' entrance to the jail, bypassing normal controls at the main gate. 'The way they let someone like me go in and out more or less as they want, and take in and out what they want is, quite frankly, ridiculous,' he said, remaining anonymous in case he was jailed on his firearms charges and ended up in Brixton.

A new dimension on the jailbreak surfaced in November when a Thames Television programme claimed that the prison officer working for Special Branch inside Brixton had not only known in advance of Quinlivan and McAuley's escape plan, but had actually discussed it with them. This intriguing dialogue had taken place when the officer was trying to gain their trust in an attempt to obtain information about the murder of a soldier at Lichfield railway station. The prisoners had asked for a gun and it was said that one could be provided, but in February, five months before the escape, Special Branch decided to abort the operation.

If all this sounded too cloak-and-dagger to be true, on 24 November the *Sunday Express* named the prison officer as thirty-two-year-old Alan Marshall and his case-handler as Detective Sergeant Keith Harrison a Special Branch officer based in Staffordshire. Marshall was fluent in Gaelic and had joined the prison service in 1986 after leaving the SAS. He was said to have told his immediate superior at Brixton about his covert activities – and the escape plot – whereupon the Governor, Reg Withers, had protested to the Home Office that such activity was going on in his jail behind his back. This had taken place in February . . . hence the source of the already admitted 'information' that an escape was being planned. The puzzle now was why had the undercover warder blown the operation? According to one of Marshall's colleagues, he had financial worries and wanted to be transferred to another area, where housing was cheaper. He was now working at Sudbury open prison, near Derby, but on sick leave. The detective sergeant had also been moved to another base.

More outrage ensued. Labour MP Ted Leadbitter, who was to name Detective Sergeant Harrison in a written Commons question later that week, said, 'I want to know whether the Home Office's secret decision to move Harrison and Marshall from their normal duties is a direct way of silencing key players in this extremely odd affair.' A Prison Officers' Association spokesman said, 'If this was a covert operation that went wrong, the people who organised it should be taking the blame, not Brixton prison officers who have been criticised for slack security.'

An investigation into the facts behind the latest furore was carried out by the Deputy Chief Constable of Nottinghamshire, Colin Bailey. Ten months later, in September 1992, and to no one's surprise, he dismissed allegations that a police or prison officer had assisted in the escape of Pearse McAuley and Nessan Quinlivan. He said that there was 'no evidence that any prison officer known to Staffordshire Police supplied any information that was of material interest' to the two prisoners. He also said there was no evidence to indicate that the police had influenced the posting of any prison officer to Brixton. Thames Television stood by their programme, saying that they had strong evidence to support the claim that a prison officer controlled by Staffordshire Special Branch had discussed escape plans with the two prisoners.

Back in August 1991, when Kenneth Baker had announced Judge Tumim's findings with regard to the escape, he had made no mention of any Special Branch involvement, although he subsequently admitted that he had been told of the involvement the morning after the escape took place. In view of its origins, it was hardly surprising that the information about the escape plan was not passed on to Brixton staff, but the protests that the Governor, Reg Withers, had been made a scapegoat now had a sharper ring.

Until the allegations of Special Branch involvement, the story that the gun used by Quinlivan and McAuley had been smuggled to them inside a training shoe was generally accepted. Talk of MI5 and undercover operations led prison officers to doubt the trainer story and questions were asked as to whether the gun had in fact been handed to the two IRA men by someone involved in the matter. The following month a prisoner put forward an altogether different version of how the gun got into the jail, in a letter to *Inside Time*, the prisoners' national newspaper.

According to 'Paul', now an inmate of Maidstone

Prison, three days before the Brixton escape an alarm bell went off in the late evening following a security camera picking up the outline of someone on top of the wall. Roll checks were made to establish who had escaped, but no prisoner was missing. The only explanation could be that, rather than an inmate breaking out of the jail, a person must have broken in, presumably to pass something on. The next morning, Friday, all cells facing the wall at ground level were searched, but nothing was found. On the Sunday Quinlivan and McAuley escaped with a gun. 'I don't really understand why they have invented this rubbish about a training shoe, why not just tell the truth?' asked the letter-writer. 'The only people who appear to be in ignorance of the facts are the "great" British public who are told only what it is deemed suitable for them to hear . . .' Nothing more was heard of this account of events.

In February 1992 a twenty-five-year-old bricklayer, William McKane, stood trial at the Old Bailey, accused of conspiring with Quinlivan and McAuley to commit murder. It was alleged that 120 pounds of Semtex explosive, bomb circuits, six guns and a hit list bearing the names of Lord Prior and Lord Mason, both former Secretaries of State for Northern Ireland, had been found in a car near to McKane's flat in Willesden, north London. McKane pleaded not guilty and was acquitted, after making some unflattering remarks about one of his alleged fellow conspirators. He said that Pearse McAuley was 'a loud-mouth and a bit of a poser, always getting into fights and having a lot to drink.' Not only this, the much-sought-after fugitive was in the regular habit of singing rebel songs in pubs and shouting, 'Up the IRA!' If this was

312

true – and McKane claimed to know – then it was astounding that Pearse McAuley was taking so long to find.

Whether by coincidence or not, Pearse McAuley and Nessan Quinlivan were both recaptured, within days of each other, in April 1993. Quinlivan was the first to fall, when Irish police acted on a tip-off and raided a lonely farmhouse in County Tipperary. He had a loaded revolver in his pocket, but was handcuffed before he could think of putting up a struggle. The following day he appeared in court in Dublin when it was made clear that charges relating to offences in the Republic would take precedence over UK matters. When Kenneth Baker, no longer Home Secretary, was told the news of Quinlivan's recapture he said, 'I am delighted'. In October 1993 Quinlivan was sentenced to four years for possessing the gun and ammunition at the time of his arrest.

Five days after Quinlivan's recapture, Pearse McAuley alighted from a lunch-time train at Dublin's Connelly railway station and was seized by detectives of the same squad that had arrested his fellow escaper. He too was carrying a handgun, loaded and cocked, in a holster under his jumper. Republican sources indicated both men had carried guns primarily to ensure that if they were caught they would be charged with an offence in the Republic, rather than face extradition, but McAuley seemed to be taking extra precautions – he had twenty bullets on him. When he appeared in court in Dublin, he waved to friends and relatives. There were no rebel songs, but as he was led away to the cells he gave a clenched fist salute and shouted, 'No problem!' In

November 1993 at the Special Criminal Court he was
sentenced to seven years for the firearms offences. At
the time of writing the British Government has made no
application for either of the Brixton escapers to be
extradited.

20   JOSEPH STEELE
The Palace Protester

Some jailbreakers hit the headlines by the manner of their escape, some through the notoriety of the crimes that put them in prison. Others become newsworthy only because of their activities while on the run. The crime for which Joseph Steele received a life sentence has been described as Scotland's worst multiple murder since the Glencoe massacre. And while his two escapes from custody – both within the space of a month – were not spectacular, the bizarre fashion of his surrenders meant that the media could not afford to ignore him.

Steele escaped to protest his innocence of the crimes which put him in jail. Other prisoners before him, Alfie Hinds the best known, have taken the same route for similar reasons. Like Hinds, Steele took advantage of his freedom to raise attention to his campaign, giving interviews to the press and demanding a fresh investigation into his case. But Joseph Steele did not wait to be hunted down. His surrender was not brought about because he was cornered and there was no other choice. Both times he escaped he stated that he would give himself up to publicise his case – and both times he did, forgoing the

315

great temptation to hang on to his liberty for as long as he was able. Such actions must add strength to his campaign.

For over a hundred years gangs and violence have flourished in Glasgow, first in the slums of the Gorbals, later in housing schemes like Easterhouse, Castlemilk and Carntyne. In such areas and among a significant number of people, the gangster is a man to be respected and feared – almost like a modern-day Jesse James or Al Capone.

Joseph Steele was not a gangster, though his family was well known to the police. His father was a safe-blower and two of his brothers, John and Jim, made a well-publicised escape from Barlinnie Jail in 1980, while serving twelve-year sentences. At twenty-one, small and bespectacled, Joe Steele was a petty criminal with no aspirations towards the big time. All this changed in the early hours of Monday 16 April 1984, when a tenement flat in the Ruchazie district of Glasgow was set alight and a family of six, including an eighteen-month-old baby, died from the effects of the fumes.

The arson attack on the Doyle family was the climax to what have become known as the Glasgow Ice-cream Wars. The troubles erupted in the early 1980s as ice-cream van owners became embroiled in violent struggles for the right to sell their wares – not only ice-cream but also stolen cigarettes, sweets, drinks and other goods – on the city housing estates. The most lucrative runs brought in up to £800 profit a week and the rivalry for control of them had already led to vans being ambushed and smashed up, business premises torched and men assaulted with knives and clubs.

Andrew 'Fat Boy' Doyle, eighteen years old and an occasional pub bouncer, ran an ice-cream van. Two months before the fatal fire his vehicle had been attacked when a masked man got out of a Volvo and blew out the windscreen as Doyle and a girl assistant were inside. The burning of his home was alleged to be just another act of intimidation, one that went wrong with tragic consequences.

From the outset Joseph Steele protested his innocence of the Doyle murders. He was implicated in the case by a man named Billy Love. On remand in Barlinnie for assault and robbery, Love decided to improve his own circumstances by telling a detective that he was responsible for the shotgun attack on Fat Boy Doyle's ice-cream van. More importantly, he said that he had overheard Steele, together with a known heavy, Thomas Campbell, and other men, discussing plans to set fire to Fat Boy's door 'to give him a fright'.

Steele was arrested six weeks after the fire, as he lay in bed. Coincidentally his alibi centred on him being in bed – with flu – at the time of the fire, an alibi corroborated by his mother and uncle. According to the detectives who arrested him, on the way to the police station Joseph Steele, a man whose whole background meant that he was under no illusions about the importance of remaining silent, suddenly blurted out, 'I'm no' the one that lit the match.' It was an unlikely utterance from a man who then refused to answer any further questions, but coupled with Billy Love's testimony, which he later retracted, it was enough to get Joseph Steele convicted of murder.

Steele and Thomas Campbell were both sentenced to life

imprisonment. The next that was heard of Joseph Steele was that he was on hunger strike and then, five years later in August 1989, he made the news when he escaped from his escort while visiting his sick mother at her home in Glasgow. After climbing through a skylight on to the roof of the tenement block, he sat astride the ridge tiles for three hours, ignoring all efforts by the police to talk him down.

The neighbours loved it. As the street was sealed off, word swiftly swept round the district and a crowd of more than 200 gathered, yelling encouragement to Steele and displaying a large, hastily-made banner which proclaimed 'JOE STEELE + T.C. IS INNOCENT'. T.C. was Thomas Campbell, whom the Scottish media had dubbed the 'Emperor of Carntyne'. Once he had made his point and the press had got their photos of the banner and the story behind his demonstration, Steele climbed back inside the building and returned to the custody of his embarrassed escort.

After that, trips home to see mother were off the agenda for a while – until April 1993, when once again Steele was allowed out of Saughton Prison in Edinburgh, and taken to Glasgow by a solitary prison officer. Once again he escaped from custody, climbing out of a bedroom window at his mother's home, but this time he went down to the ground instead of up to the roof and he did not hang about the locality to make his protest. Feeling a little guilty about leaving his escort in the lurch, he sent him a note of apology, saying he hoped the warder would not get into trouble for the escape. Five days later, after police had turned Glasgow inside out, causing no little inconvenience to the wanted man's family and friends, Joseph Steele was to be found in the most unlikely of places – over 300 miles away outside Buckingham Palace.

He was not there to visit the Queen, even though she had only recently announced the opening of her London home to the public. He was, however, hoping to attract her attention. At 3 p.m., as police of the Royal Protection Squad guarded the outside of the palace and Royal Marines the inside, Joseph Steele began his latest protest against his conviction nine years earlier of the murder of the Doyle family.

Wearing a white T-shirt with a picture of Salvador Dali's 'Christ of St John of the Cross' emblazoned on his chest, Steele strolled up to the palace's main gates, facing the Mall. Pulling a pair of handcuffs from his trouser pocket, he locked his left wrist to one of the gate's railings and then superglued his right hand to another. The police were soon on the scene, but the superglue had already set and no amount of pulling and tugging could release his right hand.

Steele nodded towards the picture on his T-shirt, telling reporters, 'I am innocent. Like Christ I have been crucified for something I didn't do.' He said that his action was a last resort and he had done it in an appeal to the Queen for help. As a police van and an ambulance were drawn up in front of him to block the view of curious sightseers, Steele pointed out that if he had wanted to escape, he would not have secured himself to the gates of Buckingham Palace. 'I have done this because I am innocent,' he said. It took fifty-nine minutes and the liberal application of solvents before the police could release him from the gate, only to handcuff him again for the short journey to Charing Cross police station.

The Buckingham Palace stunt brought a lot of attention to the campaign being conducted on behalf of Steele and Thomas Campbell. The previous year had seen the publication of a book *Frightener – The Glasgow Ice-cream Wars* by Douglas Skelton and Lisa Brownlie, which examined the case closely and brought a fresh statement from the police informer Billy Love, retracting his earlier evidence. Now he was saying that he had been frightened that he might be charged with conspiracy.

On 4 May 1993, Joseph Steele appeared at Glasgow Sheriff's Court, charged with escaping from the custody of a prison officer at his mother's home on 25 April. Outside the court 'Free the Glasgow Two' campaigners headed by Steele's mother, together with two brothers and two sisters, handed out leaflets. One brother said that an investigation by the Lord Advocate should go ahead and that a new trial date should be set or the two men freed.

Joe Steele was remanded back to Saughton Prison to continue his life sentence and await developments on the escape charge. He did not stay there long. He had made no secret of his intention to escape from prison again and he carried out his threat. This time he broke out of the jail.

On Tuesday evening, 25 May, Steele was one of about fifty inmates from C Hall, the long-termers' wing, allowed to go out of the main prison to an adjoining sports field to watch a game of football. The prison team was playing host to a local amateur league club, Captain's Cabin. Four prison officers were among the spectators who stood on the touchline, cheering the home side which by the second half was winning by seven goals to one. Such was the interest and enthusiasm for the game that none of the officers noticed five spectators – one of them Joseph Steele – slip away down a slope at the side of the pitch and head for the perimeter fence.

Saughton Prison is surrounded by a wire fence fitted with an alarm system, and beyond that an eighteen-foot wall. The sports field, however, had only a wire fence, topped with razor wire, no alarm and no outer wall. Better still, from an escaper's point of view, the corner towards which the five men ran was not covered by a security camera. Steele and the four others, three of them serving seven-year sentences, went through a hole already cut in the wire, in a matter of seconds. Yet again Joseph Steele was free to protest his innocence.

Outside the fence, the men had to scramble through brambles and undergrowth before they reached the streets of a housing estate. One of the five, lost before he had even got away, said to the first person he came across, 'I've just escaped from Saughton – which way to the motorway?' The youth he directed his question at was, unfortunately for the escaper, a prison officer's son. Thinking quickly, the youth pointed the man in the wrong direction and promptly raised the alarm.

On the football field the players had almost completed their rout of the opposition when the game was brought to an abrupt halt for a roll call to be taken. Sure enough, five spectators were missing and very soon the hole in the fence was found. Road-blocks were set up and staff urgently recalled to the jail – the loss of five prisoners was the biggest escape in Scotland for twelve years.

By 11.30 p.m. when the road-blocks were lifted, one of the escapers was back in custody. Early the following morning a second man was recaptured in Edinburgh, following a tip-off. Nothing had been seen of Joseph Steele – but he had telephoned the *Daily Record* saying that he intended to conduct his protest from outside Britain and that, having done so, he would give himself up.

This time Steele and Thomas Campbell's campaign went into a higher gear. Campbell, in Barlinnie's Special Unit after turbulent years in Peterhead and Shotts, was attracting individual attention and now organised a press conference within the unit. He had planned it and had invited journalists into the unit before Steele escaped, but on the day, when he tried to show a video in which Joseph Steele protested his innocence, the press conference was cancelled by the prison authorities.

Steele's profile was much higher this time. He followed up his telephone call to the *Daily Record* with a call to the *Scotsman* and visited Inverary Jail Museum on the west coast of Scotland, posing for photos in a T-shirt bearing the slogan 'ON THE RUN'. Moving down to London he released photos of himself taken at various sightseeing spots in the capital and was interviewed by the *Guardian*. He told journalist Duncan Campbell, 'I have to do this to draw attention to my case, otherwise nothing happens. People say that Scotland has got the finest legal system in the world, but it's no good at handling miscarriages of justice.' He said that he had gone to London so that his friends and relatives back home would no longer be raided by the police, that he had proof that a police informer gave perjured evidence against him and that a promised reinvestigation of the case by the Lord Advocate had not materialised.

★ ★ ★

From London, the fugitive whose ability to get away and stay away was causing his captors severe embarrassment, moved back to Scotland, to an uninhabited island in the Sound of Jura. There he spoke to film-maker Kevin Allen for an Open Space TV documentary about the ice-cream wars and the campaign to reinvestigate his and Thomas Campbell's case.

Amidst idyllic surroundings and while bacon sizzled on a camp-fire in front of him, Steele said he had been on the unidentified island for two weeks and had gone there, 'So my family and my friends can get peace and quiet and stop their doors getting kicked in, in Scotland and London.' Asked about parole, which he is eligible to apply for in 1994, Steele said, 'I don't take parole. Only guilty men take parole. I want my freedom. I want to see whoever killed the Doyles charged and convicted.'

The film, broadcast later on Channel 4, put forward a strong case on Steele's behalf. His sister and mother were among those interviewed, together with his solicitor, John Carroll and the already discredited police informer, Billy Love, who had signed a sworn affidavit that he had committed perjury. He now stated his hope that the wrongs he had helped bring about could be put right.

On Monday 5 July, with the police and prison authorities clueless as to where to find him, Joe Steele once more voluntarily gave himself up. Shortly before 4 p.m. he arrived outside Barlinnie Jail with a group of supporters. As prison officers watched and the Open Space crew filmed, he clambered up an eighty-foot-high pylon and began to address people gathering below. He said, 'I just want to be given a fair trial. Everybody knows I am innocent, but the authorities just won't listen to my pleas for a full investigation and retrial. I only want justice. If I was guilty I would have stayed on the run. Surely everybody must realise that now.'

Steele had been at liberty for six weeks. He had planned to surrender the following day, but kidney and liver problems caused him to bring the day forward. After ninety minutes his solicitor arrived at the foot of the pylon, which holds floodlights and security cameras, and, after speaking with him and receiving an assurance that he would get medical treatment, Steele climbed down, clearly in pain. The crowd cheered and he was led away to chants of, 'Free the Glasgow Two!' and 'The campaign goes on'.

Joseph Steele's chances of a retrial are slim. The Scottish legal system does not apparently lend itself to such procedures, even when the principal prosecution witness retracts his statement and says he was encouraged to commit perjury by the police. The two senior policemen who led the investigation into the murder of the Doyle family are dead, one by suicide. So far, the Free the Glasgow Two Campaign has brought plenty of publicity but no movement in the Lord Advocate's promised investigation – despite the interest and sympathy engendered by Steele's escapes and surrenders. Until the authorities begin to listen to him, it is reasonable to assume that Joe Steele will, given the slightest opportunity, escape yet again.

EPILOGUE

Always a Chink in the Armour

Prison security in the 1990s is at a level unimaginable in the days of Ruby Sparks and Alfie Hinds. Today, instead of high-risk inmates being placed in crumbling jails, they are concentrated in four main prisons, all controlled by state-of-the-art electronic equipment. Parkhurst on the Isle of Wight, its security enhanced by its isolation from the mainland, is the only survivor from the old convict prisons. Long Lartin in Worcestershire, Full Sutton near York and Whitemoor, opened in 1991 in Cambridge-shire, are all modern jails built for the dispersal system. At the end of 1992 there were 588 Category A prisoners in England and Wales, 79 of whom were assessed as high escape risks and 22 as exceptional.

The total had risen in a year from 460, a twenty-seven per cent increase at a time when plans were afoot to decategorize all but high- and exceptional-risk prisoners. This policy followed a post-Brixton security review aimed at focusing prison staff's attention on the smaller number of terrorists and gangsters with the intelligence, financial resources and organisational support to escape. It was felt that under the existing system staff considered some prisoners over-classified and became complacent, to the advantage of the genuinely dangerous inmate.

In recent years prison escapes have become increasingly politicised. Besides the Prison Officers' Association's long-held and much-aired assertion that they occur due to insufficient numbers of staff, the prison authorities' manipulation of publicity surrounding high-profile break-outs has at times been very noticeable. When Ronnie Pewter walked out of the Parkhurst Special Security Unit in October 1991, he merited only a short paragraph in the national press, despite being only the second prisoner ever to escape from the prison-within-a-prison. Six months later Francis Quinn, hiding in a laundry van, became the first escaper from Frankland in the jail's ten-year history, but merited little more attention than Pewter.

In February 1992 John McFayden pulled a blade on his two-man escort during a taxi journey from Full Sutton to Wormwood Scrubs and ordered the female taxi driver to take him to Euston. No details were made public as to how he had come by the blade, having supposedly undergone a thorough search before setting off. McFayden, a convicted murderer only two years into a life sentence with twenty recommended, was supposedly going to the Scrubs to see relatives.

Why was a man with so much time to serve – in addition to his life sentence McFayden had been sentenced to forty-seven years on drug offences – transferred in a taxi with only a two-man escort? The Home Office explanation was that he had been de-categorised from A to B and that it was a normal method of transfer 'used dozens of times a day'. Clearly, the lessons of Billy

Hughes' trail of carnage fifteen years earlier have not been learned.

McFayden was caught after a summer on the run, but his recapture did not make the news, just as Ronnie Pewter's had not. Perhaps the authorities wanted to avoid awkward questions about how they had got out in the first place.

The avoidance of escape publicity does not extend to alleged break-out plots that have been foiled by diligent staff. Such reports invariably involve inmates whose notoriety guarantees tabloid attention.

When, in November 1991, it was reported that grappling hooks, a rope ladder and plaited sheets had been discovered in a cell at Full Sutton, the Home Office took the unusual step of naming IRA bomber Nicholas Mullen as one of three Category A prisoners who were planning to escape. The prison Governor appeared on television, praising his staff. Earlier, the arrest of three visitors to another IRA prisoner, Martina Anderson, doing life in the women's maximum-security wing at Durham, received similar press coverage after a replica gun was found in a carrier bag. In May 1992 two hacksaw blades in the Broadmoor cell of Peter Sutcliffe, the Yorkshire Ripper, did raise questions as to how they had got there. A hospital worker was accused and cleared of planting the blades in a letter.

Reg Kray received even more break-out publicity – despite no evidence of an escape plot and the fact that he had never tried to escape during more than twenty years inside. When the authorities at Lewes Jail received an anonymous tip-off that a gun was in the jail, he was moved at short notice. At his next stop, Nottingham, the same thing happened again – this time he was on the ghost train after an anonymous telephone call that he had a gun. No gun was found at either jail, but both moves received more publicity than some recent escapes by dangerous inmates. Security was seen to be working.

Controversy and prison escapes are common partners. Usually the rows and howls of outrage occur in the aftermath, when bucks are being passed and scapegoats sought as officialdom is pressed by outside parties to offer credible explanations and to identify those responsible for the latest security failure. In the mid-1980s, however, it was the consequences of a failed escape in Scotland that brought public uproar.

Glen Hewson, a prisoner serving six years for assault and armed robbery, was one of a group of men who attempted to break out of Peterhead in January 1982. He got over the wall, but fell as he scaled the outside perimeter fence, breaking both legs. Hewson claimed his fall was caused by prison officers throwing stones and lumps of concrete at him. Four years later in the Edinburgh Court of Sessions he sued the Secretary of State for Scotland.

In March 1987 Hewson won his case. The prison staff, presumably not able to rely on the support of their superiors and afraid they could be disciplined or even prosecuted, denied throwing stones. The judge, Lord Cowie, was less than impressed by their evidence, saying that if it had been stronger he might well have doubted Hewson's credibility. As it was he awarded him compensation in the sum of £35,608.

This award was greeted with amazement in Scotland and beyond. A spokesman for the Prison Officers' Association said he could not believe that a prisoner had been awarded damages for injuries sustained in an escape attempt. He was not alone in his disbelief: those with long memories recalled another attempted escape at Peterhead, back in the days of Johnny Ramensky, when warders were armed with rifles. That man, a Glasgow bank robber, had been shot dead as he tried to get away in July 1932 and at the subsequent inquiry the warder who killed him was declared to have fired 'in the ordinary execution of his duties'. Times had changed in fifty years – the state had gone from killing would-be escapers to granting them a small fortune.

In a totally secure prison system no inmates would escape. But is such a situation realistically possible? Are Messrs Sparks, Hinds, Biggs, Blake, McVicar, Probyn, Doherty, Kendall, McAuley, Quinlivan – and all the rest – past masters whose like we will not see again? Will the steps taken in the light of Gartree 1987 and Brixton 1991, along with an £800million prison building and refurbishment programme, prevent any recurrence of the events that took these men over the wall?

History, and the opinions of experts on, and participants in, the escape business, suggest a negative answer to all these questions. In 1968 the Radzinowicz Report stated, 'Some of our witnesses suggested that prisoners would always escape . . . that there would be something very oppressive about a prison system from which there were no escapes.' The 1977 inquiry into the escape and triple murders at Carstairs State Hospital brought forth the comment, 'All fences and walls can be surmounted by determined and active men, as the history of warfare and escape shows.' In 1992, Stephen Shaw, Director of the Prison Reform Trust, wrote, 'No prison system which is humane can ever be 100 per cent secure.'

New jails can be constructed with all the latest technological equipment and devices, from X-ray machines and metal detectors to cameras, dogs, prisons-within-prisons and perimeter walls topped by electronic ganders. But if there is any flaw or weakness in any aspect of the security, a determined escaper will exploit it.

At Belmarsh, the prison/court complex in Woolwich, built and designed to hold terrorists at a cost of £104million, security looked to be in grave doubt only ten days after the showpiece jail opened in July 1991, when the building plans were found by a brewery worker in the garden of the near-by Cutty Sark public house. The Home Office was said to be embarrassed, but a spokesman was confident that the security of the new prison would not be affected. The following month a new controversy erupted at Belmarsh when the Prison Officers' Association claimed that the control room, the heart of security in any prison, was staffed by auxiliaries instead of trained officers.

The difficulties of gauging the correct degree of security for a prison became apparent when Judge Stephen Tumim took a close look at Strangeways in Manchester, refurbished after the riot of 1990. Closed-circuit cameras and double gates with electro-magnetic locks were oppressive, he said. The Prison Officers' Association seized on his comments, saying members were unhappy with the level of security which 'did not benefit the atmosphere in the prison'. They expressed a suspicion that it had been introduced 'with the privatisation of the prison in mind'.

The failure of security procedures that were believed to be foolproof has contributed to most major escapes in recent times. Often those procedures have broken down through a human element. No matter how daunting the structure of a jail or its security measures, if the people who operate the procedures are not totally reliable, security will be vulnerable. The Carstairs Report made the point that, if security is 'an attitude of mind', it must be the concern of every member of staff, but went on to say that a danger in having a general responsibility for security is that 'what begins as everybody's responsibility becomes, in time, no one's responsibility'.

Error and negligence, as successive inquiries have shown, contribute to the weakening of the system; so too does corruption. Over the years there have been instances of prison officers assisting inmates to escape, their involvement brought about by blackmail, greed or other weaknesses. Such instances have not, it must be said, been common. But can corruptibility, or other human fallibilities, be completely eradicated amidst the tensions of men and women working in volatile jails with highly manipulative, criminally sophisticated and often dangerous inmates? History suggests not.

Few escapers are at liberty for long. Most return to their home areas, to the limitations of the underworld lifestyle, get betrayed for money or police favours or are caught as a result of further crimes. Of those featured in this book, Ronnie Biggs in Brazil and George Blake in Russia are known to be alive, well and enjoying life, while it is reasonable to presume that Nikolaus Chrastny is in a similar situation, somewhere in the Third World, if not closer. Alan Reeve is in Holland, living underground and under threat of extradition back to Broadmoor, while his Dutch lawyer hopes to convince the

European Commission in Strasbourg that to return him would breach the Treaty of Rome. Two of the thirty-eight IRA men who made history by breaking out of the Maze in 1983 are still unaccounted for, while three others who have surfaced in the United States fight to remain there.

Without any doubt it will be harder for a high-security prisoner to escape in the future. As recent attempts have shown, he or she will perhaps have most chance of success in transit between court and prison, on a journey to an outside hospital, or while being moved between prisons. The statistics for this type of escape, in many cases involving violence to escorts, have risen sharply to around 100 each year. One of the most overt displays of security ever afforded a British prisoner took place on 11 November 1992 at Heathrow Airport. Machine-gun-toting police were in great evidence as Valerio Viccei, five years into a twenty-two-year sentence for the £60million Knightsbridge Safe Deposit Co. robbery, boarded an Alitalia flight, to be flown back to his native Italy where further charges awaited him.

As to the future, the opinions of two men from opposing ends of the spectrum must be considered. One is Lord Stonham, who in 1966, as a Home Office minister, spoke to reporters after a press helicopter hovered close to the roof of Leicester Prison. Twenty-one years before it was to actually happen, Stonham acknowledged that the helicopter could have been used for an escape. He also said, 'I do not think it is possible for a human mind to conceive conditions of security which another human mind could not find a way round.'

The last word goes to one of the legendary jailbreakers, Walter Probyn. Speaking to journalist Duncan Campbell of the *Guardian* in 1992, he said, 'There are two kinds of escapers: the opportunists and the planners. The first spot a sudden chance and go for it, the others are more devious and dedicated and are prepared to spend months planning their move.' No doubt recalling his own sixteen break-outs, the man they once called 'Angel Face' said prisoners have twenty-four hours a day to think about nothing else but how to escape and no matter how secure the jail they could always find 'a chink in the armour'.

BIBLIOGRAPHY

Asinof E., Hinckle W., and Turner W., *The 10 Second Jailbreak*, Michael Joseph, 1974

Biggs R., *His Own Story*, Michael Joseph, 1981

Bishop P. and Mallie E., *The Provisional IRA*, Heinemann, 1987

Bourke S., *The Springing of George Blake*, Cassell, 1970

Campbell D., *That was Business, This is Personal*, Secker & Warburg, 1990

Delano A., *Slip-up*, Deutsch, 1977

Dillon M., *Killer in Clowntown*, Arrow, 1992

Dunne D., *Out of the Maze*, Gill & Macmillan, 1988

Endle R., *Dartmoor Prison*, Bossiney Books, 1979

Fitzgerald M., *Prisons in Revolt*, Pelican 1977

Forbes G. and Meehan P., *Such Bad Company*, Paul Harris, 1982

Fordham P., *The Robbers' Tale*, Hodder & Stoughton, 1965

Hinds A., *Contempt of Court*, Bodley Head, 1966

HMSO, *Report of the Inquiry into Prison Escapes and Security (Mountbatten Report)*, 1966

HMSO, *The Regime for Long-Term Prisoners in Conditions of Maximum Security – Report of the Advisory Council on Penal Reform (Radzinowicz Report)*, 1968

HMSO, *Report of an Inquiry by HM Chief Inspector of Prisons into the security arrangements at HM Prison, Maze*, 1984

HMSO, *State Hospital Carstairs – Report of Public Local Inquiry into circumstances surrounding the escape of two patients on 30 November 1976*, 1977

Jennings A., Lashmar P., and Simpson V., *Scotland Yard's Cocaine Connection*, Jonathan Cape, 1990

Kennedy L., *A Presumption of Innocence*, Panther, 1977

Kray R., *Born Fighter*, Century, 1990

Kray C., *Me and My Brothers*, Grafton, 1988

Kray R. and Kray R., *Our Story*, Sidgwick & Jackson, 1988

Lucas N., *Britain's Gangland*, W.H.Allen, 1969

Lucas N., *The Great Spy Ring*, Mayflower, 1968

McKenzie C., *Most Wanted Man*, Panther, 1976

McVicar J., *McVicar By Himself*, Arrow, 1979

Morton J., *Gangland*, Little Brown & Co., 1992

O'Connor J., *The Eleventh Commandment*, Seagull, 1976

Probyn W., *Angel Face – The Making of a Criminal*, Allen & Unwin, 1977

Randle M. and Pottle P., *The Blake Escape*, Harrap, 1990

Read L. with Morton J., *Nipper*, Macdonald & Co., 1991

Read P.P., *The Train Robbers*, W.H.Allen, 1978

Reeve A., *Notes from A Waiting Room*, Heretic, 1983

Saunders G., *Casebook of the Bizarre*, John Donald, 1991

Short M., *Lundy – the Destruction of Scotland Yard's Finest Detective*, Grafton, 1991

Skelton D. and Brownlie L., *Frightener – The Glasgow Ice-cream Wars*, Mainstream, 1992

Slipper J., *Slipper of the Yard*, Sidgwick & Jackson, 1981

Sparks R., *Burglar to the Nobility*, Arthur Barker, 1961

Thomas J.E., *The British Prison Officer since 1850*, Routledge, Kegan Paul, 1972

Tullett T., *Inside Dartmoor*, Muller, 1966

INDEX

More Fascinating True Crime from Headline

JAD ADAMS

DOUBLE INDEMNITY
MURDER FOR INSURANCE

Extraordinary true stories of murderers who insured their victims then killed them – or attempted to.

Includes:

- **The solicitor who killed his wife and faked the scene of the crime to make her look like a drug dealer.**
- **The horse dealer who had her former lover tied in a burning car and pushed over a cliff.**
- **The shopkeeper who killed his own son for the insurance.**
- **The doctor who poisoned his mother-in-law, then his wife.**
- **The school teacher who killed a colleague and her two children.**
- **The restaurateur who insured his mother and put a bomb in her luggage.**
- **The insurance company investigator who tried three times to kill his wife.**

NON-FICTION/TRUE CRIME   0 7472 4360 3

A selection of non-fiction from Headline

THE DRACULA SYNDROME	Richard Monaco & William Burt	£5.99 ☐
DEADLY JEALOUSY	Martin Fido	£5.99 ☐
WHITE COLLAR KILLERS	Frank Jones	£4.99 ☐
THE MURDER YEARBOOK 1994	Brian Lane	£5.99 ☐
THE PLAYFAIR CRICKET ANNUAL	Bill Frindall	£3.99 ☐
ROD STEWART	Stafford Hildred & Tim Ewbank	£5.99 ☐
THE JACK THE RIPPER A–Z	Paul Begg, Martin Fido & Keith Skinner	£7.99 ☐
THE *DAILY EXPRESS* HOW TO WIN ON THE HORSES	Danny Hall	£4.99 ☐
COUPLE SEXUAL AWARENESS	Barry & Emily McCarthy	£5.99 ☐
GRAPEVINE: THE COMPLETE WINEBUYERS HANDBOOK	Anthony Rose & Tim Atkins	£5.99 ☐
ROBERT LOUIS STEVENSON: DREAMS OF EXILE	Ian Bell	£7.99 ☐

All Headline books are available at your local bookshop or newsagent, or can be ordered direct from the publisher. Just tick the titles you want and fill in the form below. Prices and availability subject to change without notice.

Headline Book Publishing, Cash Sales Department, Bookpoint, 39 Milton Park, Abingdon, OXON, OX14 4TD, UK. If you have a credit card you may order by telephone – 0235 400400.

Please enclose a cheque or postal order made payable to Bookpoint Ltd to the value of the cover price and allow the following for postage and packing:
UK & BFPO: £1.00 for the first book, 50p for the second book and 30p for each additional book ordered up to a maximum charge of £3.00.
OVERSEAS & EIRE: £2.00 for the first book, £1.00 for the second book and 50p for each additional book.

Name ....

Address ....

....

....

If you would prefer to pay by credit card, please complete:
Please debit my Visa/Access/Diner's Card/American Express (delete as applicable) card no:

Signature .... Expiry Date ....